THE ALMIGHTY I AM

PRAYERS & DECLARATIONS TO KNOW AND ENCOUNTER GOD

YOLANDITA COLÓN

Cathy,
I pray this Book
Take you Deeper!
love you
Colon

DISCLAIMER

This book does not aim to provide an exhaustive theological treatise or engage in scholarly discourse. Rather, its purpose is to kindle an ardent devotion to God in the reader, surpassing the mere intellect. As I allude to the names, attributes, and titles of God, my intention is to evoke a passionate connection with Him. I have intentionally capitalized every word referring to God to add a reverential tone when speaking about God and to distinguish between the human element from the Deity element. My hope and prayer are that as you delve into the pages of this book, you will discover a message that sparks a profound longing within you to seek and experience God through the revelation of His magnificent nature, names, and attributes. In doing so, may your pursuit of God be ignited and your encounter with Him be enriched.

CONTENTS

PART 1

LAYING A FOUNDATION OF PRAYER

1

A JOURNEY WITH GOD

*Oh, that we might know the LORD! Let us press on to know him. . . . I want you
to know me more than I want burnt offerings.*

Hosea 6:3, 6

*And this is the way to have eternal life—to know you, the only true God, and
Jesus Christ, the One you sent to earth.*

John 17:3

This book has emerged from the depths of my personal journey and intimate
communion with God, spanning numerous years. I have expanded upon the
second part of my previous book, *Revival Worshiper For The Last Days*, using
it as a fundamental starting point. This endeavor arises from a deep passion
that God has deposited in my heart, and I firmly believe it is a divine mandate
from the Father.

In recent years, my focus has been dedicated to seeking a deeper understanding of the nature of God. Through intentional study of Scriptures, I have
sought to saturate my life and deepen my comprehension of His Character.

After stepping away from a pastoral position of twenty-two years of full-time Ministry, my husband and I found ourselves in desperate need of a sabbatical. Unbeknownst to us, God had ordained an extended period of rest and seeking in our lives. During this time, God called me to engage in prolonged periods of intimate communion with Him, devoting three to six hours every morning to be alone with Him.

God gave me a strategy that enabled me to fulfill this divine instruction, empowering me to rise daily at 3:00 or 4:00 in the early morning. He even transformed my nature from being a night owl to an early bird. This was truly a Miracle! Though it presented its challenges, I faithfully adhered to this disciplined routine, with the strength and grace of His Spirit, which has now become an integral part of my life. More importantly, as I passionately studied the Scriptures and with a desperate desire to know God more intimately and encounter Him, it became what I would call a healthy addiction. His glorious nature and beautiful Presence brought so much joy, happiness, and satisfaction to my soul that it became my favorite place to be. It has become my refuge during the storms and uncertainties of life.

However, my pursuit of a deeper knowledge of God was driven not solely by the intention to write this book; I first did it for myself because I recognized that if anyone needed it, it was me. I must confess that my hunger for a greater understanding of the glorious nature of God remains insatiable and will persist until my last breath. I am completely captivated and drawn to Him forever. Within the pages of Chapter 24 of my previous book, *Revival Worshipers For The Last Days*, you will find a detailed account of my personal journey. There, I recount how I navigated through a season of depression and darkness that lasted for two years, a challenging and uncertain time. For now, I will offer a summary of this story, providing a glimpse into the transforming power of God and His mighty Nature.

For my thirty-eighth birthday I took the time to reflect and write down a historic prayer that I had desperately uttered at the conclusion of a profoundly difficult phase in my life, which had lasted almost two years. It all began when the church my husband and I had founded, through tears and sacrifices, went through a painful division. The cause of this split was a poisonous and toxic teaching given to one of our key leaders from an outside source. Regrettably, this led to a spiritual contamination as that leader embraced the destructive poisonous teachings and began to spread them to others within the congregation. This unfortunately led to a permeating confusion in the congregation resulting in people losing their focus on Jesus. The Savior and perfecter of our faith.

As a consequence, my husband and I faced numerous painful incidents. The impact was so severe that I found myself in the emergency room on several occasions, experiencing chest pain due to the overwhelming stress and anguish caused by betrayal. At times I thought I was going to die. Despite these challenges, whenever I stepped into the church, I could still sense God's mighty Presence as I led worship, sang, and ministered in my brokenness. However, the moment I returned home, everything would once again become dark and uncertain. Although the devil attempted to exploit this situation to destroy both me and my heart of worship, I came to realize that God was allowing these trials to teach me an important lesson. There was something within me that I still needed to learn, and God was using these difficult circumstances to reveal it to me.

MY AHA! MOMENT

In my historic prayer, I recounted how I came across John Paul Jackson's testimony, which resonated deeply with my own situation and captured my attention. Hearing his account provided a profound sense of identification, reassuring me that I was not alone in experiencing these challenges. It became evident that God was using such circumstances to draw His people into a personal encounter with Him, transcending mere religion.

Moved by this revelation, I found myself kneeling in my living room beside the computer, accompanied by soothing music playing softly in the background. In this sacred moment of prayer, I earnestly sought answers from God, questioning why He had permitted these trials and where He had been amidst the tumultuous events. My heart was burdened with countless unanswered questions, yearning for divine understanding and guidance.

Suddenly, a resounding voice of God echoed so clearly within my spirit, saying,

"You don't truly know Me." Astonished, I responded,

"What do You mean? I have dedicated my life to serving You. How can it be that I don't know You?"

His response struck me deeply, "Yes, everything you have known about Me has been instrumental in your journey thus far, but to embark on the next phase of your path, you need a fresh revelation of who I am and who you are in Me. To confront what lies ahead and embrace where I am leading you, you must know Me deeply."

In that profound moment, I came to the realization that I had relied heavily on my past encounters with God and the testimonies of others that I had heard or read. And, while I had been blessed with powerful experiences with God throughout my life, I had naively assumed that I already possessed a sufficient understanding of God. However, I was now confronted with the truth that I needed to grasp the significance of getting deeper into my knowledge and comprehension of God beyond religion and even ministry.

God yearned for me to know Him more intimately through His names, inherent attributes, and divine nature. I know that God knew my heart however, He desired for me to know Him on the same intimate level as He knows me. As someone once wisely expressed, "To know and be known by God" are two distinct facets. As His beloved child, God possesses an intricate knowledge of every aspect of my being, yet He passionately longs for me to pursue a deeper connection with Him. God harbors a dream, a desire for us to take genuine interest in Him, to pursue Him as a bride relentlessly seeks her Bridegroom.

Therefore, I embarked on a journey of discovering the depths of God's glorious character and embracing the sacred invitation to intimately know Him beyond the surface level. This pursuit held the potential to transform my relationship with God, enabling me to align my heart more closely with His divine purpose and enter into a profound communion that surpasses mere religion.

If you have grown up within the church, it is not uncommon to experience a deep-seated fear of being ostracized or accused of misinterpreting the Bible. There may even be a constant sense of condemnation, as if straying into heresy is just one misstep away. This fear can lead individuals to close themselves off completely from any potential new revelation from God in His word.

A powerful example of this can be found in the book of Acts (10:12-15), where God called upon the apostle Peter to bring the message of the gospel to the Gentiles. However, Peter initially resisted this divine instruction. In a vision, God told Peter to "kill and eat," but Peter defiantly responded with a resounding "NO!" He took pride in his adherence to Jewish dietary laws, fearing how he would be perceived by those who knew him. Unfortunately, this reluctance had the potential to hinder the spread of the gospel to the Gentile world, all due to Peter's religious hang-ups.

It is crucial that we exercise caution and avoid shutting the door to the Holy Spirit's new revelation. When we allow fear of the unknown, which is essentially a lack of faith, to consume us, we inadvertently seal ourselves off from the life-giving flow of the gospel. Instead of serving as vessels through which the gospel can touch and transform lives, we become stagnant repositories of what once was, resembling a museum rather than an aquarium teeming with vibrant life.

This fear-driven stance leaves us feeling like spiritual orphans within our Christian faith, stunting our growth in the knowledge and revelation of God, our loving Father.

Continuing with my recount, while I remained on my knees in prayer, a beautifully orchestrated God-aligned moment unfolded. I was enraptured as a new CD began to play, and to my surprise, I discovered that my considerate and loving husband had not only acquired this CD but also took the thoughtful step of loading it onto our computer. The CD contained the teachings of the very prophet, John Paul Jackson, whom I had previously seen on the TBN program. Its content consisted of a rich compilation of 365 names of God, an exquisite treasure awaiting my discovery.

Suddenly, my attention was captivated by this previously unknown CD. As the music played, a voice-over commenced uttering:

I am 365 names, characteristics, and attributes of God.

I am the God who shows wonders.

I am the Lord, and my voice is powerful and full of majesty.

I am Wisdom.

I am Omniscient.

I am *Jehovah-Rapha*.

As the CD played on, the utterance of each name and aspect of "The Great I AM" had a profound impact on me, gently removing the blindfold that had obscured my vision and dissipating the remnants of darkness within my being. In a moment of awe-inspiring divine alignment, I was struck with a deep realization of the vastness and magnitude of my God, a moment that would forever be etched in my memory as an "aha moment" of revelation.

Overflowing with awe, I exclaimed, "Wow! God is truly gigantic and immense! I had been unknowingly confining Him within narrow boundaries!"

In an instant, a veil was lifted, and I recognized the limitations of my previous understanding, despite serving God wholeheartedly. I had unknowingly confined myself to familiar revelations, relying on past encounters and the experiences of others that had shaped my perception since childhood. I was operating within the confines of my outdated beliefs or what the bible calls "old wineskins." I thought I already knew everything I needed to know about God. Even with a minor degree in biblical studies, intensive ministry training, and nearly a decade of ministry experience by then, I had failed to grasp the importance of intentionally pursuing an intimate knowledge of God beyond religious and even ministry itself.

Of course, I had had powerful experiences in the past with God, however those experiences had become stagnant, like old wineskins. Unbeknownst to me, I had not fully realized the significance of seeking God with undivided attention. He longed to reveal more of Himself to me, but I had been consumed with the busyness of ministry, resembling Martha rather than Mary (see Luke 10:38-42). Though I was engaged in meaningful endeavors for God, I lacked an intimate revelation of His glorious nature. I was not pursuing a deeper connection and a fresh understanding of who God truly is and who I am in Him.

It was then that I understood the personal nature of our relationship with God. He yearned to reveal Himself to me intimately and lead me into greater depths of revelation. My birthday prayer had not gone unanswered; rather, God was graciously responding and beckoning me to journey deeper into His divine truths.

A NEW BEGINNING

From that moment onward, a new chapter unfolded in my life, marking the departure of the night and darkness season. I experienced a profound paradigm shift and was infused with an insatiable hunger to delve deeper into God's glorious nature and perceive my identity through His eyes. This ignited within me an unwavering determination to explore the Scriptures, from Genesis to Revelation, in search of a myriad of names and attributes that define God. By the end of my study, I had unearthed a treasure trove of a thousand names and attributes, each one illuminating a different facet of His being.

With this newfound revelation, my worship ascended to unprecedented heights. It was infused with a fresh understanding of God and with a deeper comprehension of my relationship with Him. Prior to this revelation, my spiritual journey relied heavily on past encounters with God and second-hand knowledge. However, I realized that such an approach left me confined to old wineskins and hindered my spiritual growth. I recognized the necessity of continually pursuing a fresh revelation of God's glorious nature, allowing my understanding of Him to evolve and expand. It was a vital lesson in understanding that God is dynamic and constantly unveiling new aspects of Himself because He is a God of infinite creativity and boundless love. He longs to reveal Himself to us in ever-deepening ways, surpassing our previous encounters (see John 16:12-13).

God challenged me to seek to know Him more persistently and intentionally. He extended an invitation for me to join Him on a transformative journey to deeper places where He wanted to reveal Himself to me. That catapulted me into a hunger-driven expedition of pursuit and discovery of the glorious nature of God. Honestly. It has become an exhilarating adventure that I firmly believe will continue indefinitely, for there is always more of God to uncover and explore. (Job 26:14). The magnitude of God's greatness defies measurement, transcending the boundaries of human understanding (see Psalm 145:3; Job 26:14). The Scriptures also say that His ways and thoughts soar far beyond the limitations of our finite minds (see Isaiah 55:8–9). For now, we see but a fraction of His Majesty but one day we will behold Him face-to-face, knowing Him fully with all His splendor (see 1 Corinthians 13:12).

Despite the vastness of God's reality, He remains a personal God who desires to reveal Himself to each and every one of us. He invites us to intimately encounter His glory, extending this invitation to both the least and the greatest among us (see Hebrews 8:11). He assures us that when we call upon Him and draw near to Him in prayer, He will hear us (see 1 John 5:14). He promises that as we wholeheartedly seek Him, we will undoubtedly find Him (see Jeremiah 29:11–14). Although some mysteries are reserved solely for Him, for He is Sovereign, He has graciously chosen to reveal Himself through the Scriptures and His Spirit, providing us with sufficient knowledge to know Him, obey His commands, and become genuine worshipers (see Deuteronomy 29:29; John 4:23–24).

While crafting this book, I revisited the extensive collection of 1,200 names and attributes of God from my previous work. However, my exploration did not end there. I discovered an additional 1,700 names, attributes, characteristics, works, truths, and promises that intricately intertwine with His divine nature. The profound realization dawned upon me that the God I serve is far more magnificent and multifaceted than I had ever imagined. Our minds, finite as they are, cannot fully comprehend the depths of this awesome God, and thus embarking on a lifelong journey toward eternity becomes our ceaseless pursuit.

Throughout this journey, I felt as though God held my hand, guiding me through valleys and mountains, leading me beside streams and rivers. Together, we shared moments of tears, laughter, awe, and speechlessness. There were instances when my human mind, limited in its capacity, struggled to grasp the boundless attributes of God. Yet, with each experience and encounter, as I prayed His names, God graciously granted me glimpses of His true nature and unveiled aspects of my own being.

At times, I had to beseech God for help in overcoming the filters of my human understanding that threatened to hinder His intended messages. I persisted in pressing on, pursuing Him, waiting expectantly, and wholeheartedly trusting in His faithfulness. And every time, without fail, He came through, granting me the clarity and insight needed to receive His fresh revelations. It became evident that these filters, which can encompass preconceived notions, past traumas, disappointments, confusion, emotional pain, fears, limitations, needs, weaknesses, or even a reliance on our own understanding, must be surrendered in order to receive new revelation from the great "I AM" (see Proverbs 3:5–7). It is in our weakness that His power is made perfect, and His grace is sufficient for all our needs (see 2 Corinthians 12:9).

Ask God to empower you to understand His truths fully. He wants this more than you can ever imagine. Don't allow the filters of your human understanding to impede this thrilling new journey with God, it has the potential to become the most profound journey of your life alongside the Almighty I AM. With a heart hungry for truth and a spirit filled with curiosity, this book will become the most remarkable voyage of your life with May you be encouraged and inspired to embrace this timely tool, tailor-made for these significant times we find ourselves in—the last days.

As you embark on this journey, His Spirit will serve as your guide, teaching you the divine language and directing your steps. The Holy Spirit is our ever-present Helper. Sometimes He speaks mysteries with God as we pray in tongues, but He also wants us to speak with our understanding. We have the privilege of praying and singing both in the Spirit and with words that resonate with our comprehension. This dual approach enriches our gratitude towards God and strengthens us in the process (see 1 Corinthians 14:15–16).

Praying the language of God is a prayer that aligns with His divine Nature and speaks His words of truth. It often unveils mysteries as we pray in tongues, but He also desires that we speak with our understanding. We have the privilege to communicate with God in the language of faith and truth, a language that captivates His attention and aligns with His divine nature.

PREPARE FOR A JOURNEY WITH GOD

We do this by keeping our eyes on Jesus, the champion who initiates and perfects our faith. Because of the joy awaiting him, he endured the cross, disregarding its shame. Now he is seated in the place of honor beside God's throne.

Hebrews 12:2

We must fix our gaze upon Jesus, our Champion and the One who perfects our faith, rather than being consumed by worldly matters. Unfortunately, the essence of the gospel has been overshadowed by a list of rules and regulations, transforming it into a legalistic and inflexible religion or institution. Consequently, this has caused harm to many individuals and led them astray from God's true intentions. However, God's original desire was for us to have a personal and intimate relationship with Him, to love Him, and to be in eternal communion with Him. He longs for us to comprehend the depth of His affection towards us. It is because of His unconditional love that He sent Jesus to die and be resurrected on our behalf.

My prayer is that this book will illuminate God's initial intentions, allowing us to truly know Him and experience His love. May it propel us into a revival of holy intimacy with our Bridegroom, Jesus Christ, anchoring us so firmly in His truth that nothing could ever separate us from Him.

Our human existence is not a mere coincidence. There is an eternal purpose behind why we are here, where we are heading, and why it matters. We are embarking on a journey with the Almighty I AM. The more we acquaint ourselves with God and draw near to Him, the clearer our purpose within Him becomes, and we understand why this awe-inspiring Creator brought us into being. It is a profound journey that culminates in an eternal and intimate union with our Lord in heaven.

Knowing about God through religion is not the same as truly knowing Him through an intimate relationship. To know His names, attributes, works, and promises without a personal revelation from the Spirit of God would only be good mental and intellectual information. However, God has always desired for us to genuinely know Him and encounter His unfailing love directly, just as illustrated in the book of Hosea. He yearns for His people to intimately know Him and experience His boundless love.

Gaining a deeper understanding of His name and truths propels us to a higher level of spiritual wisdom, understanding, and experiential knowledge (*Yadah*). This leads to spiritual deliverance and transformation for ourselves and those around us. When we receive the truth through revelation, we are liberated from numerous burdens (see John 8:32). Through the Spirit's revelation of God's names, we are able to taste and encounter the magnificence and beauty of God, leaving a profound impact on us spiritually, mentally, emotionally, and even physically.

As the Spirit unveils His holy and glorious nature to us, our carnal mindset is transformed into the mind of Christ. We grow as we continue to deepen our knowledge of God (see Colossians 1:10). With an increased spiritual understanding of His Holy Nature, our mental framework shifts, and a deeper reverence and fear of the Lord take root in our hearts (see 1 Corinthians 2:9–16; Romans 12:2).

As we deepen our understanding of who God truly is, it empowers us to live a life of victory, liberated from fear and even from our own limitations. Our worries and concerns are transformed into joy and courage. With each step on this journey with God, from one level of glory to another, we are ushered into a higher realm of the supernatural that is available to us through Christ.

I have always yearned to experience more of God and draw closer to Him. However, there were moments when my mind struggled and my heart felt discouraged. The baggage of a religious legalistic background only served to hinder me, keeping me in a constant state of striving. It became challenging to process and fully embrace certain truths about God. Honestly, I often found myself questioning God when unfavorable circumstances occurred, and this hindered my ability to grasp a deeper spiritual understanding of His glorious Nature and His divine will for my life.

After many years of serving God, I believed I had a sufficient knowledge of Him, but in reality, I was barely scratching the surface. It was when God challenged me to go deeper that my perspective underwent a profound shift. I came to understand the importance of being intentional and consistent on this journey with God, not relying solely on past experiences. I understood the importance of unwavering and intentional perseverance in this journey with God, and not relying solely on past experiences with Him. Be determined with perseverance to seek, ask, and knock, and you will receive from God; you will find Him, and the doors of heaven will open for you (see Luke 11:9–10).

My husband, Herman, frequently repeats a saying: "And yet, there is MORE!" This is because there are times when we can become overly familiar and complacent with what we already know of God, mistakenly assuming we have reached a final destination. However, there is still so much more of God to discover and explore. Remember that God is ready to reveal more of Himself to us, but He requires our invitation (see James 4:8). The initiative lies in our court. If we take the necessary steps, our journey will remain on course and unstoppable.

We must embark on this journey with an insatiable hunger for greater insight and understanding of the God who lovingly created us. God cannot be confined to a church, a religion, a denomination, or a ministry. God is the All-Powerful and Almighty I AM.

Do not rely solely on past experiences and achievements, or on what you already know about Him. Instead, actively pursue fresh encounters with God and seek a deeper revelation of His character. Guard your heart against falling into the trap of familiarity or conformity. Be vigilant against the enemy's schemes to distract you from your pursuit of knowing more about God. Pay close attention to what you allow into your eyes, ears, and mind. Remember, God is a jealous God; He desires your wholehearted devotion.

Let us make the same determination as the psalmist:

I will ponder the way that is blameless. Oh, when will you come to me? I will walk with integrity of heart within my house; I will not set before my eyes anything that is worthless. I hate the work of those who fall away; it shall not cling to me. A perverse heart shall be far from me; I will know nothing of evil.

Psalm 101:2–4 ESV

Ponder this Scripture and search your heart before God:

You cannot drink the cup of the Lord and the cup of demons. You cannot partake of the table of the Lord and the table of demons. Shall we provoke the Lord to jealousy? Are we stronger than he?

1 Corinthians 10:21–22 ESV

With reverence and a deep sense of awe, our hearts should consistently long for and pursue God with purity. We must possess an inquisitive spirit, a hunger that cannot be satisfied, and an unwavering determination to see this earthly journey through to the end with resilience. Each of us moves at our own pace and walks alongside Jesus on our unique path. It is crucial not to compare our journey with that of others. Like runners on a track, we are all pursuing our individual races with Jesus. Though we may be at different points in this journey, we are all moving in the same direction with Jesus, and we are equally cherished by Him. This journey does not have to be a passive one. Humbly ask the Lord to remove any hindrances that may impede His work in your life and through you.

At times, life may become arduous, and you might encounter setbacks or obstacles that seem to block your path. However, be assured that our loving God is right there, holding your hand. As we deepen our knowledge and understanding of the great God we serve, the journey becomes smoother. We must safeguard our hearts and maintain an unyielding hunger, consistency, determination, and intentionality in our pursuit of Him. Our trust and love for Him grow exponentially as we continue on this journey until the culmination of our eternal union in heaven.

This brings to mind the words of the apostle Paul to the disciples. He assured them that he had not ceased to pray for them ever since he first heard about them. Paul fervently prayed and requested the Lord to grant them complete knowledge of His will, along with spiritual wisdom and understanding. He understood that once they reached this level of spiritual insight and understanding, their way of life would consistently honor and please the Lord, bearing abundant fruit. Paul acknowledged that throughout this journey, they would grow as they delved deeper into their knowledge of God (see Colossians 1:9–10). The same holds true for us.

2

DRAWING CLOSER TO THE ALMIGHTY
I AM

Come close to God, and God will come close to you.

James 4:8

The LORD is good to those who depend on him, to those who search for him. So it is good to wait quietly for salvation from the LORD.

Lamentations 3:25–26

Sometimes, when the concerns of life threaten to overwhelm me, I make a deliberate effort to shift my focus towards the glorious nature of God and behold His beauty. I delight in His names, attributes, and everything that He truly is. I align my mind with the obedience of Christ. I compel myself to direct my gaze towards Jesus. I consciously decide to strive to seek God above all else. I maintain control over my emotions and feelings, recognizing that God is greater than my emotions, for He knows all things. I correct my words when necessary and synchronize them with His Word.

I do this because I recognize that the power of life and death is in my tongue. Doing this helps me synchronize and align my mind and heart with His perfect will. I hide under the shadow of His wings and find in Him a hiding place from all my worries. When I do this, my emotions align with His will, and God always answers my prayers.

Praying God's words of truth can be likened to praying His language, which also helps us worship with spiritual insight. It helps us worship in Spirit and in truth. We were created to worship; therefore, worshiping Him is essential for a happy life. In Him, we find our true happiness, joy, and peace. We came from Him, and we shall go back to Him. God will empower us to overcome all challenges when we seek Him and worship Him with *all* our heart. Praises and prayers declaring His names, attributes, and truths about God and gazing at His beauty is the most effective way to worship Him.

This journey of learning more about who God is, allows us to live in communion with Him. God will empower you to learn, pray and sing His divine vocabulary. Moses and Jeremiah felt inadequate in their vocabulary, but God empowered them to speak and carry forth His mandate. The Lord empowers you to do His will, to know His ways, to understand His names, His glorious nature, His character, His word, His commandments, His promises, and His beauty.

I pray that the Lord teaches us to pray according to His Spirit and that He helps us to encounter His transforming Presence on a deeper level every day of our life. May the Lord empower us with a higher level of faith to catapult us to do greater things for Him.

Faith comes by hearing and listening to His Word. We can find much about God's glorious nature and who God is in His Word. However, we must rely a hundred percent on the help of His Holy Spirit. His Spirit is the one who reveals to us the secrets of God. And, as we pray and sing His Word, hear it, and meditate on it, God will endow us with a supernatural faith that transcends our human imagination. This is because faith comes by hearing, and fear also comes by hearing. So, to grow in our faith, we must be careful of what we are listening to. To be able to listen well, we must intentionally listen attentively and reflect on His Word. We need to allow His Spirit to reveal it to us and receive it in our hearts.

When we receive a revelation of His truth, it gives us new freedom! It releases us to enjoy life, be joyful, and reach our full potential, empowered by the Spirit of truth and freedom. We are no longer slaves of fear. We have nothing to fear because He is standing with us. We can look at the future with a smile and without any fear, only the reverent fear of God. The only stumbling block to this is when we cannot wholeheartedly believe in who He is and what He says in His Word (see Mark 11:22–25; Hebrews 11:6).

People are always evolving, but how beautiful it is when we are transformed through our intimate relationship with God and as we discover and understand more of His glorious nature. As a result, we get to be filled with Him, walk with Him, talk like Him, and feel anchored; we are grounded and secured on a firm Rock during the storms of life. This is wealth at its best!

BUT WHO DO YOU SAY I AM?

Then he asked them, "But who do you say I am?" Simon Peter answered, "You are the Messiah, the Son of the living God." Jesus replied, "You are blessed, Simon, son of John, because my Father in heaven has revealed this to you. You did not learn this from any human being."

Matthew 16:13–17

I can hear the tender heart of Jesus as He is asking His disciples, "But who do you say I am?" Reading this Scripture has moved me and caused me to weep because I can hear His heart. Jesus' desire for us to know Him is deep and strong. He wants to reveal Himself to us, His people. He wants us to know Him personally. Do you truly know God? Pause for a moment and ask yourself, *Who do I say God is? Do I truly understand God's nature? Do I truly believe in who He is and in His Word? If I do, then why do I worry? Or, why do I fear sometimes? Do I truly know God to fully trust Him?* Ponder these questions before the Presence of God and ask the Lord to help you get to the root of all these as you continue on this new journey. Ask the Holy Spirit to help you. He is more than willing; He wants you to know the Almighty I AM!

CALL ON HIS NAME

The Lord is always ready to respond to our prayers, yet we often overlook the importance of calling on His Name. Instead, we tend to reach out to friends, family members, counselors, or pastors before we turn to Him. However, it is He alone who can truly and significantly rescue us from any situation. The Lord laments,

"I was ready to respond, but no one asked for help. I was ready to be found, but no one was looking for me. I said, 'Here I am, here I am!' to a nation that did not call on my name" (Isaiah 65:1).

This passage serves as a powerful reminder that we should prioritize seeking God's help and guidance in our lives. Although it is natural to seek support from others, we should remember that God is always there, waiting for us to call upon His Name. He longs for us to acknowledge His presence and depend on Him as our ultimate source of help and deliverance. When we humbly turn to Him and seek His intervention, we will experience His faithful response and discover the depth of His love and care for us.

When we lack a true understanding of who God is, we often face setbacks and unfavorable circumstances that could have been avoided if we had a deeper comprehension of the Almighty I AM (see Hosea 4:6; Isaiah 1:3). This is because when we genuinely know God, the fear of the Lord guides us to make the right decisions throughout our lives, especially during difficult, challenging, and uncertain times. Even in our moments of weakness, God becomes the strength of our lives, and we can overcome through His power that is perfected in us. As the apostle Paul stated, when we are weak, then we are strong (see 2 Corinthians 12:9-10).

Knowing God requires great patience, waiting on Him through His Word, and meditating on His nature. It requires numerous Selah moments—moments of pause and reflection. The human mind needs time to process, and God reveals Himself to those who genuinely seek Him, desire Him, and wait upon Him. If you truly desire to know Him, seek Him with all your heart, and He will make Himself known to you. Be intentional and consistent and understand that God desires this relationship more than you can ever comprehend or desire.

3

A MYTH ABOUT KNOWING GOD

Not that we are adequate in ourselves to consider anything as coming from ourselves, but our adequacy is from God, who also made us adequate as servants of a new covenant, not of the letter but of the Spirit; for the letter kills, but the Spirit gives life.

2 Corinthians 3:5–6 NASB 1995

There is a prevailing myth that suggests that we could never truly know God unless we go to a seminary and take numerous Bible classes. However, this approach can unwittingly introduce personal biases, influenced by the backgrounds and varying levels of intimacy with God held by the professors involved. If not approached with caution, it can result in confusion and endless debates driven by pride and human knowledge, rather than being rooted in the Spirit's divine revelation found within the very words He authored.

While academic pursuits can provide valuable insights and formal education, that is not the ultimate path to knowing God. The path to truly knowing God resides in experiencing a personal encounter with Jesus and being open to the Father's revelation through our relationship with the Holy Spirit. The Holy Spirit serves as our guide, teaching us all things that he hears from the Father. These treasures are bestowed upon us solely by the Holy Spirit. It is through the work of God's Spirit that such revelation is given. God reveals Himself only to those who earnestly seek Him with a hunger in the secret place (see Proverbs 8:17; 29:13). The secret place refers to our personal time with God, the moments we spend behind closed doors alone studying His Word, praying and worshiping Him (see Matthew 6:6; 2 Kings 4:33).

I have had the privilege of learning about remarkable men and women of God, esteemed leaders in the faith, who pursued formal Bible education while treasuring their hunger for intimate communion with God even more than their acquired human knowledge. They exemplified a deep fascination with God, valuing His presence above all else and refraining from engaging in meaningless debates and unfruitful discussions that were useless and a waste of time (see 2 Timothy 2:23; Titus 3:9; James 3:13–18; 1 Timothy 6:20–21; 2 Peter 3:16–18).

Their insatiable hunger for God propelled them to become generals of revival. They treasured and pursued the simple and pure Word of God with childlike awe, recognizing that its true meaning and significance could only be fully understood with the guidance of the Holy Spirit—the very Author of this Word. He is the Context of His own Word. No one can explain or illuminate the depths of God's Word better than His Spirit, for He was there present and it was He who inspired the writers of Scripture. When you receive a genuine and profound revelation of God's Word, you will experience a revival and spiritual awakening that continually unfolds with increasing glory, for His Word is alive and transformative. As you delve deeper into the revelation of the Holy Almighty I AM, your mindset will be renewed, and you will be continually transformed into His likeness (see 2 Corinthians 3:18).

In every revival, a desperate hunger and an unwavering desire for the presence of God are crucial. Throughout history, we have witnessed revivals ignited by students on university campuses, driven by an insatiable longing for a divine transformation. These students, dissatisfied with the status quo, became vessels ready to receive the new wine of the Spirit, just as Jesus described in Matthew 9:17. They listened attentively to the voice of the Holy Spirit, choosing to pursue God above their own limited understanding. They dedicated unhurried moments in the presence of God, seeking Him with all their hearts. Through fervent prayer, passionate worship, weepings, and wailings, they immersed themselves in the Scriptures, placing unwavering faith in

God's promises. They patiently waited in God's presence, emulating the disciples of Jesus in the Upper Room.

I have also witnessed numerous young students who have veered away from the truth and faced challenges with their faith during their college years or after graduating from Bible school. The crucial distinction lies in their lack of wholehearted pursuit of God. Moreover, they approached their study of the Bible as mere textbooks, rather than recognizing it as God's inspired Word. I have observed individuals falling into the traps of religiosity, becoming familiar with spiritual matters, and succumbing to spiritual pride. Some became more focused on earthly matters rather than seeking the heavenly. Unfortunately, some lost their initial love for God's presence and His Word due to academic burdens, stress, or simply a failure to grasp the essence and message of the Bible. They ceased reading it and instead relied solely on chapel services or Sunday sermons for their exposure to Scripture.

As mentioned earlier, academia does not provide us with an intimate relationship with Jesus or bring about revival. Revival begins on a personal level, and it is through a holy intimacy with God that we are propelled into spiritual revival. When we draw near to Him with sincerity, He reciprocates and the impact is profound – personal revival that subsequently spreads to those near and far. While revival can be encouraged and discussed, true intimacy with God is cultivated as we intentionally and wholeheartedly pursue Him with a desperate hunger, seeking to know Him deeply through the guidance of His Spirit.

A heart that is hungry and yearning becomes a catalyst for revival. Sometimes this desperate hunger for the presence of God arises from our brokenness. It is through this brokenness that our hearts are opened wide to the Spirit of God, leading us into spiritual revival. In the midst of revival, our eyes are opened to the holiness and love of God in a profound way. As I share these words with you through this book, my prayer and hope is that I can ignite and stir within you a fresh hunger for God, fanning the flames of passion within your soul. I pray that you will be infused with a desperate and deep longing, prompting you to pursue a greater intimacy with God. May the Lord grant you deeper insights into His glorious nature, aided by the Holy Spirit, and may you wholeheartedly respond to His gentle nudges as you encounter this great and awe-inspiring God.

The act of reading the Bible is undoubtedly crucially important. However, it is not merely about acquiring knowledge and information, but rather about discovering the hidden treasures that can only be revealed through the guidance of the Holy Spirit. These gems of revelation unlock deeper insights into the marvelous nature and beauty of God. As we engage in this intimate exploration, we will behold the glory of the Lord with unveiled faces. This level of intimacy with our Lord equips us to overcome challenges and uncertainties, cultivating a deep trust in Him. When our focus shifts to truly knowing God and finding joy in beholding and delighting in His beauty, we gain a complete perspective on why He has graciously entrusted us with His precious Word, the Bible. It is through this pursuit that we find fulfillment and purpose, as depicted in passages such as Psalm 27:4 and 2 Timothy 3:16–17.

The purpose of the Bible extends far beyond memorizing stories, chapters, and verses. While all that is great and it has its merits, it is important not to miss the true purpose of the Bible. The primary objective of the Bible is to foster a personal and intimate relationship with God. Within the pages of the Bible, there are many hidden gems that can only be discovered by those with a hungry, seeking, and searching heart, similar to treasure hunters. We can become spiritual treasure hunters of God. Taking moments of pause and reflection, known as Selah moments, those who relentlessly pursue God can unearth these precious gems that reveal His glorious nature and beauty (see 1 Corinthians 2:10; Joshua 1:8; Luke 11:9–10; Proverbs 8:17). Through the exploration of God's character, we not only deepen our understanding of Him but also uncover our own identity and purpose on this earth. By immersing ourselves in the richness of God's Word, we embark on a transformative journey that leads us to a profound connection with Him and a greater sense of purpose.

The primary purpose of the Bible is to establish a deep and intimate relationship between God and His people. God desires a profound connection with us, envisioning us as His beloved bride and the embodiment of His church. The church is not confined to a physical building or a religious institution, but rather encompasses every individual who chooses to be united with God. God longs for a reciprocal love, as He has chosen us, and He wants us to choose Him in return. The essence of this sacred book, the Bible, and the reason we read His word is to truly encounter the Great I AM and to gain a comprehensive understanding of our identity and purpose within Him. By embracing this divine connection, we unlock the pathway to genuine happiness, joy, and peace that can only be found in a profoundly intimate relationship with God.

Simon Peter answered, "You are the Messiah, the Son of the living God." Jesus replied, "You are blessed, Simon, son of John, because my Father in heaven has revealed this to you. You did not learn this from any human being. Now I say to you that you are Peter (which means 'Rock'), and upon this Rock, I will build my church, and all the powers of hell will not conquer it. And I will give you the keys of the kingdom of heaven. Whatever you forbid on earth will be forbidden in heaven, and whatever you permit on earth will be permitted in heaven."

Matthew 16:16–19

Peter didn't need a **college** degree to grasp this truth; he discovered it through intimate communion with the Father. Only after understanding who Jesus truly was did Peter receive his divine purpose as a revivalist pastor to the nations. This incredible opportunity extends to us as well! When we receive the Holy Spirit, He dwells within us, empowering and teaching us everything we need to know. His teachings are pure, true, and sacred, unaffected by ego or confusion. It doesn't mean we can't learn from others or pursue formal education, but the untainted truth can only come through the Holy Spirit. Therefore, let us remain in **intimate** fellowship with Christ, allowing His Spirit to reveal the deep truths of God, as without Him, we are powerless **and cannot accomplish anything.** Everything we do on this earth must flow through His Spirit, filtering our learning through the absolute truth He imparts. The Holy Spirit is trustworthy, always right, reliable, and timely in guiding us (see John 15:5; 1 John 2:27).

Entering heaven cannot be achieved by mere religious affiliations or simply acknowledging Jesus as Lord. Only those who earnestly obey the Father's will and are united with His purpose, which is to truly know Him and be known by Him, will be granted entry. On the day of judgment, Jesus may have to say to some, "I never knew you; depart from me, you workers of lawlessness" (see Matthew 7:21–23).

No amount of religious traditions or rituals or esteemed positions can replace the significance of a deep, intimate relationship with Jesus for inheriting God's kingdom. Those who wholeheartedly worship and love God, engaging with His Word, are the ones who are truly known by Him (see Proverbs 8:17; 2 Timothy 3:2–4).

Our credentials, ministry work, degrees, or years of preaching the gospel do not determine our understanding of God. Although these aspects are not inherently wrong, they cannot earn us a righteous standing before God. Instead, we can encounter and know Him through the Spirit of Christ as we humbly and eagerly pursue Him. It is Jesus who empowers us to comprehend and truly know God through His Spirit's guidance.

We know that Jesus, the Son of God, has come to save us, and He has given us the power to understand so that we may know Him who is true and know that we are in Him—Jesus Christ (see 1 John 5:20). When we know God and abide in Him, we stay away from sin. We are holy in everything we do because we understand that He is a *holy* God (see 1 John 3:4–10 and 1 Peter 1:15–16). So, knowing Him helps us live in trembling reverence toward Him and stay away from sin and trouble.

As you get a bigger picture of who God is, your prayers begin to change. You learn to pray using the language of God and His truths, and you'll have an immediate connection with your heavenly Father and His heavenly resources. You can find everything you need in Him, for He is your eternal Fountain. You were created to depend on Him. All you have to do is let Him have control of your life by putting your total trust in Him. He knows everything better than you could ever know (see John 16:23–27).

The depth of our knowledge of God and our understanding of our value to Him are reflected in our private prayers. The Word of God says that His people perish for lack of knowledge. What knowledge is it talking about here? The NLT clarifies it further:

"My people are being destroyed because they <u>don't know me</u>. Since you priests <u>refuse to know me</u>, I refuse to recognize you as my priest. Since you have forgotten the laws of your God, I will forget to bless your children."

Hosea 4:6

God addressed His priests, the appointed leaders who were entrusted with the responsibility of knowing Him deeply and upholding His laws. Their role was crucial as they represented God before His people, serving as models and teachers of His Word. While there is much more to delve into regarding this Scripture verse, let's focus on a simple but profound truth.

As children of God, it is essential for us to pursue a deeper knowledge of Him, surpassing the boundaries of our religious services and our current understanding of Him. We must guard against the dangerous trap of becoming overly familiar with God and disregarding His commandments. When we fail to intimately know God and neglect to keep His laws in our hearts, it deeply affects Him. Unfortunately, this deficiency within the body of Christ has led many to live shallow Christian lives, resulting in spiritual destruction.

It is no wonder that for many, prayer may seem mundane and unexciting unless they find themselves in a crisis that compels them to their knees. The primary reason behind this prevailing shallowness and emptiness within the church is the lack of a deep and intimate relationship with God. My husband, Herman, aptly describes this as "the one-shoe gospel."

Let us not settle for a superficial faith but strive to know God intimately, fostering a profound relationship with Him. This requires a genuine desire to understand His heart and a commitment to live in accordance with His commandments. By seeking this deep connection with God, we can experience the fullness of life and avoid the detrimental consequences of spiritual emptiness.

FAMILIAR PRAYERS OF GRANDMA

While my 85-year-old grandma prayed downstairs in my house, I recognized a prayer that sounded all too familiar. I say "familiar" because I used to pray in the same way. It was the only way I knew how to pray—a prayer filled with victimhood, lacking spiritual revelation, and focused more on problems than on who God truly is. Tears would flow during those prayers, but they were driven by worries and fears. It was a prayer from an orphaned spirit, brimming with hopelessness.

This used to be the only way I knew how to pray. I lacked a deep understanding of God; my prayers were devoid of revelation and faith. I am not suggesting that our prayers must be flawless for God to hear them, for He knows our hearts. However, I believe that the language we use when we pray holds significant importance to God and in the spiritual realm that surrounds us. The effective prayer of a child of God, offered in faith, possess great power and can accomplish much more. The Word of God affirms that without faith, it is impossible to please the Lord and that those who seek Him must believe that He exists and rewards those who diligently seek Him (see Hebrews 11:6).

I often wake up at 3:00 or 4:00 a.m. to pray, read the Scriptures, journal, and spend time in God's presence. One day, while I was praying through the Scriptures and writing them down, the Lord spoke to me about my grandma. In the mornings, she would usually sit by the living room window and begin praying as we prepared her breakfast. As I listened to her praying aloud, the Holy Spirit impressed upon me the need to translate my prayers into Spanish and share them with her. From that moment on, I started translating the prayers into Spanish to bless her.

I translated the first prayer, titled "His Love" (Su Amor), into Spanish. I printed it out and handed it to her. Immediately, she asked me what it was, and I proceeded to explain it to her. I described how this prayer would assist her in praying from the perspective of being seated with Christ in the heavenly realms. I emphasized that she would be able to pray in God's language, develop a deeper knowledge of Him, and experience the power of His names. Furthermore, I explained how this would help her pray and make declarations of faith and truth. I reiterated that this approach would elevate her prayer life to another level and then left her with the prayer in her hand.

As she began reading the prayer aloud, she would occasionally pause, overcome with emotion, and weep before continuing. This pattern continued for about an hour or so. I listened attentively as she passionately prayed, and then the Spirit spoke to me, saying, "You need to continue providing this for her. I want her prayers to ascend to another level because she is my intercessor."

After some time, I returned with food to serve her, and she looked at me with still-moist eyes and exclaimed, "What a powerful prayer that was. Oh my God, it made me cry so much. I have never prayed like this before." In that moment, I realized how deeply these prayers had affected her, and I imagined the transformative impact if my parents, my family, and everyone in the world could pray in the same way.

While discussing the book I was writing with a family member, I shared this experience. She responded by saying, "We need this book because I also struggle with knowing how to pray. I often find myself at a loss for words during my prayers. I try, but I usually end up listening to a pastor on YouTube who has a program that prays for people with specific prayer requests." She went on to explain that there was a significant need for this type of prayer resource within the body of Christ. The importance of this prayer book became even more apparent to me, especially given the current times we live in.

AT THE HOSPITAL WITH MY DAD

Every time I prayed these prayers, the room was !lled with God's powerful presence. As my dad lay in his hospital bed and later at home during those weeks before he passed away and went to be with the Lord, I would pray God's names over him. Despite his pain, he would !nd comfort and fall asleep peacefully. Witnessing how God comforted my dad as I declared His names and attributes over him was a profound experience. I would often tell my family that I believed God wanted to heal Dad, and unless it was in His divine plan to bring him home, I trusted that God would heal him. When that day came, and Dad passed away, I found solace in knowing that God is Sovereign.

At one point, both my mom and dad were in the same hospital on the same "oor. My mom had contracted COVID-19, and unfortunately, I wasn't allowed to be with her. So, I wrote her a letter, printed a copy of my prayers and declarations of God's healing names and attributes, and sent it to her through a nurse.

After she was discharged, she told me that those prayers had given her strength and comfort and that she had gained a deeper under-standing of God's nature. She shared that she had even grasped some truths about God that she hadn't fully understood before. She exclaimed, "Wow. These prayers are powerful because they are pure Word of God."

Since then, she always keeps those prayers close to her so she can pray through them frequently. It dawned on me that just as these prayers impacted me and my family, they would also have an impact on you, my readers. It is my Prayer.

4
_____

THE HONOR OF HIS NAME

God is highly pleased when we think about the honor of His Name and fear Him with reverence. He listens to every detail of how we honor His Name. There is a scroll of remembrance where our name is recorded. The Lord says that we will be His people and His own special treasure. We will be spared from the day of judgment (see Malachi 3:16–18).

King David commanded his son Solomon with some important instructions as he was preparing him to build the temple of the Lord and reign in his place. The first and most important instruction his son received was to "know the God of your father and serve him with a whole heart and a willing mind" (1 Chronicles 28:9). David, a seasoned king and a man after God's heart, told his son that if he sought the Lord, he would find God. However, if he would forsake God, then the Lord would reject him forever.

FINDING VALUE IN HIS UNWAVERING CHARACTER

Have you ever found yourself in a situation where someone unjustly questioned your character? It can be a disheartening experience, leaving you feeling judged and misunderstood. We all long to be seen and understood for who we truly are. That's why it's natural to wonder how others perceive us and why their opinion holds significance.

When someone agrees with our perspective, it brings a sense of validation and affirmation. It makes us feel valued and heard, knowing that our thoughts and beliefs resonate with others. It reinforces our sense of worth and affirms that our voice matters.

In the same way, imagine how our loving God must feel when we question His character, doubting His goodness and speaking words that dishonor His nature. Just as we desire to be understood and valued, God longs for us to recognize His unwavering character, to trust in His love and faithfulness.

Reflecting on the story of Job, we see how God engaged in a profound dialogue, challenging Job's perspective and revealing His own wisdom and sovereignty. It was a reminder to Job, and to us, that even in our moments of doubt or questioning, God's character remains steadfast and unchanging.

Then the Lord answered Job from the whirlwind: "Who is this that questions my wisdom with such ignorant words? Brace yourself like a man, because I have some questions for you, and you must answer them."

Job 38:1–3

We could expand upon this further, but let us conclude by acknowledging the seriousness with which God regards His reputation, and the importance for us to do the same. As His beloved creations, it is time for us to embark on a profound journey of truly knowing Him. It is crucial that we align ourselves with our divine purpose on this earth, enabling us to reach our fullest potential and live in accordance with God's will, bringing Him pleasure.

Throughout this transformative journey, let us keep the following questions in mind, seeking to understand them in the light of His sacred Word and glorious nature:

- Who is the God revealed in the Bible?
- What are His desires for me?
- How can I deepen my knowledge and understanding of Him?
- What actions and attitudes please God, and what causes Him displeasure?
- Does He truly love and care for me?
- Can He provide help, salvation, and healing?

- How can I encounter His presence?
- How can I attune my heart to hear His voice?
- How can I draw nearer to Him and develop a close relationship?

By diligently seeking answers to these questions, we will embark on a transformative journey of knowing God intimately, experiencing His love and guidance, and living in alignment with His divine purpose for our lives.

Our ultimate pursuit should be to intimately know the God and Father portrayed in the Bible, to have a deep understanding of Christ, the eternal Word, and to be acquainted with His Holy Spirit, the Author of the Scriptures. The Word of God foretells, "For a time is coming when people will no longer listen to sound and wholesome teaching. They will follow their own desires and will look for teachers who will tell them whatever their itching ears want to hear. They will reject the truth and chase after myths" (2 Timothy 4:3–4).

One of our former church members confessed to my husband and me that after leaving our church with a few others, they would gather at a home to supposedly study the Bible. However, the troubling truth was that their intentions were not to truly study the Bible but to search for passages they could use to contradict, discredit, and attack us. Their aim was to justify and accommodate their own selfish desires. They attempted to twist the Word of God to serve their rebellious purposes. This individual was convicted by God and was the only one who genuinely repented, sought forgiveness, and returned to the church. Regrettably, this behavior is not uncommon; many individuals exploit the Bible to advance their hidden and impure agendas without any reverence for God.

However, there is a superior path. We can approach the study of God's Word with a curious and hungry heart, recognizing that we need God more than life itself and desiring a genuine knowledge of Him. We also long to discover our purpose in this earthly existence and in eternity. The Word of God becomes our daily sustenance, bringing life and joy. Moreover, as the Holy Spirit of God reveals its profound truths to us, we are equipped to nourish others with this divine sustenance.

God Himself desires to inscribe His laws in our hearts and minds so that we may please Him. His ultimate desire is for us to willingly choose Him as our God and to be His people.

"I will put my law within them, and I will write it on their hearts; and I will be their God, and they shall be my people."

Jeremiah 31:33 NRSV

Many individuals believe that the wealthy and prosperous are inherently arrogant due to their abundance of possessions and social status. However, the most dangerous form of pride is exemplified by Korah, the worship leader of Israel. God despised this spiritual arrogance to such an extent that He refused to tolerate it any longer. It acted as a cancer within His people, and as a consequence, He caused the earth to open up and swallow them alive, condemning them to hell (see Numbers 16:31-33).

Similarly, we encounter individuals who boast about their extensive knowledge of the Bible, akin to Korah. While they may possess vast amounts of information about the Scriptures, they lack a profound revelation of its true essence and have not personally experienced the message and purpose embedded within its pages. Therefore, their boasting solely revolves around the facts and figures they have memorized—the mere letters. In essence, they resemble the Pharisees of Jesus' time. Though they were well-versed in the Torah, they lacked a deeper understanding of its hidden mysteries that can only be revealed through an intimate relationship with the Holy Spirit, who serves as the Author and interpreter of this sacred text. Despite their supposed expertise in the Scriptures, they failed to recognize the Messiah's presence and were unable to receive revelation from the Spirit.

"When the Spirit of truth comes, he will guide you into all truth. He will not speak on his own but will tell you what he has heard. He will tell you about the future. He will bring me glory by telling you whatever he receives from me. All that belongs to the Father is mine; this is why I said, 'The Spirit will tell you whatever he receives from me.'"

John 16:13–15

The Pharisees were so consumed by their egos and desire for prestige that they completely missed the essence of the matter.

So, what is that essence? It is the ultimate message and purpose encapsulated within the book we know as the Bible. This sacred text exists to guide us towards a genuine experience of God and to help us comprehend our significance to Him and the reason for our creation. God desires to reveal to humanity that He is not only the most powerful being of all time, but He has also chosen us to dwell with Him for eternity. He has chosen us to enter into a deep and eternal communion with Him, akin to a divine marriage. The main reason God refers to the church as His bride is because He loves us unconditionally.

As Christ loved the church and gave himself up for her.

Ephesians 5:25 ESV

"And I will be their God, and they shall be my people."

Jeremiah 31:33 NRSV

Once you embark on this magnificent journey, you will gradually start to see through the eyes of the Spirit as Job did. You will say that you had only heard about God before, but now you have seen Him with your own eyes. You will take back everything you have said about God, and humbly kneel down in repentance (see Job 42:5–6).

5

SPIRIT-LED PRAYERS

Our feelings and emotions can easily be turned downward and subjective when we pray. There is nothing wrong with using our emotions if we channel them on the right path. However, we must remember that God is greater than our feelings and emotions (see 1 John 3:20). He knows everything. Our emotions can take us for a long ride to places we never even intended to go.

When prayers are emotionally misguided, they can be dangerous to you and others because they are not Spirit-led. Prayers can become attacks against our brethren instead of prayers to declare God's Word and blessing. We can weep and cry during a prayer (I do it all the time); however, we should do it through His Word by declaring and believing His names, attributes, character, works, promises, and praises to His Name. I see more results in my prayers when I do this.

I used to get extremely emotional to the point where, whenever I prayed, subjective feelings and negative ideas always took control of the prayer, making it difficult for me to believe God's Word or have faith in my situation. But when I bring my mind in alignment with the language of God's Word in prayer, I see and feel how my emotions and mind submit to God's Word. I take captive every thought to make it obedient to Christ. When this happens, I can still weep and cry out to God, but the difference is that my prayer is now from a different position, seated with Christ in the heavens from a higher place of authority. Despite my emotions, I can speak into any situation by declaring what God's Word says and who He is. Then, my faith starts to rise with hope because faith comes by hearing the Word of God.

My subjective thinking and emotions no longer take the lead; instead, the Spirit of God is now in full control. My prayer becomes Spirit-led. Ephesians 6:18 says we need to pray at all times in the Spirit. John 4:23–24 says we must worship in the Spirit, for God is Spirit. Therefore, praying and worshiping in the Spirit is obviously important to God. Praying in the Spirit takes a mental effort to focus on the right Spirit, the person of God, who He is, and His language. We must learn His language by praying His Word, names, attributes, works, character, and promises.

Praying through God's glorious character and nature is a language that makes an instant connection to His throne. This kind of prayer elevates our faith into the supernatural realm. It makes our prayer more about His purpose and will, and less about our ways. It is a way we demonstrate we truly depend on Him as our source to fill our every need. God is our Creator, and He longs to be involved in every aspect of our lives, and as we yield more and more to His nature in our lives, we can get a deeper understanding of who God is and how much we mean to Him.

But not everybody is ready for this, ready to see and hear and act. Isaiah asked what we all ask at one time or another: "Does anyone care, God? Is anyone listening and believing a word of it?" The point is: Before you trust, you have to listen. But unless Christ's Word is preached, there's nothing to listen to.

Romans 10:16–17 MSG

So faith comes from hearing, and hearing through the word of Christ.

Romans 10:17 ESV

When we pray the Word of God, we hear His Word, which helps us see, hear, and act. God reveals Himself to us through His Word. Then as we pray His Word, we do not just hear it but also listen and pay attention. As we meditate on His Word, we absorb His revelation like a sponge and align our Spirit with His Spirit, our mind with Christ's mind, and our will with the Father's perfect will. This empowers us to take His words and put them into action in our lives.

May the Lord help us bear the things He wants to tell us through the Spirit of Truth. May His Spirit continue to guide us into all the truth as He discloses to us what He hears the Father say (see John 16:12–15).

THE PLAN WITH PURPOSE AND CONSISTENCY

Knowing the names of God is going to take a process as your earthly senses are turned into heavenly senses. Your finite mind needs time to process the deep truths of God's nature with His names and attributes. You will need to be intentional by putting a demand on God's power and mercy.

One thing that the woman of the alabaster jar and the woman with the issue of blood, among others, had in common was their persistence and intentional demand for Jesus' power and mercy. What they did was demand the power and mercy of God, which is the key element to actually experiencing Him in a more meaningful way. Being intentional in putting a demand on God really means that you truly want this, you're going for it with all your strength, heart, and mind, and you are not giving up. It's like when you connect your cellphone to the wall outlet to demand that the electricity come into your device. In the same way, you need to intentionally connect to God's Nature with the help of the Spirit so God can give you eyes to contemplate and understand His nature and beauty. Oh Lord, give us eyes to see your glorious Divine Nature!

Your spirit needs to download and synchronize each revelational truth of who God is and how much you mean to Him. This is going to take intentional time in His Presence. Even when you go through all these names of God, you will realize that it is easy to fall into a state of familiarity or over-comfortability. What has helped me is to intentionally go back and revisit His names one by one and give my mind space to process these truths into my spirit, knowing that God wants this more than anyone. If you seek Him with all our heart, He will let you find Him (see Jeremiah 29:13). Each time you get the revelation of one of God's names and attributes, you will encounter the Almighty I AM, and you will know Him deeper.

God's names are deep and versatile; they will always get deeper and deeper in revelation. Don't ever be afraid to receive more revelation of God's nature, no matter how much you might think you know of the Bible. Even if you know the original language of the Bible, you have not arrived yet. There is still so much more to discover about our eternal, Mighty God.

KNOW GOD AS HE KNOWS YOU

Those who take intentional time to know Him deeply are the ones Jesus and heaven know. The day will come when some who think they are Christians will say, "Lord, Lord, in Your Name, *we* performed miracles, prophesied, and did many things for You." But Jesus will tell them, "I don't know you. Depart!" In reality, Jesus knows it all, but when He says, "I don't know you," He says that they operated under strange fire—unauthorized fire or anointing. These people never took the time to truly get to know the will of God and who He is. They were Marthas and did not choose the best part: to get to know Jesus as Mary did. If you don't know God, you will have no deep love for Him and He won't recognize you as an *intimate* worshiper.

This is a very scary thing; thinking of it makes me tremble. We cannot be intimate worshipers of God, let alone revival worshipers, if we operate under strange and unauthorized fire. It is one thing to sing *about* God, and a completely different thing to sing to Him in spirit and truth, genuinely *knowing* the God we are worshiping. This is what I would call worship with true and deep revelation.

When we do this, it takes a whole different meaning, approach, and level of engagement. This creates an automatic connection to the tones of the throne that bring a spirit of freedom to all. We become one with the Spirit of the Lord. The result is a revival in our lives.

This revival comes in levels. Revival starts with you first. The deeper you get to know God's glorious nature and the more united you are with His Spirit, the higher you will be able to take people to levels of revival. You will become a conduit of His glory and power to bring revival not just to your church, family, and sphere of influence but also to your city, state, country, and every corner of the world.

When you know who God is, you will be able to open a whole world of possibilities no matter how old you are or what country you are from. As you intentionally seek to know who God is, you will open your mind to a paradigm shift. Your life will no longer be about just you. It will shift to be completely about Him and what matters most to Him.

This will turn you into a true revival worshiper of the King. It will create a bonding, synchronizing, and alignment where you realize life is more than you thought it was. It is no longer about you or me but all about Him. Everything started with our Creator, and this earthly life will end with Him.

The enemy does not want us to know more about who God is because we would have a paradigm shift and be revived. But as you internalize these names of God to see who He is, you will know the truth, and the truth will set you free to be who God called you to be. Jesus is the only truth; therefore, we need to know more about the Truth—Him.

6

A LETTER FROM GOD

Read the following letter God has written to you. This is an introduction and invitation letter from God. In this letter, He is speaking from His heart directly to your heart. It is Him inviting you on a journey with Him to go deeper, get closer, and get to know Him beyond your present understanding of who He is. It is an invitation to a new and more intentional journey with Him.

Dear Child,

Knowing Me is not like a one-night stand or just one week of a honeymoon. When I enter into a relationship with you, I want to have an intimate relationship with you that will last forever. For this to happen, it cannot stop after the first time you encounter Me. This is a lifetime relationship that goes into eternity. It is a process for you; however, I take it at your pace. My Spirit is gentle and patient.

When you first encountered Me, it was an explosive encounter for you. Perhaps you got to know Me as your Deliverer, your Savior, or your Healer, and you experienced my love for the first time. You thought this was all or just enough; however, that was only your first encounter and experience of who I am. I am so much more! There is so much more I want to show you. What you have experienced of Me so far has only been a drop of a gigantic ocean of Me.

Yes, I am a Deliverer, a Savior, and a Healer, but My glorious nature can show you that I am way more than you have experienced up to this point. I have so much to share with you, but you are not ready until your heart is willing and intentional to get to know Me. You must be hungry, thirsty, and desperate to know Me. You must pursue Me every day intimately like you mean it and like you want it with all your heart.

I want you to have a genuine curiosity and to be interested in learning about who I am, how I operate, what I love and hate, how I communicate, what My decrees are, and why they are important to Me. Also, My mighty works in the history of humankind since day zero, what pleases Me, what matters to Me in the context of eternity, and why. What My character traits and nature are, and My absolute truth, My holy ways, how much I love you, why I love you so much, why I created you, My plans for your future, your final destination, and the reason for your existence. All the answers to these questions can come only as you walk intentionally with Me on this journey, seeking me above all else.

As you keep growing in knowledge and understanding of who I am, your Creator, you will know how much you mean to Me and how wide, deep, and strong My love for you has been since the day I created you. My Child, get to know Me. Come with Me on this journey; I will go with you at your pace. I will hold you by your hand and guide you into our eternal unity in heaven.

With love,

Your Heavenly Father

PART 2

PRAYING AND DECLARING THROUGH THE ATTRIBUTES OF GOD

INTRODUCTION TO THE THEMED PRAYERS

In order to fully benefit from the prayers and declarations of God's names and attributes in this book, you will need intentionality, which will help you develop consistency.

There are twenty-four prayers in this book with over 3,000 names and attributes of God. These prayers are a dialogue between you and God. You can pray those prayers in the order they are in this book, or you can choose the prayer you feel you need for your current situation. Then, you can choose one to three of the names of God who jumped out of the page and ministered to you most. Write them down, read them three to seven times, and meditate on them throughout the day. At the end of the day, take ten to thirty minutes to read the prayer you chose. Make the prayer you chose on that day your prayer and make it from your heart. You don't need to finish it if you cannot, as some are longer and so saturated with God's names and attributes that it can feel like a lot at the beginning. However, you can stay on that same prayer for a week, a month, or until you are ready to go to the next. And, of course, you will have to come back to that prayer at one point or another afterward. Just go as far as your hungry spirit leads you and as far as your understanding can handle.

When you don't understand a Name or attribute of God, read the Scripture next to it. Dig into it, research it, and most of all, ask the Holy Spirit to help you and reveal it to you (see 1 Corinthians 2:9–10).

Another way to do this is to choose one of the twenty-four prayer lists of names and attributes, go into a quiet place every morning, and meditate on one Name of God from that list. Then meditate throughout the morning on that one Name. At noon, meditate on another Name of God. And again, at dinner time, meditate on another Name of God for the rest of the evening. Let it permeate your heart and mind. Finally, right before bed, take at least ten to fifteen minutes to meditate on the three names you chose that day. It would be a great investment of time to write in your journal something the Holy Spirit revealed to you through those three names during the day. Do this as a habit, and the Holy Spirit will start to reveal to you more and more who God is.

Then, when you go through challenging times, trials, or tribulations, you will be able to understand and be aligned with the nature of God and who you have gotten to know Him to be. It will start clicking in. The Holy Spirit will bring just what you need into your mind because you have intentionally deposited into your spirit who God is. You might not be able to memorize all those names and Scriptures, but the Holy Spirit will remind you of them when you need them. It will become your spiritual arsenal against the enemy of your soul.

Once you are intentional and start with list of the names of God, you might not even get past the first Name of God for a few days. Like it happened to me with the Name "I AM WHO I AM," it literally melted me in tears of awe and reverence as the Lord gave me eyes to see and understand more of this Name. It was so profoundly impacting that I could barely process it. I could not go to the second Name for more than a week. I just kept pounding on the Name "I AM WHO I AM," and it was so deep that I am still processing it. I believe this one is the deepest in the revelation of God's nature.

When you know who God is, it's like putting wood onto the fire on the altar. The wood is your intentional effort to know God. When you align and synchronize your mind to God's nature, names, and attributes, you will start getting a deeper revelation of who God is, and your Christian life will be easier to live. God always reveals an aspect of Himself in your trials and troubled times so you can know Him better. You will be able to overcome difficulties more easily because now you are clothed with who He is. You are inside of Him, and He is inside of you.

You will get the firsthand revelation that all is good, perfect, pleasing, holy, and pure inside of Him. You will be able to see life through a different lens—through the lens of God and who He is. You will experience a paradigm shift. Then, fear will have no place in your life, because once you know Him, this truth will set you free to believe and trust in Him completely. You will feel secure in how much the God you serve loves and cares for you.

You will understand how all-powerful and glorious He is and will never want to live independently of Him. You will never want to depend on your strength or understanding for life. You will understand that everything good and bad that happens has a purpose and a destiny, that with the all-powerful and all-knowing God, there is no such thing as an accident. Our God is in control. You will discover how much power you have in your life because of Him since you've taken the time to know Him.

Before we delve into the names of God, you need to understand some very important things. You will find twenty-four powerful prayers in this section. You will have one prayer theme, followed by some featured Scripture verses to ponder. Then, there will be a list of names and attributes of God, along with verses for further study of each of God's names. The chapter will end with a powerful prayer that incorporates all the names mentioned on the list in that chapter.

This book's list is not an exhaustive list of all the available names and attributes of God; there is so much more to discover about Him, and this will be a lifelong adventure until we see Him face-to-face in heaven. However, it is a great start for this new journey. A few names and attributes of God were purposefully repeated in various chapters where it was appropriate.

I have intentionally broken the grammatical rules in this book to make a point about the person of God with a reverential tone. When the names of God are mentioned, or a word refers to God, it is purposely capitalized to emphasize who He is. For example: "God, the Creator" instead of "God, the creator," or "The One who holds all creation together" instead of "The one who holds all creation together," or "God, the Maker of all things, instead of "God, the maker of all things," And so on, you will see many uppercase letters where I want to emphasize the Deity of God.

Again, as I said before, these prayers are like a dialogue between you and God, where you are talking directly to God. So, as you begin reading the powerful names and attributes of God, keep in mind the words *You are* before each phrase. For example, "*You are* the Source of all true knowledge and wisdom," or "*You are* the God who cannot be surprised," or "*You are* God, the Alpha and the Omega."

Enjoy your new journey as you intentionally start getting to know God's nature in a deeper, more intimate way. And let's bring revival together as we pray, worship, and declare God's names, attributes, truths, works, beauty, and promises into our lives and the lives of those around us. Let's make the All-Powerful and Almighty I AM famous!

7

THE FATHER

So you have not received a spirit that makes you fearful slaves. Instead, you received God's Spirit when he adopted you as his own children. Now we call him, "Abba, Father." For his Spirit joins with our spirit to affirm that we are God's children.

Romans 8:15–16

And because we are his children, God has sent the Spirit of his Son into our hearts, prompting us to call out, "Abba, Father." Now you are no longer a slave but God's own child. And since you are his child, God has made you his heir.

Galatians 4:6–7

You are:

1. The Almighty *I AM WHO I AM* (Exodus 3:13–14)
2. God my Father (Ephesians 4:6)

3. God, Abba, Father (Mark 14:36; Galatians 4:6–7; Romans 8:15–16)
4. Abba Papa, the forgiving God (Isaiah 1:18–19; Micah 7:18)
5. God, my everlasting Father (Isaiah 9:6)
6. The God and Father of all (Ephesians 4:6)
7. God, the Father to the orphans (Psalm 68:5)
8. God, my loving Daddy (Romans 8:15)
9. God, the Father of the fatherless (Psalm 68:5)
10. The Father of abundant blessings (John 1:16; 2 Corinthians 9:8; John 10:10)
11. The Father of mercies (2 Corinthians 1:3–4)
12. The Father, tender and compassionate to those who fear You (Psalm 103:13)
13. The merciful and compassionate Father (Luke 6:36)
14. God, the righteous Father (John 17:25)
15. God, my heavenly and eternal Father (Isaiah 9:6)
16. God, the Father, the Vine Gardener (John 15:1)
17. The Father who is Spirit (John 4:23–24)
18. The Father who seeks true worshipers (John 4:23–24)
19. The Father who seeks worship in spirit and truth from me (John 4:23–24)
20. God, the Father of my spirit who gives life forever (Hebrews 12:9)
21. God, the Father of glory (Ephesians 1:17)
22. The Father who did not spare Your own Son (Romans 8:32)
23. Father, the great and dreadful God (Malachi 4:5)
24. The God of all families—present, past, and future (Exodus 12:14; Joel 1:3; Ephesians 3:21)
25. The Godhead of the divine Trinity, three in one (1 John 5:7)
26. God, the Father, Son, and Holy Spirit (Matthew 28:19)
27. The One and Only God (1 Corinthians 8:6)
28. God, the Father of Israel (Jeremiah 31:9)
29. The Father, the Author of eternal life (John 3:16)
30. The Father who never leaves or abandons me (Deuteronomy 31:6; Psalm 138:8)
31. The Father who I can always rely on (1 Peter 5:7)
32. The Father who cares for me (1 Peter 5:7)

33. The Father who is kind to me (1 Peter 5:10)
34. The Father who called me to share in Your eternal glory through Christ Jesus (1 Peter 5:10)
35. The Father who will restore, perfect, strengthen and establish me (1 Peter 5:10)
36. The God of Abraham, Isaac, and Jacob, Your memorial Name to all generations (Acts 7:32; Exodus 3:6; 15; Matthew 22:32)
37. God, the Father who knows me and chose me long ago (1 Peter 1:1)
38. The Father of great mercy (1 Peter 1:3)
39. God, the Father of my Lord, Jesus Christ (2 Corinthians 11:31; 1 Peter 1:3; Colossians 1:3)
40. The Father who reveals to me who Jesus is (Matthew 16:17)
41. Father, God of the gentiles (Romans 3:29)
42. Father, God of the Hebrews (Exodus 5:3; 7:16; Exodus 3:18)
43. God, the Father who teaches me Your Word, which is truth (John 17:17)
44. The God of Moses (Numbers 12:13; 27:22; Deuteronomy 34:5–8)
45. The Lord, tender and compassionate Father to those who fear You (Psalm 103:13)
46. God, the Father who makes me holy by Your truth (John 17:17)
47. The God of all generations (Matthew 1:17)
48. God, our Father in heaven (Matthew 6:9)
49. Father God, with a holy Name (Matthew 6:9)
50. The heavenly Father who forgives my sins (Matthew 6:14)
51. The heavenly Father who feeds the birds (Matthew 6:26)
52. The Father who values me and cares for me (Matthew 6:26–30)
53. The heavenly Father who knows all of my needs (Matthew 6:32)
54. God, the Lord of the harvest (Matthew 9:38)
55. God, the only One who can destroy both soul and body in hell (Matthew 10:28)
56. The Father who knows everything (Matthew 10:29)
57. The Father, Lord of heaven and earth (Matthew 11:25)
58. The One who answers my prayers (Matthew 18:20)
59. The One who is present with me (Matthew 18:20)
60. The Father who commands me to forgive (Matthew 18:35)

61. The One who made the male and female genders (Matthew 19:4)
62. The One who originated marriage between one man and one woman (Genesis 2:24; Mark 10:7–9; Matthew 19:8)
63. The only One who is Good eternally (Matthew 19:17; Jeremiah 33:11)
64. The God of the living, not the dead (Matthew 22:32)
65. The God of redemption (Genesis 3:15)
66. The God who took Enoch with You because he walked close to You (Genesis 5:23–24)
67. The God who empowers me to be fruitful and multiply (Genesis 9:1)
68. The One who makes me a heroic warrior (Genesis 10:8–9)
69. The God who blesses those who bless me and curses those who mistreat me (Genesis 12:3)
70. The One who declares that all the families on earth will be blessed through Abraham's seed (Genesis 12:3)
71. The Lord who gives us the impossible (Genesis 18:14)
72. The Lord who changes names according to Your plans (Genesis 17:5; 32:28)
73. God, *El Berith*, the God of the Covenants[1] (Genesis 9:12; 17:2–7)
74. The Lord, my *Peniel* experience (Genesis 32:30)
75. God, the Shepherd of all my days (Genesis 48:15–16)
76. God, the Almighty who bless me with blessings of the heavens above (Genesis 49:25–26)
77. The Ancient One who lives and reigns forever (Daniel 7:9–14)
78. The Father who loves me dearly (John 16:23–27)
79. The Father who rescues me and helps me (Psalm 124:6–8)
80. The God of the Angel-Armies (Malachi 1:6–14)
81. The heavenly Father who is perfect (Matthew 5:48)
82. The heavenly Father who gives me good and perfect gifts (James 1:17; Matthew 7:11)
83. The Father who has chosen me as Your prized possession (James 1:18)
84. The Father of the heavenly lights (James 1:17)
85. The God who speaks in righteousness (Isaiah 63:1)

86. One God and Father of all, who is over me, in me, and living through me (Ephesians 4:6)
87. The Father who blesses me when I obey (Deuteronomy 28:1–2)
88. The Father who gives me a land of blessing (Deuteronomy 27:3)
89. The Father who never breaks Your promises (Deuteronomy 27:3)
90. God, the Father of rain (Job 38:28; Leviticus 26:4; Jeremiah 5:24)
91. Father—You are, You were, and You will forever be the Lord Almighty One (Psalm 90:2, 48:14)
92. The God who knows the laws of the universe and use them to regulate the earth (Job 38:33)
93. The good Father (Luke 11:11–13)
94. The generous and compassionate Father (Psalm 126:1–6)
95. The Lord my God, Your Name is Jealous (Exodus 34:14; Deuteronomy 5:9)
96. The One who has justified me freely by Your grace through Christ Jesus (Romans 3:23–24; 8:33)
97. God, my *JAH* (Exodus 15:2)
98. God, *Jehovah* (*YHWH*), the I AM (Exodus 6:2–3; 3:14)
99. God, the One who transferred me into the kingdom of Your dear Son (Colossians 1:13–14)
100. The Father who leaves the ninety-nine for the one lost (Matthew 18:12–14)
101. The Father who delights in me (Psalm 149:4)
102. The Lord who crowns the humble with victory (Psalm 149:4)
103. God, *Jehovah-Elohai*—My God (Psalm 18:2; 31:14)
104. The One who gives children as a gift and a reward (Psalm 127:3)
105. The God whose way is perfect (Psalm 18:30; Matthew 5:48)
106. The LORD with a flawless Word (Psalm 18:30)
107. The God who never changes or casts a shifting shadow (James 1:17)
108. The Father who made my heart, and understands it (Psalm 33:15; Psalm 139:23–24)
109. The gigantic God, Giant of giants (1 John 4:4; Deuteronomy 10:17)
110. The God who goes ahead of me and will always be there with me when I arrive (Deuteronomy 31:8)

111. The Father who takes away my fears (Psalm 91:1–7; 2 Timothy 1:7; Joshua 1:9)
112. My Abba Papa, Father, and Daddy (John 1:12; Romans 8:15–16; 2 Corinthians 6:18; Galatians 4:6–7)
113. My Defender and Avenger (Deuteronomy 32:35)
114. The God who has prepared for me things that are unseen, unthinkable, and unheard of (1 Corinthians 2:9–10)
115. The Lord who weighs my heart (Proverbs 21:2)
116. My Father, the Potter, I am formed by Your hand (Isaiah 64:8)
117. The Father who knows and sees what I do in private (Matthew 6:18)
118. The One who inhabits eternity (Isaiah 57:15)
119. The LORD of heaven's armies, Israel's glorious Crown (Isaiah 28:5)
120. The God of the Hebrews (Exodus 5:3)
121. The God with seven eyes who searches and sees everything on this earth (Zechariah 4:10)
122. The God who caused us to be born again to a living hope through the resurrection of Jesus (1 Peter 1:3)
123. The Daddy of the Prodigal son (Luke 15:11-32)

A PRAYER TO THE FATHER

Father God, Abba Papa, I come before Your mighty throne in Jesus' Name. God, I recognize You are my everlasting Father and the God and Father of all. You are a perfect Father. You are the merciful and compassionate Father. I know You are the righteous Father. God the Father of the fatherless and Father to the orphans, my Daddy.

Father, I want to always bring a smile to Your face. I want to please You and do Your will. I want to cause You joy and want You to be happy that You created me. I want to depend on You as my Abba Papa. I want to bless, honor, and live for You, O Father. I want to be one with Your Spirit. God, You are the Father who joyfully sings over me with love. You made my heart, and You understand it completely. You delight in me. Father, I know You are Spirit, and I must approach You and worship You in spirit and truth. You are the Father of our spirits who gives life forever. The Father who leaves the ninety-nine for the one lost.

Father, Your way is perfect, and You are perfect in everything You do. You are the God who never changes or casts a shifting shadow. You are the LORD with a flawless word. You are my heavenly and eternal Abba Papa, Father. The Father, who is always flawless and bestows on me excellent and perfect gifts. The One who gives children as a gift and a reward. You are the God of all families—present, past, and future. You are the Ancient One who lives and reigns forever.

You are the Father who never leaves or abandons me from day one of my creation. You thought of me before I even existed. You are my loving Daddy. God, You are the Father who knows me and chose me long ago. You are the Father who knows and sees what I do in private, and You are my rewarder.

You are the Father God who goes before me and will be with me tomorrow when I arrive. You are my dear Father who takes away my fears. You are my Defender and Avenger. You are the God who has prepared the unseen, unthinkable, and unheard of for me.

You are the Father who I can rely on always. The Father who values me and cares for me. You perfectly care for me, and You are kind to me. You are the heavenly Father who knows all of my needs and gives me good gifts. The Father who loves me dearly. You are the Father who has chosen me as Your prized possession.

You are the Father of great mercy who restores, comforts, perfects, strengthens, and establishes me. You are the Lord, tender and compassionate, and a Father to those who fear You. Abba Papa, You are the forgiving and gracious God. You are the Daddy of the prodigal son. My heavenly Father who forgives my sins and commands me to forgive. Father God, You answer my prayers. You are always present with me. You are the Shepherd of all my days. God, the Almighty who blesses me with blessings of the heavens above. You are the God who blesses those who bless me, and no one can curse me because of Your blessing on my life.

Father, You teach me Your Word, which is truth; You make me holy by Your truth. God, You are the Father in heaven, with a holy Name. The only One who is good eternally. The Father and Lord who gives us the impossible. The Lord who changes names according to Your plans and will.

Father, You are the Great I AM WHO I AM. The One who inhabits eternity. You are *Jehovah (YHWH)*. My *JAH*, God, *Jehovah-Elohim*—My God. The God of Covenants. Oh, Lord my God, Your Name is Jealous. The Lord, my *Peniel* experience. Oh, Abba Daddy, I am the clay, and You are the Potter; I am formed by Your divine hands. You are the Lord who delights in me, for I am Your creation. No matter what I have to face tomorrow, You will go before me and be with me when I arrive at that situation. I have nothing to fear because I know You will not abandon me. Daddy, You are the gigantic God, the Giant of giants, the One who makes me a heroic warrior through Your Spirit. You crown the humble with victory. You are the Father who leaves the ninety-nine for the one lost. The One who transferred me into the kingdom of Your dear Son. You are the One who has justified me freely by Your grace through Christ Jesus. The God who took Enoch with You because he walked close to You. You are One God and Father of all, who is over me, in me, and living through me.

Father, You give children as a gift and a reward. You are the same God of Abraham, Isaac, and Jacob, whom You have designated as Your memorial Name for all generations. You are the same Father and God of Moses. Father God of the gentiles and the Hebrews. You are the same Father and God throughout all generations. The One who declared all the families on earth blessed through Abraham's seed.

Father, You made the male and female genders in the beginning. You are the One who originated and established a marriage between one man and one woman. Father, You are the Creator, Designer, Originator, and Establisher of the heavens and the earth and everything in them. You are the One who established all the laws of the universe and used them to regulate the world. The God who empowers me to be fruitful and multiply. Father, You bless me when I obey You. You give me the land of blessing. You give me Your wealth. Father, thank You because You never break Your promises. You are a good Father. Father, You are, You were, and You will forever be the Lord Almighty One, King of the universe.

The Father, Lord of heaven and earth. God, You are the Father of the heavenly lights, the Vine Gardener, the Father of rain. You are God, the Lord of the harvest. You are the heavenly Father who feeds the birds. Father, I trust You because You are my Provider. You have provided for me since I was in my mother's womb. The Father who created all the lights in the heavens and galaxies. God, the Father of glory. The Father who knows everything.

The God of redemption. The Father of my Lord Jesus Christ, the Author of eternal life. The Father who did not spare His own Son to save me. The tender and compassionate Father to those who fear You. The Father who called me to share in His eternal glory through Christ Jesus. Father, You revealed who Jesus is to me. You are the living God who is not dead. You always speak in righteousness. Father God, You are the only One with the power to destroy both soul and body in hell or bring us to You in heaven.

You are Deity, the One and Only God, and the Father of Israel. The LORD of heaven's armies, and Israel's glorious Crown. You are the God and the Lord of the Angel-Armies. Father, You are a great and dreadful God, the Godhead of the divine Trinity. You are three in One—God the Father, Jesus the Son, and Your gracious Holy Spirit. In Jesus' Name, amen.

---

1. W. Murray Severance and Terry Eddinger, *That's Easy for You to Say: Your Quick Guide to Pronouncing Bible Names* (Nashville: Broadman & Holman, 1997), 170.

8

HIS SON, JESUS CHRIST

Therefore, God elevated him to the place of highest honor and gave him the Name above all other names, that at the Name of Jesus every knee should bow, in heaven and on earth and under the earth, and every tongue declare that Jesus Christ is Lord, to the glory of God the Father.

Philippians 2:9–11

I once thought these things were valuable, but now I consider them worthless because of what Christ has done. Yes, everything else is worthless when compared with the infinite value of knowing Christ Jesus, my Lord. For his sake, I have discarded everything else, counting it all as garbage, so that I could gain Christ and become one with him. . . . I want to know Christ and experience the mighty power that raised him from the dead.

Philippians 3:7–10

You are:

1. The *I AM WHO I AM* (Exodus 3:14)
2. Jesus, the *I AM* (John 8:58)
3. Jesus, the VERB (John 1:1)
4. Jesus, the WORD that already existed (John 1:1)
5. Christ, the Hope of Glory (Colossians 1:27)
6. Jesus, the most powerful Name like none other (Acts 4:12; John 17:11)
7. *Yeshua*, Name above all names throughout all times (Philippians 2:9)
8. Jesus Christ, my living Hope (Colossians 1:27)
9. Jesus, the resurrecting power behind Lazarus (John 11)
10. Jesus, the One who can reverse anything without limit (John 11)
11. Jesus, the One who says, "This will not end in death" (John 11)
12. Jesus, the One who holds the keys of death and the grave (Revelation 1:18)
13. Jesus, the One who is alive forever and ever (Revelation 1:18)
14. Jesus, whose Name is alive eternally (Luke 24:23; Revelation 1:18)
15. Jesus, the Resurrection and the Life (John 11:25)
16. Jesus Christ, the Power of Resurrection and Life (John 11:25–26; Romans 6:9)
17. Jesus, the One who resurrects the dead (Matthew 8:25; 27:52; John 11:25; Daniel 12:2)
18. Christ, the One who rose from the dead (Luke 24:6–7; Romans 10:9)
19. Jesus Christ, the Resurrection and Life (John 11:25–26; Romans 6:9)
20. The God who rescues me from death (Psalm 68:19)
21. Jesus Christ, who gives us victory over sin and death by Your power (1 Corinthians 15:56)
22. Jesus Christ, the One who died and rose again (2 Corinthians 5:15)
23. Jesus, the One who died for my sins (Romans 5:8)
24. Jesus the Christ, in whose powerful Name I find life (John 20:31)

25. Jesus, the Name that brings freedom (Mark 16:17–18)
26. Jesus, whose Name is the anointing over my life (1 John 2:20, 27)
27. Jesus, whose Name is my security and protection (Psalm 121:7; John 17:12)
28. God, You are all Your names (Proverbs 18:10)
29. The One with a majestic Name (Psalm 8)
30. God, the One with endless names and attributes (Romans 1:20)
31. Jesus, whose Name is power and hope (Acts 3:6)
32. God, whose names are beyond the letters of the alphabet (John 21:25; Philippians 2:9)
33. The Commander of the Great Commission (Mark 16:14; Matthew 28:18–20)
34. Jesus, whose Name and words are sweeter than honey (Psalm 119:103)
35. The God with a Name that is Holy (Psalm 103:1)
36. The One who is interested in hearing what I say about You (Matthew 16:15)
37. Jesus, the Incarnate Truth (1 John 5:6)
38. Jesus Christ, the Absolute Truth (John 14:6; 8:32)
39. Jesus, the Son of Man (Matthew 12:8; 24:30; Daniel 7:13)
40. Jesus, the Lord over the Sabbath (Matthew 12:8; Mark 2:28)
41. Jesus, the Farmer who plants the good seed (Matthew 13:37)
42. The Son of Man who sits upon Your glorious throne (Matthew 19:28)
43. Jesus, the One who speaks words of spirit and life over me (John 6:63)
44. The Lord, the High and Exalted One who inhabits eternity (Isaiah 57:15)
45. The Lord whose Name is holy (Isaiah 57:15)
46. The Beloved whose Name is like the spreading aromatic fragrance (Song of Solomon 1:3)
47. The Lord whose Name is lovely and worthy to be celebrated with music (Psalm 135:3)
48. The One who should be praised with dancing and musical instruments (Psalm 149:3)
49. The Lord, the most beautiful Name (Psalm 27:4)

50. *Jehovah-Elohim Yeshua*—the Lord God of my Salvation, Jesus (Psalm 29:3; Matthew 16:16)
51. Jesus, the Son of God (Matthew 14:33; Matthew 8:29)
52. Jesus, the Son of the living God (Matthew 26:63; 16:16)
53. Jesus, the Christ (Matthew 16:16)
54. *Yeshua Hamashiach*, Jesus our Messiah (Matthew 1:16)
55. The Scepter of Righteousness and Uprightness (Hebrews 1:8)
56. Jesus Christ, who rules with power and justice (Psalm 45:6)
57. The Lover of righteousness who hates evil (Psalm 45:7)
58. Jesus, the *Great I AM* (Revelation 1:8)
59. Jesus Christ, the eternal King of the nations forever and ever (Psalm 10:6; 1 Timothy 1:17)
60. God, the great King of all centuries past, present, and future (1 Timothy 1:17)
61. God, the King of the saints (Revelation 6)
62. Jesus, the King of Zion (Matthew 21:5)
63. Jesus, King of the Jews (Matthew 2:2; 27:37; John 19:21)
64. Jesus, the Prince and Ruler of the kings of the earth (Revelation 1:5)
65. Christ, the head over all rule and authority (Colossians 2:9–10)
66. The One who rules with a rod of iron (Revelation 19:15)
67. Jesus, the Child in the manger (Luke 2:12)
68. Jesus, the Lord before whom every knee shall bow and every tongue shall give praise (Romans 14:11; Philippians 2:9–11)
69. Jesus, the One who will not disgrace those who trust in You (1 Peter 2:6)
70. Jesus, the Minister of the sanctuary (Hebrews 8:2)
71. Jesus, the Minister of the true tabernacle (Hebrews 8:2)
72. Jesus, the Light that enlightens the gentiles (Luke 2:32)
73. Jesus, the great High Priest (Hebrews 4:14; 10:21)
74. Jesus, the Plant of Renown (Ezekiel 34:29)
75. Jesus, the great Gift of God's unmerited favor (Romans 5:15)
76. Jesus Christ, my Lord (John 13:13)
77. Jesus, the Star out of Jacob (Numbers 24:17)
78. Jesus, the Apostle and High Priest of my profession (Hebrews 3:1)
79. Jesus, the First-Begotten of the dead (Revelation 1:5)

80. Jesus, the firstborn of every creature (Colossians 1:15)
81. Jesus, the Anointed One (2 Corinthians 1:21; Daniel 9:26)
82. Jesus, the Heir of all things (Hebrews 1:2)
83. God, the Rose of Sharon (Song of Solomon 2:1)
84. God, the Lily of the Valleys (Song of Solomon 2:1)
85. Lord, Jesus of Nazareth (Matthew 26:71; John 18:5)
86. Jesus, the exact representation of God's glorious nature (Hebrews 1:3)
87. Jesus, the image of the invisible God (Colossians 1:15)
88. Jesus, the Forerunner (Hebrews 6:20)
89. Jesus, the Mediator of a new and better covenant (Hebrews 8:6)
90. Jesus, the Mediator of grace (Hebrews 9:15; 12:24 1 Timothy 2:5; 1 John 2:1)
91. Jesus, the Promise of eternal inheritance (Hebrews 9:15)
92. Jesus, the Founder, Author, Perfecter, and Finisher of my faith (Hebrews 12:2)
93. Jesus, the Prince of life (Acts 3:15)
94. Jesus, the *Rabboni* (John 20:16)
95. Jesus, the Rabbi, Son of God, the King of Israel (John 1:49; Matthew 27:11)
96. Jesus, the great Prince of Peace, prophesied by Isaiah (Isaiah 9:26)
97. Jesus, the Prince of princes (Daniel 8:25)
98. Jesus, the good Shepherd who lays down His life for the sheep (John 10:11)
99. The Shepherd who knows Your sheep and they know You (John 10:14)
100. God, the Shepherd, and Bishop of my soul (1 Peter 2:25)
101. God, the Prince of the shepherds (1 Peter 5:4)
102. The Chief Shepherd (1 Peter 5:4)
103. The Shepherd of Your people Israel (Matthew 2:7)
104. Jesus, the Great Shepherd (1 Peter 5:4)
105. Jesus, the Prophet (John 4:19)
106. Jesus, the Promised One (Isaiah 25:8–9)
107. Jesus Christ, the last Adam (Romans 5:14; 1 Corinthians 15:45–46)
108. Jesus, the Light of the world (John 8:12)

109. The Light of the nations (Isaiah 42:6)
110. Jesus, a sign from God (Luke 2:34)
111. Jesus, the true Bread of Life from heaven (John 6:32; John 6:48, 51)
112. Jesus, the Living Bread who came down from heaven (John 6:51–59)
113. God, the Living Bread who makes me live forever (John 6:51)
114. Jesus, the Sower and Lord of the harvest (Luke 10:2; Matthew 9:38)
115. Jesus, the Manna who descended from heaven (John 3:13)
116. God, the beloved in Songs of Songs (Revelation 19:7; Song of Solomon 6:3)
117. Jesus, the God who comes from above (John 3:31)
118. Jesus, the One who comes in the Name of the Lord (Matthew 21:9; Matthew 23:39)
119. Jesus, the beloved Son of God Most High (Mark 3:17; Matthew 3:17; 17:5)
120. Jesus, the Son of the Most High (Luke 1:32)
121. God, *El Elyon*—the Lord, Most High God, and Exalted (Genesis 14:17–22; Psalm 78:35; Daniel 4:34; Acts 16:17)
122. Jesus, the chosen One of God (Luke 23:35)
123. Jesus, the Verb, in the beginning (John 1:1)
124. My Beloved One (Song of Solomon 6:1–3)
125. The Lamb and Owner of the Book of Life (Revelation 13:8)
126. The Lamb of God who takes away the sin of the world (John 1:29)
127. The God from above; You are not of this world (John 8:23)
128. Jesus of Galilee (Matthew 26:69)
129. Jesus, the true grapevine (John 15:1–8)
130. Christ, the risen One (Matthew 28:5)
131. Jesus Christ, the First to rise from the dead (Acts 26:23)
132. The Lord, my Hallelujah (Psalm 146:1–10)
133. The Lord God Most High and Exalted (Psalm 92:8)
134. God, the One who gathers (Isaiah 56:8)
135. Jesus, the righteous Branch of the Lord (Isaiah 4:2; Zechariah 3:8; 6:12; Jeremiah 23:5)
136. Jesus, the Salt of the earth (Matthew 5:13)

137. Jesus, the Master (Mark 13:1)
138. Jesus, the Pearl of Great Price (Matthew 13:46)
139. Lord, the God of the New Covenant (Jeremiah 31:31–34; Isaiah 42:6)
140. The One who is the Amen (Revelation 3:14)
141. God, the Most Famous One (Philippians 2:9; 1 Kings 8:41–42; Nehemiah 9:10; Zechariah 8:22–23; Psalm 135:13)
142. Lord, my God; You are an amazing God (Psalm 68:35)
143. Jesus, *Immanuel*—God with us (Isaiah 7:14, Isaiah 8:8–10, Matthew 1:23)
144. Lord, the great, Infallible Teacher (John 3:2)
145. Jesus, the One with the most precious blood (1 Peter 1:19; Luke 22:20; Acts 20:28)
146. Jesus, the True Vine (John 15:1)
147. The One I must abide in (John 15:4)
148. The One who makes me fruitful (John 15:4)
149. Lord, the One who rescued me from the kingdom of darkness (Colossians 1:13–14)
150. Jesus, the One who purchased my freedom and forgave my sins (Colossians 1:13–14)
151. Christ, the visible image of the invisible God (Colossians 1:15)
152. Christ, the One who existed before anything was created (Colossians 1:15–17)
153. The One who holds all creation together (Colossians 1:17)
154. Christ, supreme over all creation (Colossians 1:15)
155. Christ, supreme over all who rise from the dead (Colossians 1:18)
156. Christ, the First in everything (Colossians 1:18)
157. Christ, the Head of the body (Colossians 1:18)
158. Christ, the Head of every man (1 Corinthians 11:3)
159. Christ, the Head of the church (Colossians 1:18)
160. The Christ, the One risen from the dead (Luke 24:6–7; Mark 16:6; Romans 10:9)
161. Jesus, the only Name by which I must be saved (Acts 4:12)
162. The Lord who jealously guards the reputation of Your holy Name (Ezekiel 39:25)
163. Christ, my spiritual Rock from whom I drink (1 Corinthians 10:4)

164. God of truth and without iniquity (Deuteronomy 32:4)
165. Jesus, who finished the work the Father gave You (John 17:4)
166. Jesus, the One who brought glory to the Father here on earth (John 17:4)
167. Jesus, the Son of God who came to show us the true God (1 John 5:20)
168. Jesus, who has given me understanding so I may know the Father (1 John 5:20)
169. Jesus, the true God and Eternal Life (1 John 5:20)
170. Christ Jesus, the One who freed me from the law of sin and death (Romans 8:2)
171. The One who crowned me with glory and honor and gave me authority over all things (Hebrews 2:7–8)
172. Jesus, the One who reigns forever, Your kingdom has no end (Luke 1:33)
173. Jesus, the One with the most powerful substance, Your blood (Ephesians 1:7; Acts 20:28)
174. Jesus Christ, who existed from the beginning (1 John 2:13)
175. Christ Jesus, the Wisdom of God (1 Corinthians 1:24, 30)
176. Christ Jesus, the Redemption from God (1 Corinthians 1:30)
177. Christ Jesus, my Redeemer (Romans 3:23–24)
178. Christ Jesus, the Power of God (1 Corinthians 1:24)
179. Christ Jesus, in whom all the treasures of wisdom and knowledge are hidden (Colossians 2:3)
180. Jesus, the Sacrifice that atones my sins (1 John 2:1–2)
181. The Holy One who has given me Your Spirit without limit (1 John 2:20)
182. Jesus Christ, appointed in ages past, at the very first, before the earth began (Proverbs 8:23)
183. Jesus Christ, born before the oceans were created, before the springs bubbled forth their waters (Proverbs 8:24)
184. Jesus Christ, born before the mountains and hills were formed (Proverbs 8:25)
185. Jesus Christ, who existed before the earth was made, and the first handfuls of soil (Proverbs 8:26)

186. Jesus Christ, You were there when God established the heavens and when He drew the horizon on the oceans (Proverbs 8:28)
187. Jesus Christ, You were there when God set the clouds above and established springs deep in the earth (Proverbs 8:28)
188. Jesus Christ, You were there when God set the limits of the seas and marked off the earth's foundations (Proverbs 8:29)
189. Jesus Christ, the Architect at the Father's side (Proverbs 8:30)
190. Jesus Christ, the Father's constant delight and joy (Proverbs 8:30; Matthew 3:17)
191. Jesus Christ, who rejoiced with the world the Father created (Proverbs 8:31)
192. Jesus Christ, who rejoiced with the human family (Proverbs 8:31)
193. Jesus Christ, my Joy, all who follow Your ways are joyful (Proverbs 8:32)
194. Lord, the Blesser of those who listen, watch, and wait for You (Proverbs 8:34)
195. Jesus Christ, the Life and Favor from the Father (Proverbs 8:35)
196. Jesus, the Nazarene (Matthew 2:23)
197. The One who baptizes me with Holy Spirit and fire (Matthew 2:11)
198. Jesus, the Preacher (Matthew 4:17)
199. Jesus, the One who makes us fishers of men (Matthew 3:19)
200. Jesus, the Teacher (Matthew 4:23)
201. Jesus, the Proclaimer of the gospel of the kingdom (Matthew 4:23)
202. Jesus, the Healer of every kind of disease (Matthew 4:24)
203. Jesus, the Blesser (Matthew 5:3–12)
204. Jesus, the fulfillment of the law (Matthew 5:17)
205. Jesus, the Teacher with real authority (Matthew 7:28)
206. Jesus, the One who is willing to heal me (Matthew 8:3)
207. Jesus, the One who heals all sickness (Matthew 8:16–17)
208. Jesus, the One who casts out evil spirits (Matthew 8:16, 32)
209. Jesus, the One whom even the winds and waves obey (Matthew 8:28)
210. Jesus, the Giver of authority (Matthew 10:1)
211. Jesus, greater than the temple (Matthew 12:5)
212. Jesus, the Name of hope to the world (Matthew 12:21)

213. Jesus, the Storyteller (Matthew 13:3)
214. Jesus, the Giver of understanding (Matthew 13:11–12)
215. Jesus, who walks on water (Matthew 14:25)
216. Jesus, the One who honors my faith (Matthew 15:28)
217. Jesus, the Healer of all the sick (Matthew 15:30)
218. Jesus, who cares for our human needs (Matthew 15:32)
219. Jesus, the One who fed the 4,000-plus people (Matthew 15:37–38)
220. Jesus Christ, the Messiah (John 4:26; Matthew 1:1; 16:16)
221. The Lord who was born in Bethlehem, the City of David (Luke 2:11)
222. Christ, the Savior who was born in the City of David (Luke 2:11)
223. Jesus, the Root and Descendant/Offspring of David and Abraham (Matthew 1:1; Revelation 5:5; 22:16)
224. Jesus, the Seed of Abraham (John 8:33)
225. The Promised Seed (Genesis 3:15; John 7:42: Isaiah 25:8–9)
226. Jesus, the Son of Abraham (Matthew 1:1)
227. Jesus, the Root and Rod out of the stem of Jesse (Isaiah 11:1)
228. Jesus, the Son of David (Matthew 1:1; 9:27–28; 15:22; 20:30; 21:9, 15)
229. Jesus, the Lion of the Tribe of Judah (Revelation 5:5; Hosea 11:10)
230. Jesus, the One born of a virgin (Matthew 1:23; Luke 1:26–38)
231. The Heir to David's throne, who won the victory (Revelation 5:5)
232. The One with the title "King of kings and Lord of lords" (1 Timothy 6:15; Revelation 19:16)
233. Jesus, the Source of David and the heir of His throne (Revelation 22:16)
234. Jesus the Bright and Morning Star (Revelation 22:16)
235. Jesus, my Morning Sunrise from on high (Luke 1:78)
236. Jesus, the Son of the Blessed One (Mark 14:61)
237. Jesus, the Son of the Father (2 John 1:3)
238. Jesus, the Son of the Highest (Mark 14:62)
239. Jesus, the Savior of the world (Luke 2:11)
240. Jesus, the One who saves me from my sins (Matthew 1:21)
241. The One who builds the church (Matthew 16:18)

242. Jesus, the One who gave me power over all the powers of hell (Matthew 16:18)

243. Jesus, the One who gave me the keys to the kingdom of heaven (Matthew 16:19)

244. The One who commands me to take up my cross and follow You (Matthew 16:24)

245. Jesus, the One who will come with Your angels in the glory of Your Father (Matthew 16:27)

246. Jesus, appointed as Judge of the living and the dead (Matthew 16:27; Acts 10:42; 1 Peter 4:4–5)

247. Jesus, the One who rebukes demons and they flee (Matthew 17:18)

248. Jesus, the Provider of my taxes (Matthew 17:27)

249. Jesus, the One who loves and blesses children (Matthew 19:14–15)

250. The Lord who makes the impossible possible (Matthew 19:26)

251. God, the rewarder for my obedience (Matthew 19:29)

252. Jesus, who came to serve and give Your life in ransom for me (Matthew 20:28)

253. The Merciful Healer of the blind (Matthew 20:34)

254. The Humble King (Matthew 21:5)

255. Jesus, the Prophet from Nazareth in Galilee (Matthew 21:11)

256. The One who teaches children to praise You (Matthew 21:16)

257. The Lord who will not leave me orphaned and will come back for me (John 14:18)

258. The One who was raised to life again (John 14:20)

259. Jesus, who is in the Father, and He is in You (John 14:10; 10:38)

260. The Lord who is in me, and I am in You (John 14:20)

261. The One who reveals Yourself to me (John 14:20)

262. Jesus, the stumbling block to the religious leaders (Matthew 21:23–27; 42–46)

263. The One who said "for many are called, but few are chosen" (Matthew 22:14)

264. Jesus, the Impartial One (Matthew 22:16)

265. Jesus, the Word of Life (John 1:4; 1 John 1:1; Philippians 2:16)

266. Lord, the Light where there is no darkness at all (1 John 1:5)

267. The shining Light that darkness can never extinguish (1 John 1:5)
268. The Lord who is in the light (1 John 1:7)
269. Jesus Christ, the truly righteous One (1 John 2:1)
270. Jesus Christ, my Advocate who pleads my case before the Father (1 John 2:1)
271. Jesus, my Defender (1 John 2:1)
272. Jesus, the Sacrifice that atones for the sins of all the world (1 John 2:2)
273. Jesus, everything was created through You and for You (Colossians 1:16)
274. God, the One who is holy and true (Revelation 3:7)
275. God, the Maker of all I can and cannot see (Colossians 1:16)
276. Jesus, the Alpha and the Omega (Revelation 22:13)
277. Jesus, the First and the Last (Revelation 1:17; Revelation 22:13)
278. Jesus, the Beginning and the End (Revelation 22:13)
279. Jesus, whose Name is wonderful (Judges 13:17–18)
280. Jesus Christ, who is the same yesterday, today, and forever (Hebrews 13:8)
281. Jesus, the holy Servant, anointed by the Father (Acts 4:27)
282. Jesus, the Righteous Servant and Leader (Acts 24:7)
283. Christ, the eternal WORD (John 1:1)
284. Jesus, the Sun of Righteousness (Malachi 4:2)
285. Jesus, whose Priesthood lasts forever (Hebrews 7:21)
286. Jesus, the One who lives forever (Hebrews 7:24)
287. Jesus, the One who can save me forever (Hebrews 7:25)
288. Jesus, the One who intercedes for me (Hebrews 7:25)
289. Jesus, my eternal High Priest in the order of Melchizedek (Hebrews 6:20; 7:17)
290. Jesus, the High Priest who is holy, blameless, and unstained by sin (Hebrews 7:26)
291. Jesus, the One with the highest place of honor in heaven (Hebrews 7:26)
292. Jesus, the living One who lives forever (Revelation 1:18)
293. The God of the Holy City, the new Jerusalem (Revelation 21:2)
294. Jesus Christ, the One who is coming soon (Revelation 3:11)
295. God, the Blessed forever (Psalm 21:6)

296. The Source of all blessing (Psalm 21:6)
297. The God of cheer and joy (Psalm 21:6)
298. God, the Mighty, Awesome One (Jeremiah 20:11)
299. The Lord with a powerful and majestic voice (Psalm 29:4)
300. God, the Mighty One of Israel (Isaiah 1:24)
301. Jesus, the One who descended from heaven (John 3:13)
302. Jesus, the One who ascended to the Father (John 20:17)
303. Jesus, the Lord who holds the key of David (Revelation 3:7)
304. Jesus, the One sitting at the right hand of the Father (Mark 16:19)
305. Jesus, the Stumbling Block for the wicked and unbelievers (Ezekiel 14:3; 1 Peter 2:8)
306. Jesus Christ, the desire of all nations (Haggai 2:7; 1 John 5:6)
307. The God of the nations (Psalm 72:11; 86:9)
308. God, the Ensign and Banner for the nations (Isaiah 5:26)
309. The Lord with eyes like flames of fire (Revelation 1:14; 19:12)
310. The One with hair like wool as white as snow (Revelation 1:14)
311. The Rider of the white horse, named Faithful and True (Revelation 19:11)
312. The Lord who wears many crowns (Revelation 19:12)
313. The Lord with a Name written on You that no one understands except Yourself (Revelation 19:13)
314. The Lord who is clothed with a robe dipped in blood (Revelation 19:14)
315. The Lord whose Name is the Word of God (Revelation 19:13)
316. The One whose mouth has a sharp sword to strike down the nations (Revelation 19:15)
317. The All-Powerful God (Revelation 19:15)
318. The One who I must love with all my heart, soul, and mind (Matthew 22:37)
319. The One who commands me to love my neighbor as myself (Matthew 22:37)
320. The One who sits on the throne (Revelation 21:5)
321. The One who makes all things new (Revelation 21:5; 2 Corinthians 5:17)
322. The One whose words are faithful and true (Revelation 21:5)
323. Christ Jesus, the One I belong to (1 Thessalonians 5:18)

324. Jesus, the Chief Cornerstone chosen for great honor (1 Peter 2:6)
325. Jesus, the Chosen Living Stone, precious in God's Sight (1 Peter 2:4)
326. Jesus, a Stone in Zion, a tested stone (Isaiah 28:16)
327. Jesus, the Stone which the builders rejected (1 Peter 2:7)
328. Jesus, the One who knows the intentions of people (Matthew 22:18–20)
329. The only One worthy to open the scroll and its seven seals (Revelation 5:5)
330. The Lamb of God who was slaughtered (Revelation 5:6)
331. The One with the sevenfold Spirit of God and the seven stars (Revelation 3:1)
332. Christ Jesus, the Righteousness of God, and Savior (1 Corinthians 1:30; 2 Peter 1:1)
333. Lord, Jesus Christ, my robe of Righteousness (Psalm 132:9; Job 29:14; Isaiah 58:8)
334. Lord, whose glory is my Rear Guard (Isaiah 58:8)
335. Christ Jesus, my Sanctification (1 Corinthians 1:30)
336. Jesus, the Atoning Sacrifice for my sins (1 John 2:2)
337. The One who promised me the joy of eternal life (1 John 2:25)
338. The Holy One who gave me Your Spirit without limit (John 3:34; 1 John 2:20)
339. The Lord in whom there is no evil (Psalm 92:15; Deuteronomy 32:4)
340. The Lord, my Rock (Psalm 92:15)
341. The Lord who is Just (Psalm 92:15)
342. The One who asks me to deny myself, carry my cross, and follow You (Matthew 16:24; Luke 14:27)
343. Christ, the Power that dwells in me (2 Corinthians 12:7–10)
344. Jesus Christ, the Power through whom I can do all things (Philippians 4:13)
345. Jesus Christ, the Victor (1 Corinthians 15:54–57; Hebrews 8:1; Revelation 3:21)
346. Jesus Christ, the great Conqueror and Overcomer (1 Corinthians 15:54–57; Colossians 2:14–15)

347. Jesus, the Power that works best in my weakness (2 Corinthians 12:8–9)
348. Jesus, my *Shiloh*, my place of worship (Jeremiah 41:5; Genesis 49:10; Psalm 78:60)
349. Jesus, the Carpenter (Mark 6:3)
350. Jesus, the Way (John 14:6)
351. Jesus, the Truth (John 14:6)
352. Jesus, the Life (John 14:6)
353. Jesus, the Door to the Father (John 14:6)
354. The Fourth Man in the fiery furnace (Daniel 3:24–26)
355. The One who walks on water (Matthew 14:29; John 6:19)
356. Jesus, the Tree of Life (Genesis 2:9; Genesis 3:22–24; Revelation 22:2)
357. The One who taught me the true secret to answered prayers (Matthew 21:21–22)
358. Jesus, the One who arms me with authority to change atmospheres and circumstances by faith (Matthew 21:21–22)
359. The God who bought me with a high price (1 Corinthians 6:19–20)
360. Jesus, the Life-giving Power (John 5:26)
361. Christ, the Life-giving Spirit (1 Corinthians 15:45–46)
362. Jesus, in whom the fullness of Deity dwells (Colossians 2:9–10)
363. The One who made me complete through Christ (Colossians 2:9–10)
364. Jesus, the humble Bondservant (Philippians 2:7)
365. Jesus, my Champion who initiates and perfects my faith (Hebrews 12:2)
366. The Son of God who appeared to destroy the works of the devil (1 John 3:8)
367. The One who made me a partaker of Your divine nature (2 Peter 1:3–4)
368. The One who granted me Your precious and magnificent promises (2 Peter 1:3–4)
369. The One who granted me all things that pertain to life and godliness (2 Peter 1:3–4)

370. The One who will transform my weak mortal body into a glorious body (Philippians 3:21)
371. Jesus, the Center of everything (Galatians 2:20; Philippians 4:13; John 14:6)
372. Jesus, the Propitiation for my sins and the sins of the whole world (1 John 2:2)
373. Jesus Christ, my Secure Foundation (Isaiah 28:16; 1 Corinthians 3:11)
374. Jesus, the Reconciler (Ephesians 2:16; Colossians 1:20)
375. Jesus, the Peacemaker (Colossians 1:20; Matthew 5:9)
376. Jesus, who gave Yourself as a ransom for me (1 Timothy 2:6)
377. The Word who became flesh and dwelt among us (John 1:14)
378. The Word that became human and made Your home among us (John 1:14)
379. Jesus, full of grace and truth (John 1:14)
380. Jesus, who give me grace upon grace and undeserved blessing (John 1:16)
381. Jesus, the Offender of Pharisees and religious people (Matthew 15; Luke 11:37–54)
382. Jesus, the One with wisdom and splendor greater than Solomon's (Luke 11:31)
383. My Lord Jesus, the Love that heals (Psalm 103:2–5; Jeremiah 33:6)
384. Jesus, the Spirit of wisdom and understanding (Isaiah 11:2–3)
385. Jesus, the Spirit of counsel and might (Isaiah 11:2–3)
386. Jesus, the Spirit of knowledge and the fear of the LORD (Isaiah 11:2–3)
387. Jesus, who delights in the fear of the LORD (Isaiah 11:2–3)
388. Jesus, who never judges by appearance nor make decisions based on rumors (Isaiah 11:2–3)
389. The only Name that holds every victory guaranteed (2 Chronicles 20:15; John 16:33; 1 John 4:4)
390. The One in me who is greater than he who is in the world (1 John 4:4)
391. The Son of Man that will come in His glory with all the angels (Matthew 25:31)

392. Jesus, the gentleness that redeemed me (Psalm 18:35; Isaiah 63:9)
393. Jesus, the Glory of God (John 1:14)

A PRAYER DECLARING JESUS, THE SON OF GOD

Dear Father, I bring my life before You in Jesus' mighty Name, who is my Champion, the Author, and Finisher of my faith through the help of Your Holy Spirit. Jesus, thank You for saving my life and writing my name in the Book of Life. Lord Jesus, Your Name is power and hope for my life and my family. Jesus, in Your Name, there is freedom. Your Name is my security and protection.

Yeshua, Your Name is above all names throughout all times, the most powerful Name like none other. Lord, You are the One with endless names, titles, and attributes. Your names transcend beyond the letters of the alphabet because they existed before the alphabet. You are the One who has given Yourself a Name that no one else understands, O Lord. You are all Your names and more. Lord, Your Name is holy. Your words are sweeter than honey. My Lord Jesus, You are the Love that heals me. Jesus, Your names are majestic and wonderful. You are the One with the highest place of honor in heaven. You are Jesus the Christ. Lord, You jealously guard the holy reputation of Your great Name.

Jesus, You listen attentively to my declarations about who You are. Lord, You are the Great I AM. You are the Incarnate Truth; You are the absolute Truth. You are the Spirit of life. You are my Hope of Glory. Lord, You are the high and exalted One who lives forever.

Jesus, Your holy Name is the anointing over my life; Your Name is holy, lovely, and worthy to be celebrated and praised with music and dancing. You are the Beloved whose Name is like the aromatic fragrance that spreads everywhere, the most beautiful Name in the whole world. Your Name is far superior to the names of the angels; You are the Rose of Sharon, the Lily of the Valleys, a Plant of Renown, the great Gift, and the firstborn of every creature. Jesus, You are the exact representation of God's glorious nature. You are the image of the invisible God. You are the beloved in Songs of Songs. You are my Beloved One. You are the Pearl of Great Price. You are the Salt of the earth. Jesus, You are the Way, the Truth, and the Life; no one goes to the Father except through You.

Jesus, You are the Prophet from Nazareth in Galilee. You are called the Nazarene. The Carpenter. You are *Elohim Yeshua*—Jesus, the Son of God. You are *Yeshua Hamashiach*, Jesus Christ. You are our Messiah. You are the First-Begotten of the dead—the Prince of life. The great Prince of Peace prophesied by Isaiah. You are the Prince of princes. The Prince of the shepherds. The good Shepherd who lays down His life for the sheep. You are the Shepherd who knows who Your sheep are, and they know Your voice. Lord Jesus, You are the great and Chief Shepherd. The Bishop of my soul. The Shepherd of Your people Israel. Lord, You are the King of the Jews and Zion. Jesus, You are the King of Israel.

Jesus Christ, You are the Scepter of justice. The Rabbi, the *Rabboni*, Son of God. The Prince and Ruler of the kings of the earth. Jesus Christ, You are the eternal King of the nations forever and ever. The great King over all ages. Lord, You are the King of the saints. The Humble King. Jesus, You are the One who reigns forever; Your kingdom has no end. Jesus Christ, You are the desire of all nations. You are the God of the nations. Lord, You are the Ensign/Banner for the nations. Jesus, You are the One with the title "King of kings and Lord of lords."

Jesus, You are the child in the manger, the God who comes from above. Jesus, You are the One who comes in the Name of the Lord. Jesus, You are the Chief Cornerstone chosen for great honor, and I know I will never be disgraced because I trust in You. You are the Stone of Zion, a tested Stone that the builders rejected. You are the One who knows the intentions of people. Jesus, You are the stumbling block for the religious leaders, the wicked, and the unbelievers. Jesus, You are my Secure Foundation. The chosen Living Stone, and precious in God's sight. You are the Reconciler and the Peacemaker.

You are a light to enlighten the gentiles. Jesus, You are the Forerunner. You are Jesus, the Holy Servant and the Father's anointed One. Jesus, the Righteous Servant and Leader. You are the Apostle and High Priest of my profession. You are the Heir of all things. Jesus, You are the Mediator of a new and better covenant. The Mediator of the New Testament. Jesus, You are the Minister of the sanctuary and the Minister of the true tabernacle.

Jesus, You are called the Preacher and Teacher. You are a great, infallible Teacher. The Teacher with real authority. Jesus, You are the fulfillment of the law. Jesus, You are the Proclaimer of the gospel of the kingdom. You are the Storyteller. You are the One who gathers Your children.

Jesus, You are the son of David, the Root and Descendant/Offspring of David and Abraham. Jesus, You are the seed of Abraham, the son of Abraham. You are the Star out of Jacob. The Rod out of the stem of Jesse, the Son of Man, the Lion of the Tribe of Judah. You are the Son of the Blessed One, the Son of the Father, the Son of the living God, the Son of the Highest. Jesus Christ, You are the Messiah. The Lord born in Bethlehem, the City of David. Jesus, You are the Source of David and the heir to His throne because You won the victory. You are the One who sits on the throne. You are the Son of God Most High, the Chosen of God. Lord, You are *El Elyon*—the Lord, Most High God and Exalted. You are the Son of Man who sits upon Your glorious throne. Jesus, You are the One seated at the right hand of the Father. You are the Lord who holds the key of David.

Jesus, You are the Promised One. The last Adam. The Branch of the Lord. The Bright and Morning Star. Jesus, You are my Morning Sunrise from on high. You are the Light of the world. You are the Manna and the Living Bread that descended from heaven. You are the true Bread of Life. Lord Jesus, You are the One who descended from heaven and ascended to the Father. Lord, You are the Living Bread that makes me live forever. The Master of the universe.

Jesus, You own the Lamb's Book of Life. Jesus Christ, You are the Lamb of God who takes away the sin of the world. The only One worthy to open the scroll and its seven seals. The Lamb of God who was slaughtered. You are my sanctification, the redemption from God, my Redeemer. The God from above, You are not of this world. You are my hallelujah! The Lord God on high. Lord, You are the God of the new covenant. The One with the most precious blood. Jesus, You are the Amen. You are *Immanuel*—God with us. Lord, You are an amazing God, Jesus. You are the Most Famous One.

Jesus, You are the Sower and Lord of the harvest. You are the true Vine and I must remain in You, because You are the one who makes me fruitful. Jesus, I know that apart from You, I can do nothing. You are the One who rescued me from the kingdom of darkness. And You continue to save me from the enemy, for You are my Savior every day. Christ, the visible image of the invisible God. Jesus, You are the Verb in the beginning. You existed before anything was created from the beginning. You are supreme over all creation. Lord, You are the Maker of all I can see and cannot see. Jesus Christ, You were appointed in ages past, at the very first, before the earth began. Jesus, You are the One who holds all creation together; You are Supreme over all creation. Christ, You are supreme over all who rise from the dead. Lord, You are the first in everything; everything was created through You and for You. Jesus, You are the Alpha and the Omega, the First and the Last, the Beginning and the End. You are the same yesterday, today, and forever.

Jesus Christ, You were born before the oceans were created and before the springs bubbled forth their waters. Jesus Christ, You were born before the mountains and hills were formed. You were made before the earth, and the first handful of soil was made. Jesus Christ, You were there when God established the heavens and drew the horizon on the oceans. You were there when God set the clouds above and established springs deep in the earth. You were there when God set the limits of the seas, and You marked off the earth's foundations. Jesus, You were the Architect at the Father's side.

Jesus, You were His constant delight and great joy. You were happy with the world the Father created. You rejoiced with the human family. All who follow Your ways are joyful. Lord, You bless me with joy when I listen, watch and wait for You. Jesus Christ, You are the Life and Favor of the Father.

Christ, You are the Head of the body. You are the Head of every man. Lord Jesus, You are the Head of the church. Lord, You are my spiritual Rock from where I drink and satisfy my thirst. You are my *Shiloh*, my Worship. I know one day, every knee will bow and every tongue will have to praise You and acknowledge that You are Lord and King.

Lord, You are my Rock. Jesus, You finished the work the Father gave You and brought glory to the Father here on this earth. Jesus, You are *Jehovah-Elohim Yeshua*—Jesus, the Son of God who came to show me the true God. You have given me understanding so that I can know the Father. And now I can live in fellowship with God because I live in fellowship with You, Jesus, God's Son. You are the only true God, and You are my Eternal Life. Lord, help me stay away from anything that might want to take Your place in my heart.

Jesus, You are the only Name by which I can be saved. You saved me from my sins. You purchased my freedom and forgave all my sins. You are the Sacrifice that atones my sins and the sins of the world. Jesus, thank You for setting me free from the law of sin and death. You are the Sacrifice that atones my sins. Now You are my Advocate and Lawyer who pleads my case before the Father. Jesus, I know You intercede for me. You are my Defender. You are the One who can save me once and forever. Jesus, You are the One with the most powerful substance, Your blood. Christ Jesus. You are my sanctification, my redemption from God, and the power of God in my life. You give me grace upon grace and undeserved blessings every day.

Jesus, You love and bless children. You teach children to praise You. You are the Lord who will not leave us orphans, and I know You will come back for us one day. Oh, how I long for that day. Jesus, You are greater than the temple. Jesus, the One who makes us fishers of men. You are Lord over the Sabbath. You are the Farmer who plants the good seed.

Jesus, You are the One who builds the church, and You will come soon with Your angels in the glory of Your Father to judge all people according to their deeds.

Jesus, you walk on water and even the winds and waves obey you. Lord Jesus, I know You care for our human needs. You are the One who fed the 4,000-plus people in a moment. You are the Provider of my taxes. You are the merciful Healer of the blind. Jesus, You are the Healer of every kind of disease. You want and are willing to heal me, for You can heal all sickness. Jesus, You cast out evil spirits; You rebuke demons, and they flee, for You have given me the authority and power over all the powers of hell.

Jesus, You are the One who blesses my life and soul. Lord, You reveal Yourself to me. You taught me the true secret to answered prayers, and You always honor my faith. Lord, You make the impossible possible; everything is possible for You, and nothing is too hard for You.

Jesus, You are in the Father, You are in me, and I am in You. The One whom I must love with all my heart, soul, mind, and strength. Christ Jesus, You are the only One I belong to. Lord, You are the One who rewards my obedience. You are the One who commands me to love my neighbor as myself.

Jesus, You are the Bridegroom who will return for Your bride, the church. Jesus, Your power works best in my weakness.

Jesus, You are the One who said that many are called but few are chosen. Jesus, help me so I may be chosen by You. You are the impartial One. You don't have favorites among Your children.

Jesus, You are the Word of God. You are the Word of Life. You are Light, and there is no darkness in You because You are in the Light, and You are Light. Jesus, You are the Founder, the Author, the Perfecter, and the Finisher of my faith.

Christ Jesus, You are truly righteous. The One who is holy and true. You are the Sun of Righteousness. Your words are faithful and true. Jesus, You are the wisdom of God; You are the righteous One of God. Christ Jesus, You are the Power of God. In You are hidden all the treasures of wisdom and knowledge. You are the Giver of understanding.

Jesus, Your Name is alive forever and ever. You are the living One who lives forevermore. Jesus Christ, You are the risen One, the first to rise from the dead. You hold the keys of death and the grave. You are Christ, the One risen from the dead. You were raised to live again. The One who resurrects the dead, for You are the Power of resurrection and life.

Jesus, Your Priesthood lasts forever. You are my eternal High Priest in the order of Melchizedek, the great High Priest. Jesus, You are the High Priest who is holy, blameless, and unstained by sin. You are a God of truth and without iniquity. Lord Jesus, You are Just. You are the Lord in whom there is no evil because You are perfectly holy.

Jesus, You are the God of the Holy City, the new Jerusalem. You are the One who is coming soon. You are blessed forever, the Mighty, Awesome One. The One with the sevenfold Spirit of God and the seven stars. The Lord with a powerful and majestic voice. God, the Mighty One of Israel.

Lord, the One with hair like wool, so white as snow. Your eyes are like flames of fire.

You are the Rider of the white horse; You are called Faithful and True. Lord, You wear many crowns. Lord, the One with a Name written on You that no one understands except Yourself. You are the Lord who is clothed with a robe dipped in blood. You are the Lord whose Name is the Word of God.

Lord, from Your mouth came a sharp sword to strike down the nations, and You rule with a rod of iron. You are the All-Powerful God. Jesus, You are crowned with glory and honor and have authority over everything.

Jesus, You said that if I want to be Your disciple, I must deny myself, take up my cross, and follow You. Lord, help me do this every day of my life. Christ, You are the Power that dwells in me, and I know I can do all things through Your strength. You are the Holy One who has given me Your Spirit. The One who baptizes me with Holy Spirit and fire. You gave me Your Spirit without limit. You are the giver of authority. Jesus, You gave me the keys to the kingdom of heaven. You are my Victor and my Triumph. Jesus Christ, You are the Conqueror and Overcomer of the sin and death of the world. Now You are making all things new. Thank You, Jesus, for You have promised me the joy of eternal life. Jesus, You are the promise of my eternal inheritance.

Jesus, You came to serve others and give us Your life. Now I want to serve You and give my life to You. Jesus, You are the Name of hope to the world. You are Jesus, the Savior of the world. You are my Lord and King eternally.

I thank You, oh great King of my life, and I honor and bless Your holy Name.

I wholeheartedly praise Your great holy Name with fear and awe.

You deserve my attention, affection, reverence, adoration, and praise for all generations and forever and ever, amen and amen!

9

HIS HOLY SPIRIT

FEATURED SCRIPTURES TO PONDER

But if the Spirit of Him who raised Jesus from the dead dwells in you, He who raised Christ Jesus from the dead will also give life to your mortal bodies through His Spirit who dwells in you.

Romans 8:11 NASB1995

"But the Helper, the Holy Spirit, whom the Father will send in My Name, He will teach you all things, and bring to your remembrance all that I said to You."

John 14:26 NASB1995

You are:

1. *Ruach Hakodesh* (Yochanan [John] 3:34; Psalm 51:11 OJB)
2. The Spirit of Pentecost (Acts 1:1–4)
3. The Spirit who I must not grieve, for You are sensitive as a dove (1 Thessalonians 5:19)
4. The Holy Spirit who descended on Jesus like a dove (Luke 3:22)

5. The One whom God has sent to speak the words of God (John 3:34)
6. The Spirit who was given to me without measure or limit (John 3:34)
7. The Spirit living in me who gives life to my mortal body (Romans 8:11–14)
8. The Spirit who leads my life (Romans 8:11–14)
9. The Spirit of the Lord who is upon me (Luke 4:18–19)
10. The Spirit who has anointed me to bring Good News to the poor (Luke 4:18–19)
11. The Spirit who has sent me to proclaim that captives will be released (Luke 4:18–19)
12. The Spirit who anoints me to heal the blind (Luke 4:18–19)
13. The Spirit who anoints me to set the oppressed free (Luke 4:18–19)
14. The Spirit who proclaims through me the Lord's favor has come (Luke 4:18–19)
15. The Spirit of God who raised Jesus from the dead and who lives in me (Romans 8:11–14)
16. The Holy Spirit who comes over me, and I speak in tongues and prophesy (Acts 19:6)
17. The Holy Spirit who fills me and enables me to speak in other tongues (Acts 2:4)
18. The Spirit of Prophesy (Ezekiel 37)
19. The Spirit of God who has made me (Job 33:4)
20. The Breath of God who gives me life (Ezekiel 37; Job 33:4)
21. The Spirit who sanctifies me by Your grace (2 Thessalonians 2:13)
22. God, the Third Person of the Trinity (Matthew 28:19)
23. The Creator Spirit who hovered over the surface of the waters (Genesis 1:2–3)
24. God, the Holy Spirit, and my Intercessor (Romans 8:34)
25. God, the Holy Spirit, and my Counselor (John 14:26)
26. The Holy Spirit, the Comforter (John 14:26)
27. The Spirit of God, the One who sets me free (John 8:32)
28. The Spirit of deliverance and freedom (2 Corinthians 3:17)

29. The Spirit who gives me power, love, and self-discipline (1 Timothy 1:7)
30. The Holy Spirit, my fiercely jealous Lover (James 4:5)
31. Holy Spirit, the Unspeakable Gift (2 Corinthians 9:15)
32. God, the Spirit of adoption (Romans 8:15)
33. The Holy Spirit, the original Context of God's Word (John 16:12–15)
34. God, the Holy Spirit, a witness to us (Hebrews 10:15)
35. The Holy Spirit promised by the Father (Luke 24:49; Acts 2:33)
36. My seal of promise from the Lord (Ephesians 1:13–14)
37. The Holy Spirit, the guarantee/earnest of my inheritance (Ephesians 1:13–14)
38. The Holy Spirit, the One who revives my soul (Psalm 19:7; 119:25–26; Isaiah 57:15)
39. The Spirit of God, the Holy Ghost (Romans 5:5; Micah 3:8–10)
40. God, the Spirit who flows like a mighty river (Amos 5:24; Isaiah 66:12)
41. Holy Spirit, the Baptizer (Acts 2:38–41)
42. God, the Spirit of grace (Zechariah 12:10)
43. Holy Spirit, my Intimate Friend (James 4:5)
44. Holy Spirit, who fills me with Your spiritual fruit (Galatians 5:14, 22; Romans 12:6–10)
45. The Holy Spirit, who equips me with spiritual gifts (1 Corinthians 12)
46. God, the Spirit of holiness (Romans 1:4)
47. The Source of holiness and purity (2 Thessalonians 2:13; John 17:17; 1 Peter 1:1)
48. The Giver of grace (Zechariah 12:10)
49. God, the Spirit of the living God (2 Corinthians 3:3)
50. The Spirit of the Lord (2 Corinthians 3:17)
51. The eternal Spirit (Hebrews 9:14)
52. God, the Spirit of Truth (John 14:17, 15:26)
53. Holy Spirit, my empowerment (Acts 1:8)
54. The Spirit who empowers me to overcome (Zechariah 4:6)
55. The Lord who baptized me with Your Holy Spirit and fire (Matthew 3:11)

56. *Ruach Elohim*—the great wind and Spirit of God (Genesis 1:2; 1 Samuel 10:10)
57. The God who is Spirit (John 4:24)
58. God, Your Spirit dwells in me (1 Corinthians 3:16)
59. God, who jealously desires the spirit You have made to dwell in me (James 4:5)
60. God, Your Word is the Sword of the Spirit (Ephesians 6:17)
61. The Spirit of the Word, the two-edged sword (Hebrews 4:12)
62. The Spirit who enabled the writing of the Holy Bible (2 Peter 1:21)
63. The God who identified me as Your own and has given me the Spirit as a guarantee (2 Corinthians 1:22)
64. The Lord with the seven Spirits of God (Revelation 5:6)
65. God, the Intimate One (James 4:8)
66. God, the Author of the Bible (2 Timothy 3:16)
67. The Spirit who has made me holy (1 Peter 1:1)
68. God, the Wonderful Counselor (Isaiah 9:26)
69. The Spirit who whispers into my spirit the Father's plans (John 14)
70. The Spirit who teaches me God's divine ways (John 14:26)
71. The very definition of the fruit of the Spirit (Galatians 5:22–23)
72. God, You are gentleness (Psalm 18:35)
73. The Spirit who produces all kinds of good fruit in my life (Galatians 5:22–23)
74. The Spirit of joy and happiness (Galatians 5:22–23)
75. The Spirit of patience (Galatians 5:22–23)
76. The Spirit of kindness (Galatians 5:22–23)
77. The Spirit of goodness (Galatians 5:22–23)
78. The Spirit of faithfulness (Galatians 5:22–23)
79. The Spirit of gentleness (Galatians 5:22–23)
80. The Spirit of self-control (Galatians 5:22–23)
81. The Omnipotent Spirit of God, my Shelter and Shadow where I find rest (Psalm 91:1)
82. The Spirit who gives me rest (Isaiah 63:14)
83. God, the Spirit who empowers me (Acts 1:8)

84. The Spirit who empowered Mary to carry and deliver the Savior of the world (Matthew 1:18–19; Luke 1:34)
85. The Spirit who comforts me (John 14:16)
86. The Spirit who encourages me (John 14:16)
87. The Spirit who advocates for me (John 14:16; 15:26)
88. The Spirit, my Helper (John 14:16)
89. The Holy Spirit, who leads me into all truth (John 14:17)
90. The Spirit who will be with me forever (John 14:16)
91. The Spirit who abides with me and in me (John 14:17)
92. God, You are the air and breath in my lungs (Job 27:3)
93. The Spirit of resurrection power who lives in me (Romans 8:11)
94. The Holy Spirit who helps me in my weakness (Romans 8:26)
95. The Holy Spirit who teaches me all things (John 14:26)
96. The Holy Spirit who reminds me of the words of Jesus (John 14:26)
97. The Holy Spirit, my enabler (Acts 8:5–8, 14–17; Isaiah 61:1–3)
98. The Holy Spirit who dwells in me forever (John 14:16–17; 1 Corinthians 3:16–17)
99. The One with a Name that is Holy (Psalm 30:4)
100. The One with a Name far greater than the names of the angels (Hebrews 1:4)
101. The powerful *Shekinah* (Divine Presence) over me and in me (Leviticus 16:2 Exodus 40:35; Genesis 9:27)
102. The One who laid the Highway of Holiness (Isaiah 35:8)
103. God, the Fountain of hope (Romans 15:13)
104. The One who fills me with overflowing and uncontainable joy (Romans 15:13)
105. The One who gives me perfect peace as I radically trust in You (Romans 15:13)
106. The Spirit that makes me overflow with a confident hope through Your power (Romans 15:13)
107. The Spirit of power (Acts 1:8)
108. The Spirit of revival (Acts 1:7–8)
109. The Powerful, Eternal Spirit of God (Hebrews 9:14)
110. The Spirit of God who has sealed me for the day of redemption (Ephesians 4:30)

111. The Spirit of love (Rom. 15:30)
112. The Spirit of God who gives me great wisdom (Exodus 31:3–5)
113. The Spirit of God who gives me the ability and expertise in all kinds of crafts (Exodus 31:3–5)
114. The Spirit who reveals to me the secrets of God (1 Corinthians 2:10)
115. The Spirit who searches all things, even the deep secrets of God (1 Corinthians 2:10)
116. The Holy Spirit who empowers me to be a witness (Acts 1:8)
117. The Holy Spirit of the gospel (1 Thessalonians 1:5; 1 Peter 1:12)
118. The fearful Holy Spirit of God (Acts 5:1–10)
119. The Spirit who anoints me with a wisdom that no one can stand against (Acts 6:10)
120. The Holy Spirit who directs me into divine appointments (Acts 8:26, 29)
121. The One Spirit who baptized Your people into one body (1 Corinthians 12:13)
122. One Spirit, and we all share Your Spirit (1 Corinthians 12:13)
123. The Holy Spirit who guides and directs my life as I surrender to You (Galatians 5:16–18)
124. The Spirit who makes me more like Jesus (Galatians 5:16–18)
125. The Spirit who testifies all about Jesus to me (John 15:26)
126. The Holy Spirit who works to bring glory to Jesus Christ (John 15:26; 16:14; Acts 5:32; 1 Corinthians 12:3; 1 John 4:2)
127. The Holy Spirit who gave me new birth and life (Titus 3:4–5)
128. The One who convicts me of all sin, and righteousness (John 16:8–10)
129. The Spirit alone who gives me eternal life (John 6:62–64)
130. The One whose words are spirit and life (John 6:62–64)
131. The Holy Spirit who gives my mortal body life (Romans 8:11)
132. The Spirit who testifies with my spirit that I am a child of God (Romans 8:16)
133. The Holy Spirit who helps me in my weakness (Romans 8:26–27)
134. The Holy Spirit who prays for me with groanings that cannot be expressed in words (Romans 8:26–27)

135. The Spirit who pleads for the believers in harmony with God's own will (Romans 8:26–27)
136. God, the Spirit of power, justice and courage (Matthew 1:18; Micah 3:8)
137. The Holy Spirit, my empowerment from on high (Acts 1:8; Ephesians 3:20)
138. The Spirit who is personal (John 14:26; Romans 8:26; 1 John 5:6)
139. The Spirit who can be grieved because of my actions (Isaiah 63:10; Ephesians 4:30)
140. The Holy Spirit, the Prophet (Acts 1:16; 1 Timothy 4:1; Revelation 14:13; Acts 28:25–26)
141. The Holy Spirit who speaks to me (Acts 8:29; 10:19; 11:12; 13:2; 21:11)
142. The Spirit of the Lord who speaks through me (2 Samuel 23:2)
143. The Holy Spirit of Promise (Ephesians 1:13–14)
144. The Spirit of Christ who helps me (Philippians 1:19)
145. God, the Spirit of Christ in me (1 Peter 1:11)
146. The Seven-fold Spirit (Isaiah 11:2–3)
147. The Omnipresent Spirit of God (Isaiah 11:2–3)
148. The Spirit of the LORD (Isaiah 11:2–3)
149. The Spirit of wisdom (Isaiah 11:2–3)
150. The Spirit of understanding (Isaiah 11:2–3)
151. The Spirit of counsel (Isaiah 11:2–3)
152. The Spirit of power (Isaiah 11:2–3)
153. The Spirit of knowledge (Isaiah 11:2–3)
154. The Spirit of the fear of the Lord (Isaiah 11:2–3)
155. God, the Spirit of glory (1 Peter 4:14)
156. The Spirit who rests upon me and in me (Isaiah 11:2)
157. The Spirit I must be filled with (Ephesians 5:18)
158. The fire in my heart (Matthew 3:11; Romans 5:5; Luke 3:16)
159. The Spirit who sets my heart on fire (Matthew 3:11; Luke 3:16)
160. The mighty rushing Wind (Acts 2:1–4)
161. The Author of spiritual fire (Matthew 3:11; Luke 3:16)
162. The Spirit who has the Word as a sword (Ephesians 6)
163. The Holy Spirit who enables my ears to hear God's voice (1 Corinthians 2:12–16)

164. The Spirit who sets me free from the law of sin and death (Romans 8:1–2)
165. The Holy Spirit who gives birth to spiritual life (John 3:6)
166. The Spirit of God who washed me, sanctified me, and justified me in Jesus' Name (1 Corinthians 6:9–11)
167. The Holy Spirit who regenerates and renews me (Titus 3:5)
168. The Lord God, Omnipresent, present in all places at the same time (Jeremiah 23:23–24; Psalm 139:7–13; Acts 17:27–28)
169. The Lord God, Omnipotent, with unlimited authority and power to do what You will (Revelation 4:8; 11:17; 2 Corinthians 4:7; Mark 10:27)
170. The Lord God, Omniscient, infinite in knowledge and understanding of things past, present, and future.[1] (Psalm 44:21; Psalm 147:5)
171. The Lord God Omnificent, with unlimited power to create all things (Colossians 1:15–17; Psalm 40:5; Genesis 1:1)
172. The Lord God Omnibenevolent, supremely good (Mark 10:18; Psalm 106:1; Genesis 1:31)
173. My Hiding Place where the enemy cannot see me (Psalm 32:7)
174. The Holy Spirit who protects me and surrounds me with songs of deliverance (Psalm 32:7)
175. The Spirit who hides me in the shelter of Your Presence (Psalm 31:20)
176. The Spirit behind my spiritual songs and melodies in worship (Ephesians 5:18–19; Psalm 118:14–15)
177. The Spirit I must please, for You will give me eternal life (Romans 8:9)
178. The Spirit who is in control of my life because You live in me (Romans 8:9)
179. The Spirit I belong to forever (Romans 8:9)
180. The One who dwells in my body, the temple of Your Spirit (1 Corinthians 6:19)
181. The Spirit who is like a gentle dove (Mark 1:9–12)
182. The Holy Spirit whom I fellowship with; You are with me (2 Corinthians 13:14)
183. God's deposit of guarantee in my heart (2 Corinthians 1:21–22)

184. The Holy Presence who fills me with joy and gladness (Psalm 68:3)
185. The Spirit who gives me ears to listen to and understand what You say (Revelation 2:7)
186. My Encouragement (Acts 9:31)
187. The Spirit who commands me to prophesy life into dried bones (Ezekiel 37:9–14)
188. The One who resurrects lifeless situations back into life (Ezekiel 37:9)
189. The One who can resurrect an exceeding great army from dry bones (Ezekiel 37:10)
190. The Spirit who brings God's mercy to us (Hebrews 10:29)
191. The Spirit who gives life (John 6:63)
192. The Spirit of God who made me (Job 33:4)
193. The Breath of the Almighty that gives me life (John 6:63; Genesis 1:26–27; Isaiah 42:5; Job 33:4)
194. The Holy Spirit who manifests in my life (1 Corinthians 12:7–11; John 6:63; Ephesians. 5:18; Acts 2:1–4)
195. The Holy Spirit, the Power of Resurrection who lives in me (Romans 8:11)
196. The good Spirit who leads me on level ground! (Psalm 143:10)
197. The gentle Spirit who instructs me (Nehemiah 9:20; Psalm 143:10)

A PRAYER DECLARING HIS HOLY SPIRIT

Father, I come before You in Jesus' Name and through Your wonderful Holy Spirit. Father God, Your Holy Spirit is Your own Spirit, the Third Person of the Trinity. You are *Ruach Hakodesh*, the Holy Spirit. Spirit of God, You are the Creator Spirit who hovered over the surface of the waters during creation. You are a creative and innovative Spirit. You are the Source of holiness that purifies my soul.

You are the Giver of grace; Your grace is like an ocean where I feel safe.

O Holy Spirit of God, thank You for being my intercessor; thank You for Your love and mercy. Holy Spirit, You are the Counselor and the Comforter of my soul.

You are the eternal Spirit of God, by whom Christ offered Himself to God as a Perfect Sacrifice for my sins. Holy Spirit of God, You are the powerful One who raised Jesus from the dead, and things that have died prematurely and dried up because of the enemy's activities will now resurrect and come back to life in Jesus' Name.

You are the Spirit who commands me to prophesy life into dried bones. You are the Sovereign Lord who says: "Come from the four winds, O breath, and blow on this lifeless situation and blow into these dry bones, so that they may live again." You are the One who can resurrect an exceeding great army out of these dried bones because Your breath is the essence of life.

Holy Spirit of God, You set me free and gave me the spirit of freedom and liberty. You are the Spirit who gives me power, love, and self-discipline. You are my fiercely jealous Lover. I delight in You, and You give me my heart's desires. I belong to You; I'm Yours forever. Holy Spirit, You are my Unspeakable Gift; You are the Spirit of adoption, the Spirit of Christ in me.

Holy Spirit, You are the context of Your Word. You are the Author of the Bible. You inspired different men and women to write the holy and powerful words. You reveal God's secrets to me. You are a witness to me and through me.

You are the Spirit of the fear of the Lord; You fill me with the knowledge of You. You are the Spirit of holiness of the living God, the Spirit of the Lord. You are the Spirit I must always please, for You give me eternal life. Take total control of my life, oh Holy Spirit of God. You live in me, and I belong to You forever. You are mine, and I am Yours.

You are the eternal Spirit who has always been in existence since day zero and will continue to exist through eternity. You never die or cease to exist. You are Omnipresent, You are present in all places all the time. You are an Omnipotent God with unlimited authority to bring into existence whatever You want and will. You are the all-powerful Invincible One. You are Omniscient, the infinite, All-Knowing One. You are Omnificent, the unlimited powerful Creator. You are Omnibenevolent, a supremely good God. You are the Spirit who was given to me without measure or limit.

You are the Spirit of Truth. O Holy Spirit, teach me Your truths so I may be wise. Grant me Your discernment to make wise choices in everything I do and say every day. for I want to do everything that pleases You with reverent fear and trembling.

Holy Spirit, You are the very definition of the fruits of the Spirit. You are always gentle and patient with me.

Holy Spirit, You fills me with Your fruit and equip me with spiritual gifts. You are the Spirit of God who gives me great wisdom, ability, and expertise in all kinds of things according to Your assignment and call over my life. You empower and equip me with the intelligence to create winning strategies for the ministry, my job, my business, and my home.

Oh, Spirit of God, Holy Ghost, You are God, the Spirit who flows like a mighty river, my Baptizer. You baptize me with Your Holy Spirit and fire. You dwell in me forever. You have baptized Your people into one body. You are one Spirit, and we all share Your same Spirit. You are the same Spirit who dwells in a child as also in an adult. You are the Spirit of grace, my Intimate Friend, who whispers God's will into my ears. Lord, You are the One whom God has sent to speak the words of God into my life. Spirit of God, You are my empowerment from on high. You enable and endow me to do what is impossible through Your holy power. You are the Holy Spirit who gives me a new birth and life. Your words are spirit and life. Holy Spirit, I want to please You, and I know I will obtain eternal life from You. For You alone give me eternal life. You give my mortal body life and health with your lovingkindness. You are the fire in my heart. You ignite me with the holy passion that enables me to do more for You.

Lord, Your Word is the sword of Your Spirit. You are the Spirit of the Word, the two-edged Sword. Lord, You are the God who identified me as Your own and You sealed me with the Holy Spirit as a sacred deposit in my heart. Holy Spirit, You are the earnest of my inheritance. You are the promise of the Father to me. I love to fellowship with You, I know You are always with me. Father, Your Spirit dwells in me and You jealously desire the spirit You have made to dwell within me. Oh Holy Spirit, my body is Your temple; help me keep it filled with Your Spirit always.

Mighty Holy Spirit of God, You are my Wonderful Counselor. You are the Holy Spirit who guides me and directs my life as I surrender to You. The Holy Spirit who directs me into divine appointments today. You are the Spirit who reveals to me the secrets of God. You search all things, even the deep secrets of God. Holy Spirit, You speak to me what You hear from Jesus and the Father. You are the Holy Spirit, the Prophet. Holy Spirit, You speak to me and through me. You are the Spirit who whispers the Father's plans for my life into my spirit. It is You who teaches me the divine ways of God. You are the Spirit of counsel and might, wisdom and understanding, and the Spirit of knowledge over me.

Holy Spirit of God, You are the One who lays the highway of holiness before me so I may walk in it, and You sanctify me to walk in holiness with You. You are holy and I must be holy to walk with You in communion. Lord, I know I can do nothing without You, and I depend on Your empowerment so I may walk in communion with Your Holy Spirit.

Holy Spirit, You produce all kinds of good fruit in me so I may be an effective follower of Christ and be productive and fruitful in Your kingdom. You are the Holy Presence that fills me with joy and gladness. You are the Spirit of eternal joy and happiness in my life. I know I cannot find this happiness and joy anywhere else. It does not exist outside of You. You are the Fountain of joy, my Fountain of hope. Holy Spirit, You are the One who fills me with overflowing, uncontainable joy. The only One who gives me perfect peace when I trust in You. You are the Power from on high that continually makes me overflow with a confident hope.

Lord, I declare that You are the Spirit of patience in me, You are the Spirit of kindness in me, You are the Spirit of goodness in me, You are the Spirit of faithfulness in me, You are the Spirit of gentleness in me, You are the Spirit of self-control in me.

The Omnipotent Spirit of God, my Shelter and Shadow where I find rest. You are the Spirit who gives me rest. You are my Hiding Place where the enemy cannot see me. You protect me in the day of trouble; You surround me with songs of deliverance. You hide me in the shelter of Your Presence, safe from those who conspire against me. You shelter me in Your Presence, far from accusing tongues.

You are the Holy Spirit of Promise. Spirit of God, You empower me to do God's will and to do everything I must do. You are the Spirit who sanctifies me by Your grace. You are the same Holy Spirit who empowered Mary to carry and deliver the Savior of the world. The Holy Spirit, my enabler and my empowerment. You empower me to be a witness. The Spirit who anoints me with a wisdom that no one can go against. You are the Spirit who has the Word as a sword. Holy Spirit, You enable my ears to hear God's voice.

Holy Spirit, You comfort and encourage me. You are the Spirit who advocates for me, my Helper. You help me with my weakness. You are the Holy

Spirit who leads me into all truth. The Spirit who will be with me forever. You are the Spirit who abides with me and in me. Spirit of God, You are the air and breath in my lungs. You are the Spirit of resurrection power who lives in and through me.

Your Spirit leads my life. You are the Spirit of the Lord who is upon me. You have anointed me to bring Good News to the poor, to proclaim that captives will be released. You anoint me to heal the blind and to set the oppressed free. You proclaim through me that the Lord's favor has come. You are the same Spirit of God who raised Jesus from the dead and lives in me. You are the Holy Spirit who fills me and enables me to speak in other tongues. You are the Spirit of Prophecy, You come over me and I prophesy. You are the Spirit of God who has made me. You are the Breath of God who gives me life.

You are the Spirit of Christ who helps me. You are the Holy Spirit who intercedes for me according to the will of God; You pray for me with groaning that cannot be expressed in words. You are gentle and compassionate with me. Holy Spirit, You teach me God's divine ways. You always teach me everything, and You remind me of the words of Jesus. You make me more like Jesus.

You are the Spirit who testifies all about Jesus. You work to bring glory to Jesus Christ. You are the Holy Spirit of the gospel, the Spirit of Pentecost. You are the Spirit who testifies with my spirit that I am a child of God.

Holy Spirit, I know You are a Person, and therefore You are personal. Endow me so I can know You personally. Reveal Yourself to me. Spirit of God, I know You can be grieved by my actions. Help me obey you, I want to please you in everything. I want you to take delight in me.

You are *Ruach Elohim*—You are the Great Wind and Breath of God. You are the seven Spirits of God. Holy Spirit, You are the One with a holy Name. You are the Spirit who has made me holy. You are the fearful Holy Spirit of God. You are the powerful *Shekinah* and Divine Presence over me, the Spirit of Glory in me. You are the Spirit of power, *Dunamis*; Your Spirit rests upon me and in me. You are the Spirit I must be filled with continually. You are the One who convicts me of all sin and God's Righteousness. You have set me free from the law of sin and death.

You washed me, sanctified me, and justified me in Jesus' Name. Your Spirit gave birth to my spiritual life. You regenerated and renewed me. Holy Spirit, You are the One who revives my soul and sets my heart on fire. You are the Author of spiritual fire. You are the Spirit behind my spiritual songs and melodies. You are the Spirit of the latter-day prophetic worship.

You are the Spirit who gives me ears to listen and understand what You are saying. You are the mighty rushing wind with a breaker anointing. You are my Encouragement. Your holy Presence is what I long for and desire with all my heart. You are the Spirit of revival!

Come, Holy Spirit, come! Blow over me and revive my soul today!

---

1. Walter A. Elwell and Barry J. Beitzel, "Omniscience," *Baker Encyclopedia of the Bible* (Grand Rapids, MI: Baker Book House, 1988), 1588.

10

THE SOURCE, ORIGIN, AND OWNER
OF ALL

And the One seated on the throne said, "Behold, I make all things new." Then He said, "Write this down, for these words are faithful and true." And He told me, "It is done! I am the Alpha and the Omega, the Beginning and the End."

Revelation 21:5–6 BSB

For everything comes from him and exists by his power and is intended for his glory. All glory to him forever! Amen.

Romans 11:36 NLT

You are:

1. The God who spoke the world into existence, It appeared at Your command (Psalm 33:9)
2. God, the Maker of all things (Jeremiah 10:16)
3. God, the Alpha, and the Omega (Revelation 21:6; 22:13)
4. God, the First and the Last (Revelation 21:6; 22:13)

5. God, the Beginning and the End (Revelation 21:6; 22:13)
6. Father—You are, You were, and You will forever be the Lord Almighty One (Psalm 90:2, 48:14)
7. The Source of all true knowledge and wisdom (Daniel 2:21; Colossians 1:9–10)
8. The God who cannot be surprised (Ezekiel 11:5; Genesis 3:5)
9. God, the Creator of the visible and invisible (Colossians 1:15–18; Romans 1:20–23)
10. God, the Creator of thrones, powers, rulers, and authorities(Colossians 1:15–18)
11. God, with invisible qualities, eternal power, and divine nature (Romans 1:20)
12. God, *Jehovah-Elohim*—God is the All-Powerful Creator of the universe (Genesis 1:1–3; Deuteronomy 10:17; Psalm 68; Mark 13:19)
13. The King of Creation (Genesis 1; Psalm 8)
14. The Lord God who made the earth and the heavens (Genesis 2:4)
15. God, the Fountain of living waters (Jeremiah 2:13)
16. God, the Source of the water of life, who gives freely to all who are thirsty (Revelation 21:6)
17. God, the Source of all true wealth (Proverbs 10:22; Deuteronomy 8:17–18)
18. God, the Source of all life (Psalm 68:26; 87:7)
19. The Lord, the God of all humanity (Jeremiah 32:27)
20. The Lord, Creator of everything and (who) made all things (Colossians 1:16)
21. God, the Inventor and Creator of the great heavenly lights (Genesis 1:14, 16; Psalm 136:7; James 1:17–18)
22. The God, the Source of all light (Job 38:24; Revelation 22:5)
23. The One who knows where the light comes from, and where the darkness goes to (Job 38:19)
24. The God who laid out the path for the lighting (Job 28:26; 38:24–25)
25. The Lord who made the earth with great power and with outstretched arm (Jeremiah 32:17)

26. The God who has made everything perfect in its time (Ecclesiastes 3:11)
27. God, who made me for Your delight (Psalm 100:3; Isaiah 43:21; Psalm 138:8)
28. The One who made me fearfully and wonderfully complex (Psalm 139:14)
29. The God who knew me before I was formed in my mother's womb (Jeremiah 1:5; Isaiah 49:5)
30. The One who saw me before I was born, from conception (Psalm 139:16)
31. The God who consecrated me before I was born (Jeremiah 1:5)
32. The One who made and wove all the delicate inner parts of my body (Psalm 139:13)
33. The God who took me out of my mother's womb (Psalm 71:6)
34. The One who knows everything about my past, present, and future (Psalm 139:13–16)
35. The God who did a marvelous workmanship in my creation (Psalm 139:14)
36. The Lord who made the heavens skillfully by Your wisdom (Psalm 136:5)
37. The Lord who made the heavens by Your Word (Psalm 33:6)
38. The Lord who made Your army by the breath of Your mouth (Psalm 33:6)
39. God, the Maker of all things (Jeremiah 51:19; Ecclesiastes 11:5)
40. The Lord God my Maker (John 54:5–8; Isaiah 43:15; Psalm 95:6; Job 36:3)
41. The God who formed me for Your delight (Isaiah 43:7, 21; 49:5; Psalm 119:73)
42. The God who makes all things new (Revelation 21:5; 2 Corinthians 5:17–18)
43. Father, the great God who formed all things (Colossians 1:16)
44. God, who before You no other god was formed, nor will there be after You (Isaiah 43:10)
45. The God who formed me into Your image and likeness (Genesis 1:27)
46. God, my eternal Owner (Jeremiah 3:14)

47. The God who owns all our ways (Daniel 5:23)
48. The God who holds my breath in Your hands (Daniel 5:23)
49. God, the Inventor of my personality (Genesis 1:26–28; 2 Peter 1:3–4)
50. The God who can give me the ability to play music for You (Psalm 150:1–5; Genesis 4:21; Psalm 43:4)
51. God, my energy and vitality (Ephesians 3:16; Judges 16; 1 Samuel 30:6)
52. The God who counts all my hairs (Luke 12:7)
53. The God who gives me creativity (Exodus 35:35)
54. God, my reason to live (Philippians 1:21; Romans 14:8)
55. Lord, the Fountain of life (Psalm 36:9)
56. God, my Fountain of rejuvenation (Psalm 103:5; Psalm 91:16; Romans 8:11; Isaiah 40:31)
57. God, the Source of joy and happiness (Isaiah 9:3; Psalm 47:1; 86:4)
58. God the Source of all my Joy (Psalm 43:4)
59. Jesus, the beginning of God's creation (Revelation 3:14; John 1:1)
60. Christ, the One who *existed* from the beginning to end (1 John 1:1; 1 John 2:13; Colossians 1:15–17; Proverbs 8:22)
61. The ever-present God, before the earth and world were birthed (Psalm 90:2)
62. The God who was before the mountains were born (Psalm 90:2)
63. Jesus, everything was created through You and for You (Colossians 1:16)
64. The One who holds all creation together (Colossians 1:17)
65. Christ, Supreme over all who rise from the dead (Colossians 1:18)
66. Christ, Preeminent in everything (Colossians 1:18)
67. The Lord God of the mountains and hills (1 Kings 20:28; Psalm 36:6)
68. God, the Uncreated, Self-existent God (Exodus 3:14; Genesis 21:33; 1 Timothy 6:16; Colossians 1:15)
69. The Master and Possessor of the heavens and the earth (Genesis 14:19)
70. God, the Origin of everything (Genesis 1:1)
71. The Originator of all things (John 1:1–5)

72. The Origin of origins (Genesis 1:1)
73. The Origin of my creation as a human (Genesis 1:27)
74. God, who originated my life, my Originator (Genesis 1:26–27; 5:1–2)
75. God, the Origin of my spirit—You are my Origin; I was Originated in the midst of Your throne (Genesis 1:26–27; 2:7; Psalm 139:13–18; Job 33:4; Ecclesiastes 12:7)
76. God, who created me for Your glory (Isaiah 43:7)
77. God, who created me to worship You eternally (1 Peter 2:9; Isaiah 43:7)
78. God, who was before the day was (Psalm 90:2)
79. The Creator and Designer of all DNA (Genesis 2:7, 21–24)
80. The God and Architect of the ark of the covenant (Exodus 25:10–22)
81. The Designer of the ark who saved Noah and his family from the flood (Genesis 6:14–18)
82. My Designer (Genesis 1:26)
83. My reason to live (Romans 14:8)
84. God, the Creator of every living creature that moves (Genesis 1:21)
85. God, the Creative One (Ephesians 3:9)
86. God, the Creator of all things (Ephesians 3:9)
87. God, the Creator and Designer of humankind (Genesis 1:26–2:25)
88. God, the Creator of the earth (Genesis 1:1)
89. God, the Divine Inventor and Creator of innovation (Revelation 21:5; Exodus 31:2–11)
90. God, the Creator of all true worship (Revelation 4, 5:9–14; Juan 4:23-24)
91. The Creator and Designer of the tabernacle of David (Acts 15:16–17)
92. God, the All-Self-Sufficient, Self-Sustained, and Self-Created (Exodus 3:14; John 5:26; Acts 17:24)
93. The Creator of all heaven and the earth (Genesis 1:1; Genesis 14:19; Psalm 146:6; Daniel 4:37)
94. God, the Faithful Creator (1 Peter 4:19)

95. God, Creator of all angelic beings and spirits (Revelation 5:11)
96. The God and Creator of the angels, cherubim, and archangels (Colossians 1:16; Genesis 2:1; Job 38:4–7; Jude 9; Genesis 3:24)
97. God, the Creator, and Owner of silver and gold (Haggai 2:8–10; Genesis 2:11–13)
98. The Creator and Blesser of the fruits and vegetables (Genesis 1:11; Leviticus 26:4)
99. The Creator, and Owner of all the lands of the world (Genesis 1:9–10)
100. The God and Creator of the creeks, rivers, and lakes (Genesis 1:6–10; 2:10–14; Psalm 65:9; Revelation 22:1)
101. God, the greatest and best Artist of all time (Genesis 1–2:4; Job 40:15–41:34)
102. God, the Master, Chief musician of all times (Psalms)
103. God, the Creator of music (Psalm 32:7; Isaiah 6:1–7)
104. God, the Author, and Creator of sounds and rhythms (Psalm 150:3–6)
105. God, the Creator of colors and fragrances (Genesis 9.13–16; Revelation 4.3; 10:1)
106. The God who creates and forms the mountains (Amos 4:13)
107. God, the Creator and Owner of all the birds (Genesis 1:20; Psalm 50:11)
108. Jesus, by you *all things* were created in heaven and earth (Colossians 1:16; Ephesians 3:9)
109. God, the great Composer of songs of love (Song of Solomon 1; Zephaniah 3:17; Job 35:10 Psalm 42:8)
110. God, the best Singer forever (Zephaniah 3:17)
111. God, the Father who sings joyful songs over me with love (Zephaniah 3:17)
112. The Lord who rejoices over me with gladness (Zephaniah 3:17)
113. God, the Author of all authors (Hebrews 12:2)
114. My Father, the Author of eternal life (John 3:16)
115. Jesus, the Source of eternal salvation for all who obey You (Hebrews 5:9; Hebrews 2:10)
116. The Source of divine healing (Exodus 15:26; 1 Peter 2:24; Luke 7:1–17)

117. Jesus, the Founder, Author, Perfecter, and Finisher of my faith (Hebrews 12:2)
118. God, the Author of peace (1 Corinthians 14:33; John 14:27)
119. God, the Author and Governor of the day and night (Psalm 74:16)
120. The God who built all things (Hebrews 3:4)
121. The God of the living (Mark 12:27)
122. The God of the spirits of all flesh (Numbers 27:16)
123. The God of all flesh (Jeremiah 32:27)
124. The God of the whole earth (Psalm 57:5; Isaiah 40:21–31)
125. The God of my parents (Matthew 22:32; Genesis 31:42)
126. Jesus, the firstborn of every creature (Colossians 1:15)
127. Lord God, who lives from eternity to eternity (1 Chronicles 16:36)
128. The God who kept the sea inside its boundaries as it burst from the womb (Job 38:8–9)
129. The God who clothed the ocean with clouds and wrapped it in thick darkness (Job 38:8–9)
130. God, the Maker of ice (Job 37:10; 38:29–30; Psalm 147:17)
131. God the One who gave birth to the frost of heaven (Job 38:29)
132. God, the divine Architect of all (Psalm 19)
133. Jesus, Appointed Heir and Lawful Owner of all things (Hebrews 1:2)
134. The God who owns the mountain peaks (Psalm 95:4)
135. The God who owns the cattle on a thousand hills (Psalm 50:10)
136. God, the Owner of all that exists—past, present, and future (Psalm 24:1)
137. God, the Owner of the entire earth and all it contains (Ephesians 4:6; Psalm 24:1; Job 41:11)
138. The Lord who owns greatness (1 Chronicles 29:11)
139. The Lord who owns the power (1 Chronicles 29:11 Psalm 62:11; Proverbs 8:14)
140. The Lord who owns the victory (1 Chronicles 29:11)
141. The Lord who owns the majesty (1 Chronicles 29:11)
142. The Lord who owns the riches (1 Chronicles 29:12)
143. Lord, the Author of the New Covenant (Jeremiah 31:31–34; Isaiah 42:6)
144. Lord, the One who builds Your Church (Matthew 16:18)

145. Jesus, the Head of the Church (Ephesians 5:23; Colossians 1:18)
146. Lord and God of the church (Matthew 16:18; 1 Corinthians 1:2)
147. God, the Master Planner of all nations and kingdoms (Isaiah 14:26; Jeremiah 10:7)
148. God, the One who was before Abraham, Isaac, and Jacob (Acts 3:13)
149. The God of all generations (Genesis 17:7; 9:12)
150. The God and Master of heaven and earth (Psalm 146:6; Genesis 14:19)
151. The great Engineer of the world (Genesis 1–5)
152. The Great Architect of Noah's ark (Genesis 7)
153. The God of the rain and snow (Job 37:6; Leviticus 26:4; Psalm 147:16)
154. The God who sends the rain on the earth in its season (Psalm 104:13; Job 5:10; Deuteronomy 11:14; Zechariah 10:1; Leviticus 26:4; Jeremiah 5:24)
155. God, the Father of rain (Job 38:28; Jeremiah 5:24)
156. The One who created a channel for the torrents of rain (Job 38:25)
157. The God who made the laws for the rain (Job 28:26)
158. The God of the spring and summer (Genesis 8:22; Deuteronomy 11:34; Psalm 104:10; Zechariah 10:1)
159. The God of the fall and winter (Job 37:5–6)
160. The Lord, whose earth is full of Your possessions (Psalm 104:24)
161. The God of the water I drink (Genesis 1:2; Isaiah 49:10)
162. The God of the islands (Genesis 1:9-10; 2 Peter 3:5; Ezekiel 26:18; Psalm 97:1)
163. The God of the flowers (Song of Solomon 2:12; Luke 12:27)
164. The God of the cascades and waterfalls (Isaiah 41:18; 61:11; Psalm 42:7)
165. The God who makes the sun and the moon shine (Jeremiah 31:35; Genesis 1:16–18; Psalm 8:3; 136:7–9; 148:3)
166. The God and Creator of the rocks and stones (Exodus 24:4; Deuteronomy 8:7–9; Psalm 31:3)
167. The God and Creator of the twelve pearly gates (Revelation 21:21)

168. The God and Creator of every kind of precious stone (Revelation 21:19)
169. The God of the beautiful butterflies (Genesis 1:20)
170. The God of my pets (Psalm 50:10–11; 145:9)
171. The God of all the animals of the world (Psalm 50:10–12; Genesis 1:20–26; Proverbs 12:10)
172. The God of mountains, hills, ravines, and valleys (Ezekiel 6:3; Proverbs 8:25; Psalm 50:10–12)
173. The God of the beach and the sand (Genesis 22:17)
174. The Lord God who made all sorts of trees grow up from the ground (Genesis 2:9; Leviticus 26:4)
175. The God and Creator of the beautiful trees that produce delicious fruit (Genesis 2:9; Psalm 104:16; Leviticus 26:4)
176. The Creator of seeds (Genesis 1:29)
177. The Creator of green plants (Genesis 1:30)
178. The Creator and Provider of our food (Genesis 1:29; Ecclesiastes 2:24; Psalm 145:15)
179. The God who planted the cedars of Lebanon (Psalm 104:16)
180. The Creator of the garden of Eden, the first garden (Genesis 2:8)
181. The God of the Tree of Life (Genesis 2:9; Genesis 3:22–24; Revelation 22:2)
182. The God of the wind (Psalm 107:25; Luke 8:25; Genesis 8:1–2)
183. God, the One who creates the wind (Amos 4:13)
184. The One who knows the home of the east wind (Job 38:24)
185. The God of the mountain mines of copper (Deuteronomy 8:7–9; Jeremiah 17:3)
186. The God who owns the stones of iron (Deuteronomy 8:7–9)
187. The Origin and definition of Perfect Beauty (Psalm 50:2; 27:4; Ezekiel 27:3)
188. The God who shines in glorious radiance (Psalm 50:2)
189. The God who is my place of relaxation (Mark 6:31; Psalm 46:10; Matthew 8:24; Psalm 3:5; 23:1–6; 127:2)
190. God, the Strength of the strong (Psalm 46:1; 81:1; Judges 16)
191. The God of numbers and symbols (Numbers 10:10)
192. The very definition of perfect peace (John 14:27)
193. The One who is Way more than we know of You (John 21:25)

194. God, the only essential One! (John 15:5)
195. Christ, the Supreme over all creation (Colossians 1:15)
196. God, the Maker of all things I can and cannot see (Colossians 1:16)
197. The King of all kings, Lord of lords, and God of gods (Revelation 17:14; 19:16)
198. Christ the Creator of thrones, kingdoms, rulers, and authorities in the unseen world (Colossians 1:16)
199. The Creator and Designer of all babies (Jeremiah 1:5; Psalm 139:13–24)
200. The Lord who enables even barren woman to become pregnant and give birth (Ruth 4:13; Genesis 29:31; Genesis 30:22–24; Genesis 18:9–14; Luke 1:37)
201. The Creator and Designer of holy sex, it was your idea (Genesis 1:27–28)
202. God, the Author and Creator of the genders of man and woman without mistake (Genesis 2:4–25)
203. The Creator and Author of the man's body designed without mistake (Genesis 2:7; 5:1–2)
204. The Creator and Author of woman's body designed without mistake (Genesis 2:22; 5:1–2)
205. The God who never errs or makes a mistake (Numbers 23:19; Isaiah 46:9; Philippians 1:6; James 1:17; Hebrews 13:8)
206. God, the Creator and Establisher of marriage between one man and one woman from the beginning (Genesis 2:18, 22–24; Matthew 19:8; Romans 1:24-28)
207. The Origin of blessing (Genesis 1:22, 28; 22:17; Ephesians 1:3)
208. God, the Creator and Owner of all diamonds, precious stones, and gems (Ezekiel 28:13; Isaiah 54:12)
209. God, the Architect and divine Designer of nature (Genesis 1; Romans 1:20)
210. The One who formed and established the earth (Jeremiah 33:2; Psalm 93:1)
211. The One whose Name is the Lord (Jeremiah 33:2)
212. God, the Creator of the Leviathan on the sea (Psalm 104:25–26; Job 41:1)

213. God, the Creator of the great sea creatures (Genesis 1:21)
214. The God of the great sea filled with small and great animals (Psalm 104:25–26)
215. The God of all the animals in the waters, skies, and earth (Genesis 1:20–25)
216. The God and Lord of thunders (2 Samuel 22:14)
217. The Creator of law (Exodus 31:18; Galatians 3:1–29)
218. The God who defines what is good and what is not good (Genesis 1)
219. The God of the new beginnings (Genesis 1:1)
220. The King and Author of creation (Genesis 1)
221. The Giver of skills to play musical instruments (Genesis 4:21)
222. The Giver of expertise in the forging tools of bronze and iron (Genesis 4:22)
223. The God who gives the skill to raise livestock (Genesis 4:20)
224. The God who placed all the animals on the earth, sky, and sea in my power (Genesis 9:2)
225. The God who created and provided food, grain, and vegetables for my livelihood (Genesis 9:3)
226. The Creator and Designer of the rainbow and all its colors (Genesis 9:13–14; Revelation 4:3; Ezekiel 1:26–28)
227. The One who designed the rainbow as a sign of Your covenant of mercy with all earth (Genesis 9:13–14)
228. The God who laid the foundation of the earth and set its dimensions (Job 38:4–5)
229. The One who gives birth to the dew (Job 38:28)
230. The One who causes the dawn to know its place (Job 38:12)
231. The God of the stars (1 Corinthians 15:41; Isaiah 40:26; Matthew 2:2)
232. God, the One who can direct the movement of the stars (Job 38:31; Isaiah 40:26)
233. The God of Mars and Jupiter (Acts 14:8–18; 17:22–23)
234. The God of the sun and the moon (Genesis 1:14–16; Psalm 74:16)
235. The God who made the moon to mark the seasons (Psalm 104:19)
236. The One who can direct the constellations through the seasons (Job 38:32)

237. The One who can guide the Bear with her cubs across the heavens (Job 38:32)
238. The Maker of the Pleiades with its seven stars (Amos 5:8)
239. The Maker of the Bear and Orion, the Pleiades and the constellations of the south (Job 9:9)
240. The One who binds the cluster of the Pleiades or loosens the cords of Orion (Job 38:31)
241. God, the One who knows the laws of the universe and use them to regulate the earth (Job 38:33)
242. The Creator of the universe's galaxies (Psalm 8:3; Hebrews 11:3; Job 26:7)
243. The God who created Behemoth, who eats grass like an ox (Job 40:15)
244. The God who commands the sun to start a new day (Job 38:12)
245. The Maker of this new day in which I must rejoice and be glad in it (Psalm 118:24)
246. The God of my ancestors, who have given me wisdom and strength (Daniel 2:23)
247. The Origin of where everything comes from (Romans 11:33–36)
248. The God of Sinai (Psalm 68:8)
249. The Owner of all authority (Ephesians 1:21–23; Matthew 10:1; John 14:12)
250. The One who put all creation under my authority through Jesus Christ (Genesis 1:28; Romans 16:20; Matthew 16:13–20; 21:21–22; Luke 10:19; John 14:12; Psalm 8:4–8; 91:13; Hebrews 2:8)
251. The Creator and Owner of the floodgates of the heavens (Malachi 3:10–12)
252. The One who makes springs pour water into the ravines (Psalm 104:10)
253. The One who makes the streams gush down from the mountains (Psalm 104:10)
254. The God of streams and springs (Deuteronomy 8:7)
255. The God with no equal (Isaiah 40:12-31)

A PRAYER DECLARING THE SOURCE, ORIGIN, AND OWNER OF ALL

Father, I approach Your throne of grace in the Name of Jesus and by Your grace through the Holy Spirit. You always hear my prayers and answer them. I recognize that you are the origin and the fountain of love, mercy, protection, and providence. I acknowledge that You are the Originator of all things and apart from you I can do nothing.

Lord, no matter what challenges come my way this day, I will always recognize You as the Source, the Fountain, and the Origin of everything good. You know it all, so I depend on You for every situation. You are much more than what I think to know of you. You are the One who made this day. You are the Origin of blessing. Lord, You are the only essential One for everything in my life.

I can ask You for Your wisdom and knowledge because You are the Source of all true wisdom, knowledge, and understanding. You made the heavens skillfully by Your wisdom. Father, You are the God of all humanity.

Father, You are the great God who formed all things that exist. You are the One who makes all things new. You are my Owner. You are the One who owns all our ways. You commanded the sun to start a new day since my days began. You are the Maker of this new day; I will rejoice and be glad in it.

You are the Origin of everything, the Source of all beginnings. You hold my breath in Your hands. You are the Fountain of life. In You, I find rejuvenation for my body, soul, and spirit. You are my never-ending Fountain of joy and happiness. You are the Source of all my joy. Lord, pour new joy over my life today.

Lord, You are my energy, vitality, and health. You count all the hairs on my head. You give me anointing for creativity. You are the Inventor of my personality. Lord, You are my Designer, my reason to live. God, You created me for Your glory, to worship You eternally. I worship Your great Name today and forever!

Lord, You are the King and Author of creation. The God of the new beginnings. The Origin of where everything comes from. Father, You are the creative One, the God of all creations. The faithful Creator. Lord, You are the Creator and Designer of humankind.

God, You are the Architect and divine Designer of nature. You are the One who created, formed, and established the earth. You made the earth with great power and with an outstretched arm. You laid the foundations of the earth and set its measurements. You made the heavens by Your Word. Lord, You are the God and Creator of heaven and earth. You are the Creator of the visible and invisible things. The Creator and Maker of everything that exists. In You and through You, all things remain. You are the Master and Possessor of the heavens and earth.

Lord Almighty, You are the Creator of the universe galaxies. The God of the stars. You are the God of Mars and Jupiter, the sun and the moon. You made the moon to mark the seasons. You are the Maker of the Pleiades with its seven stars. You are the Maker of Orion and the Bear, the Pleiades, and the constellations of the South. The One who binds the cluster of the Pleiades or loosens the cords of Orion. God, the One who can direct the movement of the stars. The One who can direct the constellations through the seasons. The One who can guide the Bear with her cubs across the heavens. How amazing are You!

The God who kept the sea inside its boundaries as it burst from the womb, clothed it with clouds, and wrapped it in thick darkness. You are the Creator of the Leviathan of the sea. You created *Behemoth*, who eats grass like an ox. You are the Creator of the great and small sea creatures and every living creature that moves. You are their God.

God, the Father of rain and snow. The One who created a channel for the torrents of rain. The God who made the laws for the rain. You are the One who sends the rain on the earth.

The One who gives birth to the dew. The One who causes the dawn to know its place. You are the Inventor and Creator of the great heavenly lights. The Source of light. The One who knows where the light comes from and where the darkness goes to—the God who laid out the path for the lighting.

You are the Maker of ice. You gave birth to the frost of heaven. God, You know the laws of the universe and use them to regulate the earth with dominion. You are the God and Lord of thunder.

The God of all the animals in the waters, skies, and earth. Father, You placed all the animals on the earth, sky, and sea in my power. You are the Creator of the mountains and the valleys. The God of the mountain mines of copper. You are the God who owns the mountain peaks and owns the cattle on a thousand hills. The God of the hills, the God of the beach, and the sand. You are the God and Creator of the first garden and the Tree of Life. Lord,

You planted the cedars of Lebanon. You were before the mountains were born.

You are the God of the wind; You created the wind and know where the east wind blows. You are the Creator of all winged birds. The Creator of beautiful butterflies such as the Monarch butterfly. The God of all the animals. You are even the God of my pets.

You are the God of the spring and summer, fall and winter. The God who makes the sun and the moon shine. The God of the islands. The God of the flowers. The God of the cascades and waterfalls. The God and Creator of the rocks and stones. You are the God and Creator of the twelve pearly gates. God, You are the Creator and Owner of all diamonds, every kind of precious stones, and all the gems. You are the Creator and Owner of silver and gold. You own the stones of iron. You are the Giver of expertise in the forging tools of bronze and iron—the God who gives the skill to raise livestock.

Father, You are the uncreated, self-existent God. You are The all-self-sufficient, self-sustained, and self-created God. You are the divine Architect of all, Father, You are and will forever be the Lord Almighty! You are my *Jehovah-Elohim*, the God who is all-powerful, Creator of the universe. Lord, You are the Author of eternal life. Father, You are the Author of peace. The very definition of perfect peace.

Father, You are the One who is from the beginning. You are the Author and Governor of the day and night. The God who built all things. God, the Owner of all that existed in the past, present, and future. You own the entire earth and all it contains. You own the greatness; You own the power. Lord, You own the victory, the majesty, and the riches. Father, You are the Source of all true wealth. Lord, the earth is full of Your possessions.

Lord, You are the God and Creator of the beautiful trees that produce delicious fruit, the Creator of seeds and green plants. You created and provided food, grain, vegetables, and fruits for my livelihood and benefit. Lord, You have been the Provider and Source of my provision since the day I was created and every day of my life. Father, You are the Creator and Owner of all lands. Lord, You are the Creator of the creeks, rivers, and lakes. You are the God of the water I drink.

You are the God of the living, the God of the spirits of all flesh. You are the God of the whole earth. The God of my parents and ancestors who have given me wisdom and strength. God, You are the One who was before Abraham,

Isaac, and Jacob. You are the God of all generations. You are the Master Planner of all nations and kingdoms.

Lord, You were formed from the beginning, before anything else was created, supreme over all creation. You existed before all things. Jesus, everything in the heavenly realms and on earth was created through You and for You, and You hold all creation together. You are the Maker of things we can and cannot see.

You are King of all kings, Lord of lords, and God of gods. You made Your army by the breath of Your mouth. You created for Yourself the thrones, powers, kingdoms, rulers, and authorities in the unseen world. You are the former of all things; the Alpha and the Omega; the First and the Last; the Beginning and the End. God, the Maker of all I can see and cannot see. Jesus, You are the Author of the new covenant. The One whose Name is the Lord. You are the Creator of law. The God who defines what is good and what is not good, and no one can change it.

Jesus, You are the Source of eternal salvation for all who obey You. You were the Appointed Heir and Lawful Owner of all things. Lord Jesus, You are supreme over all who rise from the dead. You are the first in everything. You were before the day was. You are God from beginning to end. Jesus, the first-born of every creature, Your existence is from eternity to eternity. You are the Author and Finisher of my faith. You are the Doctor of doctors, the Source of divine healing. The One who created all the earthly ingredients for medicine. The One who enables scientists with knowledge and power to create and invent.

Lord, You are the One who builds Your church. Jesus, You are the head of the church. Lord, You are the God of the church. You are the Source of living waters, the Source of the water of life. You give freely to all who are thirsty. God, You are the Source of all life.

Lord God, before You, no other god was formed, nor will there be after You. You are the God and Creator of all angelic beings, spirits, cherubim, and archangels.

Father, You are the God and Architect of the ark of the covenant. The Creator of the floodgates of heaven. You are the Creator of all true worship, the Creator and Designer of the tabernacle of David. You are the greatest and best Artist of all time. You are the Master and Chief Musician of all times, the Creator of music. The Creator and Giver of skills to play musical instruments.

It is You who gives me the ability to play music for You. Father, You are the great Composer of songs of love. The best Singer ever, the Author and Creator of sounds and rhythms. You gave me vocal chords so I can sing, worship, and proclaim Your names.

You are the Author of all authors and Composer of all composers. You are the Creator of colors and fragrances. You are the Creator and Designer of the rainbow with all its colors. The One who designed the rainbow as a sign of Your covenant of mercy with all earth after the flood.

The divine Inventor and Creator of innovation. You are the great Engineer of the world. You are the Architect and Designer of Noah's ark, who saved Noah and his family from the flood. You are the God of numbers and symbols. You are the God of Mount Sinai.

Lord, You fearfully and wonderfully made me. You are my Maker. You knew me before You formed me in my mother's womb. You created me in Your image and likeness. You made me for Your delight. No matter what I do, You can never be surprised, for You know it all—past, present, and future. Father, You are the Creator and Designer of my DNA. Lord, You are the Origin of my creation, my spirit originated in the midst of Your throne. You are my Origin. Lord, You are a God of covenants. The Creator, Author, Founder, and Establisher of marriage between one man and one woman.

You are the Creator and Designer of holy sex. You are the Author, Creator, and Designer of the genders of men and women without mistake because You are a perfect Creator. You created men and women's bodies perfectly and designed them without mistake. You are the excellent Creator and Designer of all babies. You consecrated me before I was born. You made all the delicate inner parts of my body, knit me together, and shaped me in my mother's womb. Lord, You know me inside and out; You know every bone in my body. You know exactly how I was made, bit by bit, how I was sculpted from nothing into something special for You. Thank You for making me so wonderfully complex! Your workmanship is marvelous and that I know very well. You saw me before I was born, and You know everything about me from conception to birth, even now, and into my future. I worship You in awe. You are breathtaking!

Lord, You are the Origin of beauty, the Perfection of beauty, the definition of perfect beauty, the embodiment of beautiful perfection. You made everything perfect in its time. Lord, You are the God of tranquility and, therefore, my place of relaxation. You are the strength of the weak and the strong.

O Lord, my God, Your majestic Name fills the earth! Your glory is higher than the heavens. Lord, when the night comes, I look at the sky and see the work and signature of Your fingers. You set in place the moon and the stars. And when I see this Lord, I wonder and ask myself, What am I, a mere mortal, that You should think about me, that You should care for me?

Lord, You are the Owner of all authority. You put all creation under my authority through Jesus Christ. God, You are such a marvelous God! You are super amazing! Everything started with You, and all will end on this earth with You. Your plans for me were made before the foundation of the earth. You had me in mind all along through eternity. O Lord, my Lord, Your majestic Name fills the earth!

I will worship Your great Name for eternity! In Jesus' Name, amen and amen.

11

HIS AMAZING LOVE

Beloved, let us love one another, for love is from God, and whoever loves has been born of God and knows God. Anyone who does not love does not know God, because God is love. In this the love of God was made manifest among us, that God sent his only Son into the world, so that we might live through him. In this is love, not that we have loved God but that he loved us and sent his Son to be the propitiation for our sins. Beloved, if God so loved us, we also ought to love one another. No one has ever seen God; if we love one another, God abides in us and his love is perfected in us.

1 John 4:7–12 ESV

And may you have the power to understand, as all God's people should, how wide, how long, how high, and how deep his love is. May you experience the love of Christ, though it is too great to understand fully.

Ephesians 3:16–19

Lord, You love me like I am Your child. You are:

1. God, the Author and Creator of love (1 John 4:19; 1 John 4:8)
2. God, full of tenderness and affection toward me (Philippians 1:8)
3. he God who loves me unconditionally (Romans 5:8; Ephesians 2:8)
4. God, the Father who sings joyful songs over me with love (Zephaniah 3:17)
5. The Father who loves me, because I believe in and love Jesus (John 16:27)

Lord, You love me with an incredible love. You are:

1. The One with an extraordinary love, my amazing incredible Lover (John 3:16; Romans 5:8; Song of Solomon 1:8–14; Psalm 139:14; 1 John 4:8, 16)
2. The high God, You are breathtaking! (Psalm 139:14)
3. The God who breathes Your *Ruach* over and into me (John 20:22)
4. The Lord who is in me, and I am in You (John 14:20; 17:23)
5. My matchless Lover (Psalm 45; Song of Solomon 1:2–4; 5:16)
6. The Lover whose love is better than wine (Song of Solomon 1:2–4)
7. My King-Lover, You are mine and I am Yours (Song of Solomon 1:4, 12; 2:16; 5:16)
8. God the Author of divine romance (Jeremiah 31:3; Revelation. 19:7; 21:2, 9; Psalm 45:11)
9. God, whose unfailing love is better than life itself (Psalm 63:3)
10. The very definition of love and kindness (John 3:16;1 John 4:8)
11. The God who is Love (1 John 4:8)
12. The God whose love is deeper than the ocean; it has no limits or boundaries (Psalm 36:5–7)
13. The Lord, my new love song (Psalm 89:1; 98:1; Job 35:10)
14. The Lord, the Song of my heart (Psalm 40:3; Ephesians 5:19)
15. God, the beloved in Songs of Songs (Song of Solomon 6:3; Revelation 19:7)

16. God, my first love forever (1 John 4:19; Romans 5:8; Revelation 2:4)
17. The God who loves the godly (Psalm 146:8)
18. The One who is altogether lovely (Song of Solomon 5:15)
19. God, the lovely wreath over my head (Proverbs 4:9)
20. God, the agape Love (John 3:16; Romans 3:5)
21. The God who understands my heart always (Proverbs 24:12; Psalm 44:21; 139:1-6)
22. The God who sees me (Proverbs 24:12; 139:1-6)
23. The loving and gentle God (John 3:16; 1 John 4:19)
24. The God of unity (Juan 17:11; 13:35; Ephesians 1:10)
25. God, the Composer of songs of love (Zephaniah 3:17; Song of Solomon)
26. The God of *Selah* (Psalm 3:2–4; 24:6; 62:7–8)
27. The Lord who has countless precious thoughts about me, they outnumber the grains of sand (Psalm 139:17–18)
28. The God whose ways are perfect, who loves justice (2 Samuel 22:31; Matthew 5:48; Psalm 10:14–18)
29. The God who has called me by name and says, "You are Mine." (Isaiah 43:1; 49:1)
30. The Lord whose smile brings forth life into my soul (Proverbs 16:15)
31. The God who deserves to be praised for His great love (Psalm 107:8)
32. God, the divine Lover of my soul (James 4:5)
33. The God who jealously desires the spirit in me (James 4:5)
34. The Lord who declared to me, "You are Mine." (Isaiah 43:1)
35. Lord, the intimate God (James 4:8; John 15:15)
36. The Lord, my only eternal inheritance (Psalm 16:5)
37. The Lord, my Cup of Blessing (Psalm 16:5)
38. My lovely Poem, O King (Psalm 45:1)
39. The most handsome and elegant of all (Psalm 45:2)
40. My Royal Husband who delights in my beauty (Psalm 45:11)
41. My eternal Bridegroom, my Maker (Isaiah 54:5; Hosea 2:16,19–20)
42. My only Lord (Psalm 45:11)

43. The God who loves those who love You (Proverbs 8:17)
44. The Lord, whose Name is a spreading sweet fragrance, a pleasant perfume (Song of Songs 1:2–4)
45. The King who brings me into Your inner chamber (Song of Solomon 1:2–4)
46. The God of spiritual intimacy (James 4:8; John 15:5–15; Song of Solomon 2:10–13; Revelation 3:20)
47. The God who is my Confidant and Best Friend (John 15:15)
48. The high God, You are breathtaking! (Psalm 139:13–14)
49. The Lord whose faithful love never ends (Lamentations 3:22; 1 Corinthians 13:8)
50. The One whose loving waves and surging tides sweep over me (Psalm 42:7)
51. The Lord who pours Your unfailing love upon me (Psalm 42:7)
52. You are my song at night (Psalm 42:8)
53. The God who has precious thoughts about me, that outnumber the grains of sand (Psalm 139:17-18)
54. My Creator who is with me every morning when I wake up (Psalm 139:18)

Lord, You show me your love with actions. You are:

1. The God who loves me with an everlasting love (Jeremiah 31:3–4)
2. The God who has drawn me to Yourself with lovingkindness (Jeremiah 31:3–4)
3. The God who saved me by grace when I believed in You (Ephesians 2:8)
4. The God who gave me the free loving gift of salvation (Ephesians 2:8)
5. The God who gives me long life and satisfaction (Psalm 91:16)
6. The God who pursues me with Your goodness and mercy all the days of my life (Psalm 23:6)
7. The God who keeps Your promises of unfailing love (Daniel 9:4)
8. The God who is in love with me (John 3:16; Romans 8:35, 37–39; Psalm 5:11–12)

9. The Lord who quietly calms all my fears with Your love (Zephaniah 3:17)
10. The Lord God, slow to anger, abounding in lovingkindness and truth (Exodus 34:6–7)
11. The Mighty Savior who delights in me with gladness (Zephaniah 3:17)
12. The Lord God whose unfailing love continues forever (Psalm 117:2)
13. The Lord, whose faithful love endures forever (Psalm 136:1)
14. The God whose steadfast love is eternal for those who fear You (Psalm 103:17)
15. The God who loves me and gave Yourself for me (Galatians 2:20)
16. The Father who loved the world sacrificially, giving Your only Son (John 3:16)
17. The God who crowns me with an everlasting love and tender goodness (Psalm 103:4)
18. The God who claims me as Yours, and calls me by name (Isaiah 43:1)
19. The Lord who makes me acceptable in Your sight (Psalm 19:11–14)
20. The Lord who practices steadfast love, justice, and righteousness in the earth (Jeremiah 9:24)
21. The God who forgives and forgets (Isaiah 43:25)
22. The Lord who gives me a crown of beauty and blessing instead of mourning (Isaiah 61:3)
23. The Bridegroom who will return for Your bride, the church (Matthew 9:15; 25:1–13; Revelation 19:7)
24. The God of total forgiveness (Romans 3:23; Psalm 130:3–4)
25. The One who guards my soul (Proverbs 24:12)
26. The Lord who will not abandon Your people, for that would dishonor Your great Name (1 Samuel 12:22)
27. God, the One who is still present with me when I wake up every morning (Psalm 139:18)
28. The One who puts my tears in Your bottle and registered them in Your book (Psalm 56:8)

29. The King who enchants me with the fragrance of Your love (Song of Solomon 1:3)
30. The Lord who delights in me with love (Psalm 18:19; 149:4)
31. The God who never rejects me, nor will You ever (John 8:11; Isaiah 49:15)
32. The God who never criticizes me (John 8:11)
33. The God who overlooks my weaknesses (2 Corinthians 12:8–10)
34. The Lord who is my strength when I am weak (2 Corinthians 12:8–10)
35. The God of second chances (John 8:11)
36. The God who comforts me with Your unfailing love (Psalm 119.76)
37. The God who gives me rest because I am loved by You (Psalm 127:2)
38. The Lord who gives me a sense of belonging (Jeremiah 30:22; Isaiah 43:1; 1 John 4:4)
39. The One who formed me and called me by name (Isaiah 43:1)
40. The Lord who gives me a sense of significance (John 3:16; Romans 5:8)
41. The God who gives me dignity (Job 40:10; Psalm 148:14, Genesis 1:27)
42. The God who draws near to me when I seek You (James 4:8)
43. The Lord who protects all those who love You (Psalm 145:20)
44. The God who exercises and delights in lovingkindness over the earth (Jeremiah 9:24)
45. The One who takes care of every detail of my life (Psalm 37:23; 47:11)
46. The God who works with my shortcomings and weaknesses patiently (Exodus 4:1–8; 4:10–14)
47. The One who captivates me with Your sweet Presence (Psalm 27:4; Exodus 33:14–15)
48. The delight of my life (Psalm 37:4)
49. The Giver of my heart's desires (Psalm 37:4)
50. The God who will never abandon me (2 Corinthians 4:8–9, Psalm 23:4, Romans 8:35, 37)
51. The Lord who loves me and calls me precious (Isaiah 43:4–5)

52. The Father who loves me dearly & profoundly (John 16:23–27)
53. The Lord, my Best Friend (John 15:13–15)
54. The Lord with a steady and unwavering love that never ceases (Lamentations 3:22)
55. The Lord who places Your hand of blessing over my head (Psalm 139:5)
56. The God who is on my side (Psalm 56:9)
57. The God with a precious unfailing love (Psalm 36:7)
58. The God who took Enoch with You because he walked close to You (Genesis 5:23–24)
59. The Lord who makes my heart Your home as I trust in You (Ephesians 3:17)
60. The Lord who makes my roots grow down into Your love to keep me strong (Ephesians 3:17)
61. The One who gives me the power to understand the magnitude of Your love (Ephesians 3:18)
62. The God of lovingkindness that is from everlasting to everlasting on those who fear You (Psalm 103:17)
63. The God of lovingkindness and faithfulness (Psalm 92:2; Psalm 101:1–2)
64. The One with a magnificent, unfailing love and forgiveness toward me (Numbers 14:19)
65. The God with a priceless unfailing love toward me (Psalm 36:7)
66. The One I can take refuge under the shadow of Your wings (Psalm 36:7)
67. The Lord who weeps and laughs with me, my Best Friend (Genesis 21:6; Luke 6:21; Psalm 126:2–3; Jeremiah 33:11; Isaiah 53:3–4)
68. The One whose unfailing love is as vast as the heavens (Psalm 36:5)
69. The God who provides a daughter-in-law better than seven sons (Ruth 4:14–15)
70. The God who restores our youth and cares for us in our old age (Ruth 4:14–15)
71. The God who knows me well (Isaiah 37:28a; Psalm 139:15–18)
72. The Lord who loves the righteous (Psalm 146:8)

73. The One who runs after me (Psalm 23:6; Luke 15:3–10; Luke 19:10)
74. My Lord Jesus, the Love that heals (Psalm 103:2–5)
75. The LORD who protects all those who love You (Psalm 145:20)

A PRAYER DECLARING HIS AMAZING LOVE

Father, I come before You in Jesus' Name, thanking You for Your amazing love. I know that you love me profoundly, just like your Son, Jesus. You loved me and gave Yourself for me. You sing over me with love because You are full of tenderness and affection toward me, and You love me unconditionally. You loved and saved me by Your grace when I believed and loved You, Jesus. You gave me Your free loving gift of salvation, and You give me long life and satisfaction in You.

You are the Author and Creator of love. Your love never ends. Father you sing joyful and happy songs over me with love. You pursue me with Your goodness and precious unfailing love all the days of my life, and you keep Your promises of incomparable love towards me. Your love is better than life itself. The Lord Almighty, and all-sufficient God.

You are my loving Father, the One who is still with me when I wake up every morning since day one of my creation. You formed me, called me by name and gave me purpose. You delight in me and rejoice over me with gladness. Oh Lord, You are the delight of my life, the Most Precious One! You are breathtaking Lord!

You love me like an extraordinary Lover. You are my eternal incredible Lover. Your love and kisses are better than wine; Your name is sweet. You are the King who captivates me with Your aromatic fragrance of your loving Presence. You are the King who brings me into Your inner chamber. You breathe Your *Ruach* over me and into me. You are in me, and I am in You. You are my matchless Lover and Author of divine romance. My King-Lover, You are mine and I am Yours. You are my eternal Royal Bridegroom who delights in my beauty. I am Your bride, the church. I am waiting for your return because I know that you will come back for me. Lord, You are in love with me, and I am in love with You. You love me with everlasting love. You have drawn me to Yourself with Your unfailing love.

Father, You are love and the very definition of love and kindness. Your love is deeper than the ocean; it has no limits. Lord, You make my heart Your home for I trust in You. You are my new love song, the song of my heart. You are the Beloved in Song of Songs and my beloved too. You are my first love. Jesus, You are altogether lovely. You are an intimate God. You put a lovely wreath over my head. My Lord King, You are my Cup of Blessing, my lovely Poem, the most handsome of all, my only Lord.

When I am troubled, You quietly calm me with Your love. You keep track of all my sorrows, O Lord. You have collected all my tears in Your bottle. You have recorded each one in Your book. I know You are on my side because I trust in you. I know you like it a lot when I trust you.

Lord, You see and know me better than I know myself. When I fail You, You are slow to anger, overflowing with loyal love and faithfulness toward me. You are the God of total forgiveness, the definition of perfect, loving justice. Your eternal love continues eternally because I fear You. You crown me with an everlasting love and tender goodness. You give me new life in Your love. You make me acceptable in Your sight; You forgive and forget my sins. You are the God of second chances.

You make me a diadem of beauty. You are the One who guards my soul. You will not abandon me, for that would dishonor Your great Name. You never reject me, nor will You ever. You never criticize me, You overlook my weaknesses because of Your love, and You are my strength when I am weak.

You work with my shortcomings and weaknesses patiently. You are the God who comforts me with never-ending love. You give me rest because You love me. Lord, You declared me as Yours and called me by name. You give me a sense of belonging, significance, and dignity. You make my roots grow deep in Your love to keep me strong. You are the One who gives me the power to understand the magnitude of Your love because Your love is so deep and infinite. You crown me with Your steadfast love and mercy, which gives me hope for a better future. O Lord, You are the God of lovingkindness and faithfulness from everlasting to everlasting for those who fear You. I know You take delight in me. Lord, thank You for having such marvelous steadfast love and forgiveness toward me.

You zealously desire the spirit in me. Lord, You draw nearer to me when I seek You with all my heart. You protect me because I love You, and You love me with everlasting love. Your lovingkindness toward me is eternally unending. You are the same God who took Enoch with You because he walked close to You. You are a God who seeks to have an intimate relationship with me. You are the God of spiritual intimacy. You weep and laugh with me; You are indeed my Best Friend and my Confidant.

Lord, You take care of every detail of my life. You are the Giver of my heart's desires. Lord, You always understand my heart because You know me well, inside and out. You know where I am, and when I come and go. You know my thoughts and You know my heart. Lord, because of Your great love, You will never abandon me. You love the godly who love and honor Your Name. You've always been a loving God who loves me with an agape love, a selfless, sacrificial, and unconditional love. I take refuge in the shadow of Your wings, and You protect me with love.

Lord, You are the Composer of songs of love. You are my only eternal inheritance. Lord, You have so many precious thoughts about me.

Father, Your smile brings forth life into my soul. You are the divine Lover of my soul. You love those who love You eternally. You love me and have called me precious to You. My Lord, You deserve to be praised for Your great unfailing love. You are the One who calms my fears. You are the God who can provide a loving daughter-in-law better than seven sons. You will restore my youth and You will take care of me in my old age.

You are the perfect Father who loves me deeply more than an earthly father can ever do. Lord, thank You for Your steady and unwavering love that never ceases. Father, place Your hand of blessing over my head and bless me and my family today and forever. You are my *Selah*, I will pause and reflect on Your love on this day. Thank You for Your amazing love Jesus, amen!

12

HIS DIVINE WISDOM AND GUIDANCE

FEATURED SCRIPTURES TO PONDER

He said, "Praise the name of God forever and ever, for he has all wisdom and power. He controls the course of world events; he removes kings and sets up other kings. He gives wisdom to the wise and knowledge to the scholars. He reveals deep and mysterious things and knows what lies hidden in darkness, though he is surrounded by light."

Daniel 2:20–22

If You need wisdom, ask our generous God, and he will give it to You. He will not rebuke you for asking.

James 1:5

You are:

1. The Lord whose instructions are perfect to revive my soul (Psalm 19:7)

2. The God who has the answer for everything (Jeremiah 33:3; Daniel 10:12; Luke 1:37)
3. The God who makes all things work out according to Your plan (Ephesians 1:11)
4. Jesus, the Way (John 14:6)
5. Jesus, the Truth (John 14:6; 8:32)
6. The God who leads me down the right paths for Your Name's sake (Psalm 23:3; Isaiah 48:17)
7. God, the Spirit of wisdom and understanding (Exodus 31:3; Isaiah 11:2; Colossians 1:9)
8. Lord, the Spirit of prophecy (Revelation 19:10)
9. God, the great Guide of my life (Isaiah 33:22)
10. The God who makes the simple wise (Psalm 19:7)
11. The Lord who took me out of a life without direction to give me a land to possess (Genesis 15:7)
12. The God who makes my way perfect (Psalm 18:32; James 1:4)
13. The God who makes me as surefooted as a deer (Psalm 18:32–33)
14. The God who sets me secure upon high places on mountain tops (Psalm 18:33)
15. The God who enables me to stand on mountain heights (Psalm 18:32–33)
16. The One who has given me Your shield of victory (Psalm 18:35)
17. God, the Spirit of counsel and might (Isaiah 11:2–3)
18. The God who frees me from all fear and doubt (Isaiah 41:10)
19. The God who is always with me and never abandons me (Psalm 94:14; John 8:29)
20. A Friend who is closer than a brother (Proverbs 18:24)
21. The God who inspires me with thoughts of innovation (Mark 2:21–22)
22. God, the lamp who lights my way (Psalm 119:105)
23. The Lord who is so good to all, all the time (Psalm 34:8; 135:3; 145:9; 2 Chronicles 5:13)
24. The Lord whose faithfulness continues to all generations (Psalm 100:5)
25. God, the great Giver (John 3:16; Ephesians 2:8–9)
26. The God who never sleeps (Psalm 121:4)

27. God, the Preparer of my place in heaven (John 14:3)
28. The God who gives me much more than all I can ask or think (Ephesians 3:20)
29. God, the Lord my Maker (Psalm 95)
30. God, the Lord my God (Deuteronomy 1:6,19–20)
31. The God who is for me, in me, and over me (Acts 17:28; John 17:23)
32. The God of lovingkindness that endures forever (Psalm 136; Psalm 101:1–2)
33. The God who makes all things new (Revelation 21:5; Isaiah 43:18–19)
34. The God who teaches me what is good (Isaiah 48:17)
35. The God who makes everything beautiful for the right moment (Ecclesiastes 3:11)
36. God, my secret intelligence (Ephesians 3:4; Deuteronomy 29:29)
37. The God who reveals great and hidden things (Jeremiah 33:3; 1 Corinthians 2:10; Deuteronomy 29:29)
38. God, the Giver of all revelation (Revelation 1:1)
39. The God of mysteries, you possess secrets that no one knows (Deuteronomy 29:29; 1 Timothy 3:16)
40. The God who works in mysterious ways (Isaiah 55:8–9)
41. God, who gives me insight (2 Timothy 2:7)
42. God, my Revelation, my Light (Psalm 27:1)
43. God, the One who gives wisdom abundantly and without reproach (Ecclesiastes 2:26)
44. Christ, the Power and Wisdom of God (1 Corinthians 1:24)
45. The God of divine purpose (Job 42:2; Romans 8:28; Proverbs 19:21)
46. The God of my destiny (Jeremiah 1:5; Isaiah 55:11)
47. The God who knows everything (1 John 3:20; Psalm 69:5)
48. The God who knows the past, present, and future (Isaiah 43:18)
49. God, the Shepherd's Rod (Psalm 23:4)
50. The God who instructs my heart (Psalm 16:7)
51. The Lord who directs my steps (Psalm 37:23; Proverbs 3:5–6; Psalm 32:8)
52. The God who delights in every detail of my life (Psalm 37:23)

53. The Spirit that takes me from one degree of glory to another (2 Corinthians 3:18; Psalm 84:7)
54. Lord, the only wise God (Romans 16:27)
55. God, the Guide of my youth (Jeremiah 3:4; Proverbs 2:17)
56. The God who knows the human heart (Proverbs 15:11)
57. The God who tests my heart and character (Psalm 105:19; 139:23)
58. The God who searches the mind and the heart of humans (Romans 8:27; Jeremiah 17:10; Psalm 44:21)
59. The God who searches out the thoughts and intentions of everyone (Revelation 2:23)
60. The Lord who examines the motives of people (Proverbs 16:2; Psalm 7:9)
61. The God who reveals Your thoughts to humans (Amos 4:13)
62. The God who speaks from heaven (Hebrews 12:25)
63. God, the only wise God, there is no other like You (Romans 16:27; Jude 25)
64. God, the Solution to everything (Philippians 4:6)
65. God, the only One who satisfies my soul (Psalm 63; 107:8–9)
66. God, my everything in everything (1 Corinthians 15:28)
67. The God who reveals Yourself to whomever You desire (Matthew 11:27; Luke 24:32; Ephesians 1:17–18)
68. God, the Spirit who guides and instructs me into all truth (John 16:13)
69. The God who tests us and refines us as silver and gold is refined (Psalm 66:10; Malachi 3:3; Zechariah 13:9: 2 Corinthians 3:18)
70. The God who refines me in the furnace of suffering (Isaiah 48:10)
71. The One who enables me with pure, peace-loving, and gentle wisdom (James 3:17)
72. The Lord who fills me with mercy and the fruit of good deeds (James 3:17)
73. The God who gives wisdom to the wise (Daniel 2:21)
74. The God who empowers me with Your wisdom and strength (Daniel 2:23)
75. The God who knows all my works through eternity (Acts 15:18; Revelation 3:8)

76. The God who speaks into my life (Matthew 4:4)
77. God, the Giver of dreams and visions (Numbers 12:6; Daniel 1:17)
78. The God who speaks in my dreams and visions at night (Job 33:15; Numbers 12:6)
79. The God who opens my ears to listen (Isaiah 50:4)
80. The God who opens my eyes to see and understand (Psalm 119:18)
81. The Solution to all my challenges (Matthew 7:7; James 1:5; Philippians 4:13; John 15:5)
82. The God who is greater than my emotions (1 John 3:20)
83. The God who is greater than my understanding (Isaiah 55:9)
84. The gracious Spirit who leads me on level ground (Psalm 143:10)
85. The God who teaches me to do Your will (Psalm 143:10)
86. The gentle Spirit who instructs me (Nehemiah 9:20; Psalm 143:10)
87. The Lord who gives the right answer to my plans (Proverbs 16:1)
88. The Lord who determines my steps (Proverbs 16:9)
89. The Lord who made everything for Your divine purposes (Proverbs 16:4)
90. The God who gives me complete knowledge of Your will (Colossians 1:9)
91. The God who empowers me to honor and please You (Colossians 1:10)
92. The God who gives me spiritual wisdom and understanding (Colossians 1:10)
93. The Source of all true knowledge and wisdom (Daniel 2:21; Colossians 1:9–10)
94. The God who helps me grow as I get to know You better and better (Colossians 1:10)
95. The God who leads, guides, and restores me for Your Name's honor (Psalm 23:3; 31:3)
96. God, my total trust (Psalm 143:8; 22:4)
97. The God of my future and destiny (Jeremiah 29:11; Psalm 37:37)
98. The God of divine revelation (Matthew 13:11)

99. The Father who teaches me Your Word, which is truth (John 17:17)
100. God the Light by which I see (Psalm 36:9)
101. The God who commands me not to depend on my understanding (Proverbs 3:5)
102. The God who revealed Your ways to Moses (Psalm 103:7)
103. The God who is familiar with all my ways (Psalm 139:3)
104. The Lord who tells me remarkably unknown secrets I do not know about things to come (Jeremiah 33:3)
105. The God of true wisdom and power (Job 12:13; 28:28)
106. The God who owns counsel and understanding (Job 12:13)
107. The One who owns all strength and wisdom (Job 12:16)
108. The God who does nothing unless You reveal it to Your servants, the prophets (Matthew 13:11)
109. The Lord who holds me by my hand so I may not stumble or fall (Psalm 37:24)
110. Christ Jesus, in whom all the treasures of wisdom and knowledge are hidden (Colossians 2:3)
111. The One who shows me the way of life (Psalm 16:11)
112. The Lord who established the world by Your wisdom and understanding (Jeremiah 10:12)
113. The Power behind my faith (Romans 10:17)
114. The God of my origin and destiny (Job 1:21; Jeremiah 1:5)
115. The God who speaks with signs (Exodus 4:1–8)
116. The God who teaches me what I am to do (Exodus 4:15–16)
117. The God of wisdom (Proverbs 1:3–4; James 1:5)
118. The God who teaches me to live a disciplined and successful life (Proverbs 1:3–4)
119. The God who gives insight (Proverbs 1:3–4)
120. The God who gives knowledge and discernment to the young (Proverbs 1:3–4)
121. The foundation of true knowledge (Proverbs 1:7)
122. The Lord who grants me wisdom (Proverbs 2:6)
123. The Lord from whose mouth comes knowledge and understanding (Proverbs 2:6)
124. The Knowledge that fills me with joy (Proverbs 2:10)

125. The God who owns counsel and sound wisdom (Proverbs 8:14)
126. The God of understanding (Proverbs 8:14)
127. The God who owns Common sense and success, Insight, and strength (Proverbs 8:14)
128. The God who gives wisdom to the kings to reign and make impartial decrees (Proverbs 8:15)
129. The God who helps rulers lead and nobles make righteous judgments (Proverbs 8:16)
130. The Holy One, knowledge of You results in good judgment (Proverbs 9:10–11)
131. Lord, Your wisdom multiplies my days and adds years to my life (Proverbs 9:10–11)
132. The Lord who gives the right answer to my plans (Proverbs 16:1)
133. The Lord who made everything for Your own purposes (Proverbs 16:24)
134. The Lord God, no one can measure the depths of Your understanding (Isaiah 40:28)
135. The God who has all wisdom and power (Daniel 2:20–22)
136. The One who gives me wisdom and makes me wiser (Daniel 2:20–22)
137. The God who gives me knowledge (Daniel 2:20–22)
138. The God who reveals deep and mysterious things (Daniel 2:20–22)
139. The God who knows everything that is hidden (Daniel 2:20–22)
140. The God who controls the course of world events (Daniel 2:20–22)
141. The God who understands and knows the way of wisdom (Job 28:23)
142. God, the One who gives intuition to the heart and instinct to the mind (Job 38:36)
143. The One who is wise enough to count all the clouds (Job 38:37)
144. The God of divine purpose (Job 42:2)
145. The One who uncovers mysteries hidden in darkness, and brings light to the deepest gloom (Job 12:22)
146. The One I depend on for everything (John 15:5; Philippians 4:13)

147. The Strength through whom I can do everything (John 15:5; Philippians 4:13)
148. The One who grants a treasure of common sense to the upright (Proverbs 2:7)
149. The Shield to those who walk with integrity (Proverbs 2:7)
150. The One who guards the paths of the just (Proverbs 2:8)
151. The One who protects those who are faithful to You (Proverbs 2:8)
152. The Lord who helps me understand what is right, just, and fair (Proverbs 2:9)
153. The Lord who helps me find the right way to go (Proverbs 2:9)
154. The God who is great and rich in wisdom and knowledge (Romans 11:33)
155. The God of unsearchable judgments and unfathomable ways (Romans 11:33)
156. The Origin from where everything comes and exists by Your power for Your glory (Romans 11:33–36)
157. The One who opens my mind to understand the Scriptures (Luke 24:45)
158. The mighty God who does not despise anyone (Job 36:5)
159. The God who is mighty in power and understanding (Job 36:5)
160. The one who guides all the nations of the world (Psalm 67:4)

A PRAYER DECLARING HIS WISDOM AND GUIDANCE

Father God, I come before Your Presence in Jesus' mighty Name. I draw near to You on this day by Your merits and sacrifice on the cross and through Your Holy Spirit. Thank You with anticipation for Your wisdom and guidance You are giving me today. You always have the answer for everything, even the hardest things. You are the God who makes all things work out according to Your plan. You are wise enough to even count all the clouds and stars.

You have all wisdom and power in Your hands. You understand and know the way of wisdom in everything. You control the course of world events; You know everything that is hidden. You are the God who reveals deep and mysterious things. You give intuition to my heart and instinct to my mind.

You are a God of divine purpose. You are the Spirit who guides and instructs me into all truth every day of my life. Lord, instruct me, for Your instructions are perfect and always revive my soul. You are the God of divine revelation and the Giver of dreams and visions; therefore, give me Your dream and Your vision for my life today, this week, this month, and this year.

Father, You reveal Yourself to whom You desire in Your sovereignty, and love those who love You.

Lord, search my mind's thoughts and my heart's intentions to see whether I am seeking after You and going after Your will. I know You are a God who works all things after the counsel of Your own will and for Your divine purposes.

Jesus, when I need Your direction and I don't know which way to go, all I need to do is go through You, because You are the perfect Way, Truth, and Life. So, as I enter Your Presence, which is the Way, the Truth, and the Life, You take away all fears of the future because You are my Eternal Security, and my life is hidden in Your merciful and loving hands. Give me wisdom and empower me to understand and comprehend Your divine nature. Give me eyes to see and ears to hear, endow me so I can process Your truths and Your will.

You guide me in the paths of righteousness. You are the Spirit of wisdom, understanding, and prophecy, the Giver of all revelation. Lord God, no one can measure the depths of Your understanding. You are the One who gives wisdom to kings and presidents to reign and lead nations, and You make unbiassed decrees. You help rulers lead, and nobles make righteous judgments. You make the simple wise. O Lord, You know my human heart; make me wise. I know that the knowledge of You will empower me to make a good and sound judgment that will multiply my days and years of life.

God, You are the Spirit of counsel and might. You are the One who frees me from all fear and doubt; You make my way perfect by teaching me Your ways. You are the lamp that lights my way. Lord, when I cry out to You in prayer, You reveal to me remarkably unknown divine truths that I was unaware of, and You reveal to me future events that we don't know of.

You are the Shepherd's Rod who leads me beside peaceful streams. You guide me along the right path. Lord, You lead, guide, and restore my strength for Your Name's honor. You are the One who instructs me every day. You speak to me from heaven. You direct my steps, and You delight in every detail of my life, even the smallest and most "insignificant" things, because You love us. You know everything.

You have been my Guide, Knowledge, and Discernment since my youth. You have tested my heart and character throughout my life. Lord, You are the One who tests me and refines me as silver and gold. You refine me in the furnace of life's sufferings and life's challenges. You purify, mold, and form me more and more into Your glorious image, so I may look more like You. Lord, enable me to walk in Your pure, peace-loving, and gentle wisdom on this day.

Lord, You are the true highest intelligence, my secret intelligence. You give me insight; You are my revelation because You are the God of divine power and wisdom. You give me divine purpose through Your wisdom. My destiny is found in You because Your Presence is my origin and my destiny. I came from You, and I shall go back to You. You are my sweet home. You know everything, yes, absolutely everything. You know everything about my ancestors' past, present, and future. You are my all in all; You are the divine Solution to everything I need and desire. You are a mighty God who does not despise me. The God who is mighty in strength of understanding.

Father, You have provided me with all I need to live a godly life through my knowledge of Your Son. You give me spiritual wisdom and understanding to honor Your Name and please You in all I do. You bestow on me a treasure of common sense. You help me understand what is right, just, and fair. You help me identify the right way to go. You open the understanding of my mind and You give me the ability to understand Your Word and hear Your voice in my heart. Empower me to understand the mysteries in Your Word. Reveal to me the things that are hidden and hard to understand for humans. Lord, I know You have the power to do this and more.

You are the Shield to those who walk with integrity. The One who guards the paths of the just. You protect those who are faithful to You. You are great and rich in wisdom and knowledge—the God of unsearchable judgments and unfathomable ways. You are the Origin from where everything comes and exists by Your power and for Your glory.

You are my Friend, closer than a brother. You are always with me and never abandon me. Father, You are so good to me all the time. You are trustworthy because Your faithfulness continues through all generations. Lord, You make all things new and fresh. You are writing a new page daily with wisdom in my heart. Lord, You are the only One who satisfies my soul.

Thank You because You are the One who gives me innovating ideas for my business, ministry, and day-to-day endeavors. Lord, You are the only wise God;

there is no one like You. Lord, You are the great Guide in my life. You took me out of a life without direction to give me a land of blessings to possess.

Lord, You make me as surefooted as a deer, enabling me to stand on high places on mountain tops. You train my hands and strengthen my arms for each day's battle, and You have given me Your shield of victory.

Father, You are the great Giver who never sleeps. I know Your lovingkindness endures forever in me and over me. Thank You for giving me much more than all I can ask or think. Thank You for preparing my place in heaven where we will spend eternity together, where there will be no longer be pain, sickness, loneliness, or any other earthly need. We will be together for all eternity. You are my safe place, my place of origin from where my soul originated. You are my beloved Father, Creator of my spirit. You uphold me with Your gentleness.

Father, You know all my works through eternity; I ask for Your merciful favor and grace over my life. Lord, You are the One who directs my steps. You hold me by my hand so I may not stumble or fall. You are my Maker, and You know me better than anyone else. Lord, You reveal Your thoughts to me. You grant me and empower me with Your wisdom and strength.

From Your mouth comes knowledge and understanding that fills me with joy. You speak into my life through Your Word and Spirit. You speak through signs. You are a God who works in mysterious ways. You make Yourself known through visions and dreams. You are the One who opens my ears to listen to Your voice and opens my eyes to see and understand Your will for my life.

I have treasured Your Word in my heart so I might not sin against You. Oh, gentle and gracious Holy Spirit, instruct me, guide me, and lead me in Your divine heavenly ways.

Father, You possess every desirable counsel and sound wisdom. Teach me Your Word, which is truth. You are the Light by which I see. Lord, I will not depend on my own understanding but Yours. I will lean on You for knowledge and understanding, for You are my Tree of Life. Lord, keep me from leaning toward the tree of the knowledge of good and evil so that I will never rely on my own understanding but solely on Yours. Lord, do not allow me to go my own way, nor to make me independent of your wisdom. You are the strength and power through whom I can do everything. I know apart from You, I cannot do anything but with you I can do everything.

Lord, help me listen to what You say and treasure Your commands. Tune my ears to Your wisdom and help me concentrate on Your divine understanding. Lord, I cry out for insight, wisdom, and understanding. I seek them as if they were silver and hidden treasures so that I may comprehend what it means to fear You and obtain knowledge of You. I know You are the One who grants wisdom! From Your mouth comes knowledge and understanding. You grant a treasure of common sense to the upright. You are a Shield to those who walk with integrity. You guard the paths of the just and protect those who are faithful to You. Lord, help me understand what is right, just, and fair, and help me find the right way to go. Let Your wisdom enter my heart, and knowledge fill me with joy, so that my wise choices will watch over me and Your understanding will keep me safe.

I know You are familiar with all my ways and deeply know me more than anyone in this world. O Lord, my God, true wisdom, power, strength, counsel, understanding, and intelligence belong to You.

You are a God who is great and rich in wisdom and knowledge. You are the One who opens my mind to understand the Scriptures.

You are the Solution to all my challenges. You help me understand You are greater than my emotions; therefore, my emotions bow before You in obedience. Lord, You are greater than my understanding. You are the Source and foundation of all true knowledge and wisdom that I can depend on. Lord, teach me what I am to do on this day and going forward. Teach me and empower me to live a disciplined and successful life according to You. I know You take delight in blessing me because Your love for me is great.

Father, I know You made everything beautiful in its own time. Lord, give me a deeper knowledge of You and make me wiser so I can always honor Your great Name. So, I can also influence the world to honor Your great Name.

You have the correct answer to my plans for You are the One who determines my steps. You made everything for Your own divine purposes. It is Your delight to give me complete knowledge of Your will for my life. You enable me to produce every kind of good fruit in honor of Your Name. Fill my life with mercy and compassion.

You help me grow as I get to know You better and better. You guide me along the right paths with Your truth.

Father, I give You my total trust and put my future and destiny in Your hands going forward from this day on. You do nothing unless You reveal it to

Your servants. Jesus, in You is hidden all the treasures of wisdom and knowledge, and You established the world by Your own wisdom and understanding.

Jesus, I depend on You to show me the way of life because You are the Way, the Truth, and Life. You are the Power behind my faith. Guide me on this day, and empower me to produce the fruit of Your Spirit throughout this day. Enable me to overcome life's challenges and shortcomings so that I can grow, flourish, and thrive in my relationship with You and others from this day forward. Grant me Your favor and grace, and the blessing of Your wisdom, knowledge, understanding, revelation, discernment, and direction to make the right decisions in a timely manner every day.

Synchronize my will to Your will, and don't let me go astray from it! Lord, open the doors that need to be opened and close those that are a waste of my time, energy, and life on this earth. Holy Spirit, dwell in me and guide me in all my decisions over this day and going forward. I commit everything before You, Lord and King of my life. I trust Your guidance, protection, and providence for all my family needs—spiritually, physically, mentally, intellectually, emotionally, and financially. Thank You for Your mighty divine guidance, my beloved Father. In Jesus' mighty Name, amen!

13

HIS HEALING POWER

Trust in the LORD with all your heart; do not depend on your own understanding. Seek his will in all you do, and he will show you which path to take. Don't be impressed with your own wisdom. Instead, fear the LORD and turn away from evil. Then you will have healing for your body and strength for your bones.

Proverbs 3:5–8

"I will give you back your health and heal your wounds," says the LORD.

Jeremiah 30:17

My Emotional Healing. You are:

1. My Lord Jesus, the Love that heals me (Psalm 103:2–5; Jeremiah 33:6)
2. The One who seated me in the heavenly realms with Jesus (Ephesians 2:6)

3. The God who comforts those who are cast down (2 Corinthians 7:6)
4. The Lord whose Presence and words are healing to my soul (Psalm 41:4)
5. The God who wounds and heals (Deuteronomy 32:39)
6. God, *Jehovah-Rohi*—the Lord my Shepherd/Pastor (Psalm 23:1)
7. God, the Spirit of Power (Matthew 1:18; Micah 3:8)
8. The God of my strength (2 Samuel 22:33)
9. God, my Helper (Psalm 54:4)
10. The God who cries with those who cry (Romans 12:15; John 11:35)
11. The God who answers my cry (Psalm 34:17; Jeremiah 33:3)
12. The God who wipes away all my tears (Revelation 21:4)
13. God, my Battle Cry (Isaiah 42:13; Ephesians 6:10)
14. The Lord whose ears are attentive to my cry (Psalm 34:15)
15. God, the health of my countenance (Psalm 43:5)
16. God, the Giver of all abundant life (John 10:10)
17. The God of the little ones (Matthew 18:10)
18. The God who has a count of all my hairs (Luke 12:7)
19. The God who arms me with strength and power (Psalm 18:32)
20. The Lord who gives strength to Your people (Psalm 29:11)
21. God, the strength of the poor and needy in distress (Isaiah 25:4)
22. The One who renews my youth like the eagle's (Psalm 103:5)
23. God, the Rock of my strength and my glory (Psalm 62:7)
24. God, the Almighty in strength (Job 9:4)
25. The God with incredible greatness in power (Ephesians 1:19)
26. The God of all comfort (2 Corinthians 1:3)
27. The God who establishes me with power (2 Corinthians 1:21; Isaiah 40:10)
28. The God whose Spirit dwells in me (Romans 8:9; John 14:17)
29. The Giver of rest and sweet sleep (Matthew 11:28; Psalm 4:8)
30. The God who gives rest to those who are weary and burdened (Matthew 11:28–30)
31. The God who restores my soul (Psalm 23:3)
32. God, my Restorer (Isaiah 58:12; Acts 3:21; Psalm 23:3)

33. The God who guides me along paths of justice for the love of Your Name (Psalm 23:3)
34. God, my Rest (Psalm 62:1)
35. God, the Strength of my heart and my Portion forever (Psalm 73:26)
36. The God of sufficient and sustaining grace (2 Corinthians 12:9–10)
37. The One who heals me and lifts my head with honor (1 Samuel 2:30; Psalm 3:3; John 12:26)
38. The Lord who heals my heart (Psalm 147:3)
39. The God of consolation (Jeremiah 31:13)
40. The God who is greater than my emotions (1 John 3:20)
41. The God who comforts me with Your unfailing love (Psalm 119.76)
42. The God who strengthens me to do all things through Christ (Philippians 4.13)
43. The God of peace that surpasses all comprehension (Philippians 4:7)
44. The one who guards my heart and mind with peace in Christ Jesus (Philippians 4:7)
45. The God who is close to the brokenhearted (Psalm 34:18)
46. The Lord who heals the brokenhearted and binds up their wounds (Psalm 147:3)
47. The Lord who saves those who are crushed in spirit (Psalm 34:18–19)
48. The LORD who lifts up those who are bowed down (Psalm 146:8)
49. The Sun of Righteousness who rises with healing in its wings (Malachi 4:2)

My Physical Healing. You are:

1. The One who heals me by Your wounds (1 Peter 2:24)
2. The God who heals me by Your powerful Word (Psalm 107:20)
3. The God who heals all my diseases (Psalm 103:3; Exodus 15:26)
4. The God who gives me health and healing (Jeremiah 33:6)

5. Jesus, the One who heals every kind of disease and illness (Matthew 4.23)
6. The God who can heal all the sick (Matthew 8:16)
7. The God who snatched me from the door of death (Psalm 107:20)
8. The God who never fails me (1 Peter 4:19)
9. The Lord who restores me to full health (Psalm 41:3)
10. The Lord who sustains me when I am sick (Psalm 41:3)
11. Jesus, the great Physician (Jeremiah 8:22)
12. God, *Jehovah-Rapha*—the Lord my Healer (Exodus 15:26; Acts 9:34)
13. The God who heals my body (Proverbs 3:8; Jeremiah 33:6; Psalm 41:3)
14. The God who strengthens my bones and tendons (Proverbs 3:8; Ezekiel 37:4-10)
15. The God of health (Jeremiah 30:17)
16. My Divine Health and Wellness (Jeremiah 30:17; 1 Corinthians 6:19–20; Psalm 30:2)
17. The God of maximum power over all and over everything (Revelation 15:8; Psalm 147:4–5; Romans 9:5)
18. The God who gives me sight to see (Proverbs 29:13)
19. The God who works miracles among Your People (Galatians 3:5)
20. The God of great wonders beyond measure (Job 5:9; Psalm 77:14; 1 Timothy 1:14)
21. The God of countless miracles (Job 5:9; Psalm 77:14)
22. The God of signs, wonders, and mighty miracles (Hebrews 2:4; Psalm 13:4; Deuteronomy 6:22)
23. The God who did wonderful works to be remembered (Psalm 111:4)
24. The God of the impossible, nothing is too difficult for You (Luke 18:27)
25. The God who delivers the demon-possessed and oppressed (Matthew 8:16)
26. The God who casts out evil spirits with a simple command (Matthew 8:16)
27. The God of powerful decrees (Exodus 18:20; 2 Chronicles 34:31)

28. The God who declares new things before they happen (Isaiah 42:9)
29. The Owner of the key of David (Revelation 3:7)
30. The Lord who keeps me alive (Psalm 54:4)
31. The Lord who is my life eternally (Psalm 42:8)
32. God, the air and breath in my lungs (Genesis 2:7; Job 27:3; Ezekiel 37:9; Psalm 150:6)
33. The God who helps me and rescues me from death (Psalm 56:13)
34. The Life-Giving Light of my soul (Psalm 56:13)
35. The God who is always with me, right beside me (Psalm 16:8)
36. The One who calms my fears (Isaiah 43:4–5)
37. The Lord, my life-giving Fountain (Proverbs 14:27)
38. The Lord who gives power to the weak and strength to the powerless (Isaiah 40:29)
39. The One in whom I find new strength to soar high on wings of eagles (Isaiah 40:31)
40. The One who hears my cry and restores my health (Psalm 30:2)
41. The Doctor of doctors, the Source of divine healing and miracles (Exodus 15:26; 1 Peter 2:24; Luke 7:1–17)
42. Jesus, whose power works best in my weakness (2 Corinthians 12:8–9)
43. The God who holds the breath of my life in Your hands (Job 12:10)
44. The God in whom all humanity finds shelter (Psalm 36:7)
45. The Fountain of life (Psalm 36:9)
46. My Fortress in times of trouble (Psalm 37:39; 62:2)
47. The Lord who rescues the godly (Psalm 37:39)
48. The One who keeps me from falling into the pit of death (Psalm 30:3)
49. The One whose anger lasts only a moment (Psalm 30:5)
50. The One whose favor lasts a lifetime (Psalm 30:5)
51. The One who converts my weeping into joy (Psalm 30:5)
52. The One who takes sickness away from me (Exodus 23:25–26)
53. The LORD who opens the eyes of the blind to receive their sight (Psalm 146:8; Luke 7:21–23)
54. The Merciful Healer of the Blind (Matthew 20:34; Luke 4:18–19)

55. The King of our bodies (1 Corinthians 6:19–20; 1 Timothy 4:8; Genesis 2:7)
56. The King of our divine health (3 John 2; Psalm 105:37; Joel 3:10)
57. The Healer of all demon-possessed, epileptic, or paralyzed (Matthew 4:23–25)
58. The One who make the lame walk, cleanses the lepers, and make the deaf hear (Luke 7:21–23)
59. The One who raises up the dead (Luke 7:21–23)
60. He who commands me: get up and walk! (Acts 3:6; John 5:1–18; Mark 2:1–12)

A PRAYER DECLARING HIS HEALING

Father, I stand before Your throne through Jesus Christ, my Savior. You raised me with Christ and seated me in the heavenly realms with Jesus Christ, and from this position, I pray to You. Lord, I am believing with confidence and certainty that You are the truth. You are the God of great wonders beyond measure. The God of countless and marvelous miracles. You did wonderful works to be remembered forever. You are the God of signs, wonders, and mighty miracles—yesterday, today, and forever. Therefore, on this day, You are still as powerful as You have always been because You reign over everything for eternity. Your throne is immovable and invincible, and Your words are faithful and true, worthy of being trusted.

Father, I find my strength inside Your grace; submerge me in the ocean of Your grace. You comfort those who are cast down, and You heal the wounds of the brokenhearted. Lord, Your sweet and powerful Presence and words of truth heal my body, soul, and spirit.

My body is Yours, the temple of Your Holy Spirit who dwells in me and is with me. Since my body is Your temple, this temple has to be free from disease and bondage. Because where Your Spirit is, there is freedom, healing, wholeness, joy, and peace.

Holy Spirit, You are my deliverance because where You are present, there is freedom. Holy Spirit of God, release me from all bondage of sickness in the Name of Jesus. You are the Spirit of power and might; therefore, You are my Strength and Helper. You are always close to those who are suffering. You never reject a broken and contrite heart. O Lord God, heal my heart today.

You are my *Jehovah-Rohi*—the Lord, my Shepherd, my Pastor. I have all I need in You. You let me rest in green meadows and lead me beside peaceful streams. Lord, it is You who renews my strength. I know You guide me along the right paths, bringing honor to Your Name. When I walk through my darkest valley where there seems to be no hope, I don't have to be afraid.

I know You will always protect and comfort me as You guide me to the brighter side. There I will see Your shining glory upon my face.

You give power to the powerless and strength to the weak. Lord, You heal me when I am brokenhearted and bind up my wounds because You are my Abba Papa and You love me unconditionally. You cry with those who cry, and You are the One who answers my heart cry, for You are my Battle Cry. You promise to answer my cry and to reveal great and mighty things that I am unaware of when I call on You.

I know Your ears are attentive to my weeping prayers because You are a good Daddy. You turn my weeping into joy. You are my Fortress in times of trouble; You take sickness away from me. You are the Heartbeat in my heart and the Fountain of my life. You are the One who keeps me alive! Lord, You keep me from falling into the pit of death. The God in whom all humanity finds shelter. You always rescue the godly. Father, I know Your anger lasts only a moment, but Your favor lasts a lifetime.

In the middle of my distress, You armed and established me with Your strength and power so I can be renewed and comforted in You. You are my Rock of Refuge, my Strength, and my Glory. Your Holy Spirit dwells in me powerfully. You are the mighty in strength and the God with incredible greatness of power.

Father, You are the One who gives me rest and sweet sleep every night. You are the God who gives rest to those who are weary and burdened. You restore my soul and guide me along paths of justice for the love of Your Name. You are my rest—the One who restores my soul.

You are always sufficient and enough for me. You sustain me by Your grace. Your power is perfected in my weakness; it is You who makes me strong. You are the One who heals my heart and lifts my head with honor for Your sake. My Lord, You are the God of consolation, and You are greater, higher, and more valuable than my emotions. Thank You because You comfort me with Your merciful and unfailing sweet love.

Lord, You restore my soul. You strengthen and empower me to do all things through Your power and strength. You are the one who guards my heart and mind with peace in Christ Jesus, which surpasses all human comprehension.

Lord, touch my body and heal me by Your stripes on the cross, Your precious blood, and Your mighty Name.

Heal my mind and my emotions from all past trauma. Erase all painful and traumatic memories from every cell in my life. Jesus, in Your mighty Name and by my own decision, I ask You to close the doors of trauma in my life. I renounce all anger, confusion, hatred, perplexity, spiritual deafness, stubbornness, bitterness, resentment, feelings of failure, and the spirits of rejection and abandonment in my life. I dethrone, disavow, and throw them out of my life forever in the Name of Jesus Christ. I now declare myself healthy, free, and restored mentally and emotionally, physically and spiritually, in Your powerful Name, and by Your blessed blood.

Jesus, send Your powerful Word, and I will be healed, set free, and restored in You.

You are the one who commands me on this day to *get up and walk*. I get up from all disease and walk in your powerful faithful Word. I decide to believe you no matter what my body says, because you are True to your Word and your Word is Truth.

Transform and renew my mind and emotions so they are filled with Your fragrant love and sweet peace.

I know You are the God who heals all "my" diseases and bestows divine health upon me. You heal all diseases and illnesses, regardless of their names, since Your Name is above the names of all diseases, and they are no match for Your tremendous Name. Jesus, You delight in healing the sick and restoring their broken hearts. Your kingdom has come, and at the mention of Your Name, the blind see, the lame walk, lepers are cured, the deaf hear, the dead are raised to life, and the Good News is spread to the poor.

You are a great physician. Jesus, right now, snatch me from the door of death by Your mighty Name and holy and powerful blood. Lord, You never fail me, nor will You ever. Sustain and restore me to full health because You are the God of health, and there is no sickness or evil in You. In You, all is perfect. O Lord, I hide in You.

You are my *Jehovah-Rapha*—the Lord, my Healer. You heal my body and strengthen my nerves, neurons, bones, and tendons. You are my divine health and wellness; You work miracles among Your people. You are the God of maximum power over all and over everything. You give me sight to see and ears to hear, vocal cords to worship, feet to walk like a gazelle, and hands to serve You. You give me a sound mind and heart to live a life worthy of You. You created me perfectly in You and for You.

Lord, You are my Eternal Life, and You give me abundant life. You are the air and breath in my lungs, Holy Spirit. You are the One who holds the breath of my life in Your hands; You renew my youth. In You, I find new strength to soar high on the wings of eagles. I will run and not grow weary; I will walk and not faint because of Your strength. You are the Strength of my heart and my Portion forever.

Your life-giving light helps and rescues my soul from death. You are always with me, right by me, Lord. Your love calms my worries. Lord, You are the Source and life-giving Fountain of my life; the health of my countenance. You know the number of my hairs, O Sovereign God. You are the God of the little ones.

You are the God of the impossible; nothing is too difficult for You. Lord, You deliver the demon-possessed and oppressed. You cast out evil spirits with a simple command because You are the Maximum Power of the universe. Your powerful decrees cannot be revoked.

You declare new things before they happen. You are the One who owns the key of David. What You open, no one can shut; and what You shut, no one can open. You have given me the authority to command, forbid, bind, decree, declare, allow, and release in Your Name. Jesus, You said with absolute authority that the powers of hell will not be able to conquer me because I am Your church, your holy temple. You have given me the keys to the kingdom to declare things into existence according to Your Word. Father, Your Word says that if two of us agree concerning anything on earth, You will do it for us. I stand and agree with Your promises through faith, which is confidence in what we hope for and assurance of what we do not see. I know I will see it manifested just in time, for You are never late.

Father, listen to my cry and restore my health. Lord, because Your Word says that whatever we command on earth will be commanded in heaven, I command life and healing to enter my body, mind, and soul in Your Name. Send Your mighty army of angels to bring Your miraculous healing over my health in Jesus' glorious Name.

Lord, You are the God who declares new things before they happen, the God of the impossible, and nothing is too difficult for You. Lord, You are the God who never fails us. Lord, You are the Creator of our bodies and organs. You give us our health and healing because You are the great physician and the best in the universe.

You are the Source of healing. You are the Healer and Deliverer of all demon-possessed, epileptic, or paralyzed, and You make the blind receive their sight. You make the lame walk, and You cleanse the lepers and make the deaf hear. All diseases and illnesses run from Your mighty Name and powerful blood. You raise up the dead, because You are the Resurrection and Life. You are the Healer of every kind of disease and illness, no matter what doctors or science say, because life is in Your hands only. Our breath belongs to You. Lord, I stand firm, believing what You say in Your Word. You are the God of absolute truth. You are our divine Healer, and You want to heal me and see me well.

Your Name is above all names, above the names of any disease. Lord, You are the God of maximum power who heals us by Your powerful Word.

Jesus, You are the Doctor of doctors, the Source of all divine healing. Therefore, in Your Name, I release Your divine healing over my body and command it to be healed, reborn, restored, and strengthened.

Holy Spirit, flow through my breath and completely revive my lungs and immune system with the swift wind of Your loving Spirit.

Lord, comfort me with Your unfailing love and sweet, peaceful Presence as You work the healing in my body. Lord, I know You can do anything, and no one can stop You. Open my eyes to see Your wonderful works.

Lord, You are greater and higher than my human emotions and thoughts. Jesus, You are the One who sustains me during the times of weakness, and You restore me to full health. Oh Father, even though I might be weak right now, I know Your power works best through my weakness as this makes me depend more on You. Through my weakness, Your power becomes more evident in my life. I know through this situation, You are showing me that Your grace is enough for me and Your power is stronger when I feel weak. I know my weakness pushes me to my knees and drives me to depend on Your strength rather than my human strength or abilities. Lord, help me not to focus on my situation but appreciate the gift of Your glorious power dwelling in my life. Help me understand that the weaker I feel, the stronger I become through Your power. Lord, I make myself vulnerable before You and let You take control of my situation.

Jesus, You said that apart from You, I can do nothing. Therefore, unite my thoughts and words to Your Word of truth and make Your declaration of wholeness over my life. I unite my spirit with Your Spirit into one Spirit. Jesus, I can now do everything through You because You give me strength and empower me to be strong and wholesome.

Lord, I know that nothing is impossible for You, and nothing is too difficult for You—without faith, it is impossible to please You. You want me to believe Your Word and pray with sincerity, knowing that You will answer and reward me because I seek and trust You. Lord, I know faith is confidence in the things we hope for, as well as certainty, assurance, and conviction about things I don't see yet, but will see. Lord, I believe Your Word because You are the Way, the Truth, and the Life.

In Jesus' Name, I release Your peace over my emotions and mind, which surpasses all human comprehension. Jesus, guard my heart and mind inside of You with Your loving peace. Thank You in advance for Your healing work and loving Presence over my life and my family. In Jesus' Name, amen and amen!

14

HIS PROVISION, WEALTH, AND PROSPERITY

Yours, O LORD, is the greatness, the power and the glory, the victory and the majesty; for all that is in heaven and in earth is Yours; Yours is the kingdom, O LORD, and You are exalted as head over all. Both riches and honor come from You, and You reign over all. In Your hand is power and might; in Your hand it is to make great and to give strength to all. Now therefore, our God, we thank You and praise Your glorious Name... For all things come from You, and of Your own we have given You.

1 Chronicles 29:11–17 NKJV (emphasis mine, from NLT)

"These things dominate the thoughts of unbelievers, but your heavenly Father already knows all your needs."

Matthew 6:32

You are:

1. The God of the rich and the poor (Proverbs 22:2; 1 Samuel 2:7)
2. The God who makes some poor and others rich (1 Samuel 2:7)
3. The God who multiplies my blessings greatly (Genesis 17:2–3)
4. The Father who changed my name and promoted me to higher levels (Genesis 17:5)
5. The God who makes me extremely fruitful (Genesis 17:6)
6. The Lord, my inheritance and possession (Ezekiel 44:28)
7. God, the One who empowers us to make riches (Deuteronomy 8:18)
8. God, the Manna who descended from heaven (John 3:13)
9. The Lord who prepares a wonderful future for those who love peace (Psalm 37:37)
10. The Lord who honors those who honor Your Name (1 Samuel 2:30)
11. God, the Creator and Owner of silver and gold (Haggai 2:8–10; Genesis 2:11–13)
12. The Blessing that makes true wealth (Proverbs 10:22; Deuteronomy 8:17–18)
13. The Lord God of recompense (Jeremiah 51:56)
14. The God of rewards (Hebrews 11:6; Colossians 3:23–24)
15. The God who will Reward my actions (Revelation 22:12; Genesis 15:1; Genesis 17:8)
16. The God of wealth and prosperity (Isaiah 66:12; Proverbs 8:18)
17. The God of opportunities (Ephesians 5:16)
18. The great God whose understanding is infinite (beyond comprehension) (Psalm 147:5)
19. God, my Inventor (Genesis 5:1)
20. God, the divine Inventor and Creator of innovation (Revelation 21:5; Exodus 31:2–11)
21. The God who gives riches (Ecclesiastes 6:2)
22. The God of blessings, the Blesser (Numbers 6:24–26)
23. The God with dominion over the universe (Genesis 1:26; Colossians 1:15–18)

24. God, the Creator of the universe (Genesis 1:1–31)
25. God, the Spirit of knowledge (Isaiah 11:2; Daniel 5:12)
26. The God, the Author of all knowledge (Proverbs 1:7)
27. The God who is perfect in knowledge (Job 36:4; Psalm 18:30)
28. God, the One who prospers me (Psalm 106:5)
29. Jesus, the Appointed Heir of all things (Hebrews 1:2)
30. The God who made me fellow heir with Christ (Romans 8:17)
31. Jesus, the Living Bread who came down from heaven (John 6:51–59)
32. Jesus, the door through which I must enter for salvation and blessing (John 10:9)
33. My Gate and Door to a better life on earth and beyond (John 10:8–10)
34. The One who gives me a rich and satisfying life (John 10:10)
35. The God who gives food to the hungry (Psalm 146:7; Proverbs 30:8)
36. The God who supplies the food in my house (Genesis 1:29; Ecclesiastes 2:24; Psalm 111:5; 145:15)
37. My Great Shepherd provider, I will lack nothing (Psalm 23:1)
38. God, *Jehovah-Jireh*—the Lord my Provider (Genesis 22:13–14; Matthew 6:25–34)
39. The God who honored me by anointing my head with oil (Psalm 23:2–5)
40. The One who makes my cup overflow with blessings (Psalm 23:2–5)
41. The Source of my exceeding joy and great happiness (Psalm 43:4)
42. The God who gives me all things abundantly for my enjoyment (1 Timothy 6:17)
43. The God who gives food to every living thing (Psalm 136:25)
44. The God who makes all things new (Revelation 21:5; 2 Corinthians 5:17–18)
45. The God and Creator of the twelve pearly gates (Revelation 21:21)
46. The God and Creator of every kind of precious stone (Revelation 21:19)

47. The God who fed me all my life until this day (Genesis 2:16; Philippians 4:19; Deuteronomy 8:3)

48. The God who fills all in all (Ephesians 1:23)

49. The God who reveals secrets and mysteries to me (1 Corinthians 2:10; Deuteronomy 29:29)

50. The God of success (Proverbs 16:3; Psalm 20:4)

51. God, the Inventor of the highest intelligence (Psalm 94:11; 1 Corinthians 3:20; 1 King 10:24; James 1:5)

52. God, my Everything in everything (1 Corinthians 15:28)

53. God, the Solution to everything (Philippians 4:6)

54. God, the only One who satisfies my soul (Psalm 63; 107:8–9)

55. The Blesser from the beginning to eternity (Deuteronomy 28; Numbers 6:24–25)

56. The Father who knows all my needs always (Matthew 6:32–33)

57. The Father who gives me everything I need when I seek You above everything else (Matthew 6:33)

58. The Lord who owns the riches (1 Chronicles 29:12)

59. The God who opens Your hand to satisfy the desire of every living thing (Psalm 145:16)

60. The God who waters the earth and blesses its bountiful harvest of grain (Psalm 65:9–10)

61. God Most High who fulfills Your purposes for me (Psalm 57:2; Romans 8:28)

62. The God who crowns the year with abundant harvests and goods (Psalm 65:11)

63. The Lord who will give me an inheritance that will last forever (Psalm 37:18)

64. The Lord, the Source of honor and wealth (1 Chronicles 29:12; Proverbs 8:17–21)

65. The God who always makes a way where there is no way (Isaiah 43:16)

66. God, my best Teammate (Romans 8:14; Galatians 5:17–18)

67. God, the Champion of all time (Isaiah 19:20–21; Jeremiah 20:11; Colossians 2:14–15)

68. The God who gives me creativity (Exodus 35:35)

69. The God who declares new things before they happen (Isaiah 42:9)
70. The God who plans with heaven's hosts to bless me and prosper me (Psalm 35:27; 84:11; 3 John 1:2)
71. The God who supplies all my needs according to Your riches in glory (Philippians 4:19–20)
72. The God who satisfies the thirsty and fills the hungry with good things (Psalm 107:9)
73. The Giver of blessings (Genesis 12:2; 1 Chronicles 4:10)
74. The God who prospers my life (Jeremiah 29:11)
75. The best Blessing of all blessings (Psalm 73:26; Numbers 6:24–26)
76. The Creator and Owner of all diamonds and gems (Ezekiel 28:13)
77. The One who builds and protects my home, my business, my ministry, and my city (Psalm 127:1)
78. The One who blesses my city (Psalm 127:1)
79. The One who blesses my home (Psalm 127:1)
80. The Lord God, my Sustainer (Psalm 54:4)
81. The Owner of the earth and all that it contains (1 Corinthians 10:18–26)
82. The God who fills my life with good things (Psalm 103:5)
83. The God who sustains me so I may not lack anything (Nehemiah 9:20; Psalm 23:1; Philippians 4:19)
84. The God who blesses the work of my hands (Job 1:10)
85. The God who increases my possessions (Job 1:10)
86. The Lord who gives and the Lord who takes away, I bless Your Name (Job 1:21)
87. The God who restores my fortunes (Jeremiah 33:7)
88. The God who never abandons the godly (Psalm 37:25; 28)
89. The One who empowers me to possess the land of blessing (Psalm 37:11, 22; 29)
90. The Lord who delights in every detail of my life (Psalm 37:23)
91. The Lord who takes care of the godly (Psalm 37:17)
92. The One who makes me live safely in the land and prosper (Psalm 37:3)

93. The God who gives me my heart's desires when I delight in You (Psalm 37:4)
94. The God who fills my life with blessings (Psalm 103:5)
95. The God who renews my youth like an eagle (Psalm 103:5)
96. The God who waters the mountains from Your upper chambers (Psalm 104:13)
97. The God who causes the grass to grow for the cattle (Psalm 104:14–15)
98. The God who causes vegetation to grow so we can have food (Psalm 104:14–15)
99. The God who provides my food in due season (Psalm 104:27; Psalm 145:15)
100. The God who sends the manna from heaven (Nehemiah 9:20)
101. The God who prospers those who fear You (Exodus 1:21)
102. The Giver of all good things (Psalm 16:2)
103. The Lord, my only inheritance (Psalm 16:5)
104. The Lord, my Cup of Blessing (Psalm 16:5)
105. The Lord, the Provider for my human needs (Matthew 6:25–34)
106. The God who brings me to a good and spacious land to prosper me (Exodus 3:8–10)
107. The God who transfers wealth from the wicked to Your people (Exodus 3:21–22)
108. The God who gives land to Your people to possess it, for You are Lord (Exodus 6:9; Genesis 13:17; 15:7; 17:8; 35:12)
109. God, the One who holds success in store for the upright (Proverbs 2:7)
110. The Lord who has riches and honor as well as enduring wealth and justice (Proverbs 8:18)
111. The Lord whose gifts are better than the purest gold (Proverbs 8:19)
112. The Lord whose wages are better than sterling silver (Proverbs 8:19)
113. God, the Father who gives me good and perfect gifts (James 1:17)
114. The Lord who rewards those who love You with wealth (Proverbs 8:21)
115. The Lord who will not let the godly go hungry (Proverbs 10:3)

116. The Lord who showers the godly with blessings (Proverbs 10:6)
117. The Lord whose blessing makes me rich, and it does not come with sorrow (Proverbs 10:22–23)
118. The One who grants my hopes (Proverbs 10:24)
119. The Lord who protects the property of widows (Proverbs 15:25; 2 Kings 8:3-6)
120. The God who works in me to give me the desire and power to do what pleases You (Philippians 2:13)
121. The Lord whose strength spills over into joy (Colossians 1:11; 1 Samuel 30:6)
122. God, my insurance to safety and prosperity (Psalm 37:3–5)
123. The Lord who gives my heart's desires as I delight in You (Psalm 37:3–5)
124. The One who helps me in everything because I trust You (Psalm 37:3–5)
125. The One who helps me in times of need (Hebrews 4:16)
126. The Lord, the Owner and Giver of riches, silver, and gold (Genesis 13:2)
127. The God who knows the interpretation and meaning of my dreams (Genesis 40:8)
128. The Lord, the Possessor of heaven and earth (Genesis 14:19)
129. The Lord who creates (*Rehoboth*) open space for me to prosper in this land (Genesis 26:22)
130. The Lord who resurrects and brings back to life my dead dreams (Genesis 18:14)
131. The God who is not limited by my age (Genesis 18:14)
132. The God who is with me and causes everything I do to succeed (Genesis 39:23)
133. The God who reveals strategies for survival (Genesis 41:33–36)
134. The God who makes me fruitful in the land of my affliction (Genesis 41:52)
135. The God who fulfills my dreams (Genesis 42:8–9)
136. The One who provides for the ravens when their young cry to God in hunger (Job 38:41)
137. The God who restores my fortunes and gives me double for my trouble (Job 42:10–11; Jeremiah 33:11)

138. The One who opens the windows of heaven over me (Malachi 3:10)
139. The One who pours out a flood of blessings over me (Malachi 3:10; Isaiah 32:20)
140. God, the Almighty who blesses me with blessings of the heavens above (Psalm 139:5)
141. The One who places Your hand of blessing over my head (Psalm 139:5)
142. Lord of all the earth, who owns wealth and riches (Micah 4:12–13)
143. The God who blesses those who bless me and curses those who curse me (Genesis 12:3)
144. The One who declares that all the families on earth will be blessed through Abraham's seed (Genesis 12:3)
145. The Creator and Giver of skills to play musical instruments (Genesis 4:21)
146. The Giver of skill in the forging of bronze and iron tools (Genesis 4:22)
147. The God who gives the skill to raise livestock (Genesis 4:20)
148. The Fountain of all resources in heaven (Zechariah 13:1; Philippians 4:19–21)
149. The God who cares for people and animals alike (Psalm 36:6)
150. The God who feeds us from Your abundance (Psalm 36:8)
151. The One who lets me drink from the river of Your delights (Psalm 36:8)
152. The Blesser of my bread and water (Exodus 23:25–26)
153. The God who owns the cattle on a thousand hills (Psalm 50:10)
154. The God and Creator of the trees that produce delicious fruit (Genesis 2:9; Psalm 104:16)
155. The Creator of seeds and green plants (Genesis 1:29–30)
156. The Creator and Provider of our food (Genesis 1:29; Psalm 111:5)
157. The One who sends rain and snow from heaven (Isaiah 55:10; Psalm 147:8)
158. The One who waters the earth, making it bring forth and sprout (Isaiah 55:10)

159. The One who gives seed to the Sower and bread to the eater (Isaiah 55:10)
160. The One whose Word goes out of Your mouth and shall not return empty (Isaiah 55:10)
161. The One whose Word shall accomplish its purpose successfully (Isaiah 55:11)
162. The One who makes the mountains sing and the trees clap their hands (Isaiah 55:12)
163. The Rebuker of the devourer (Malachi 3:11)
164. The One who gives me power to get wealth (Deuteronomy 8:17–18)
165. The richest One in the world (1 Chronicles 29:11–17)
166. God, the Wealth of heaven (Ephesians 2:4–6)

A PRAYER DECLARING HIS PROVISION

Father, on this new day, I come before Your mighty throne in Jesus' Name and through my Helper, Your Holy Spirit. You are the God who crowns the year with abundant harvests and goods. I want to thank You for what You have already done and what You have done but have not yet manifested. Lord, I know You know everything, and You are intimately aware and acquainted with every one of my needs. I know You are never late. You are the Father who is always mindful of my needs and completely aware of them. You are always with me in times of need. Lord, thank you because I know that you delight in every detail of my life. I know that you really care about me and take care of me because your love me profoundly. You are the God who is with me and causes everything I do to succeed because of Your deep love for me and because I love You.

You know the interpretation and meaning of all my dreams, from childhood until now. You are the One who resurrects and brings my seemingly dead dreams back to life. My age does not constrain or limit You because all I need is You and Your empowerment. Thank You, Lord, for You are the God who makes my dreams become a reality. All You do in my life is perfect because You are the God of perfection, and You flawless in all You do, God Almighty.

Father, You multiply my blessings greatly. You are the God of the rich and the poor. I know You are the Fountain of all resources in heaven for everything we need on this earth. Lord, You are my inheritance and possession. You are my Manna from heaven. You prepared a wonderful future for me because I love Your peace. You are the only One who satisfies my soul. You are the Blesser from the beginning to eternity. You reveal strategies for survival on this earth. You make me fruitful in the land of my affliction.

You are the One who provides for the ravens when their young cry to You in hunger, and it is You who feeds the birds of the sky and the fish of the sea.

You are the God and Creator of the beautiful trees that produce delicious fruit. You are the Creator of seeds and green plants. You are the Creator and Provider of our food. I have nothing to worry about, for You own the cattle on a thousand hills. The One who sends rain and snow from heaven. You water the earth, making it bring forth and sprout. You are the One who gives seed to the sower and bread to the eater.

The One who ensures that Your words will not be returned empty when spoken. The One whose Word shall accomplish its purpose successfully. The One who makes the mountains sing and the trees clap their hands. You cause the grass to grow for the cattle. You cause vegetation to grow year-round so we can have food. You provide my food in due season. Lord, You are the One who feeds the hungry. Lord, thank You for You are the Blesser of my bread and water since my conception. You have provided food for me and my family every day since I was in my mother's womb. You've fed me every day of my life till now and will continue until my last breath. Since the beginning of time, you have provided food for all living things throughout all human history.

You are the eternal Owner of silver and gold. Father, You are the Source of all true wealth and prosperity. You are the Lord of recompense and rewards,

You will Reward me according to my actions on this earth. You are my eternal great Reward. You are the God of opportunities. The great God with an infinite understanding who knows everything. You are my Inventor. You are the divine Inventor and Creator of all past, present, and future innovations. Lord, give me the anointing to be innovative in my business or ministry. You are the Lord of all the earth, the possessor of all wealth and riches. You are the One who gives true riches to those You please. You are the One who declares that all the families on earth will be blessed through Abraham's seed. Lord, You are the God of blessings, the Blesser of my life and my family. Lord, place Your hand of blessing over my head on this new day.

My Father, You are the only One with dominion over the universe. The

Creator of the universe and galaxies. You are the Spirit and Author of knowledge, and the one who knows everything clearly and perfectly. Therefore, You are the One who prospers me. Father, You made Jesus and appointed Him heir of all things, and You made me fellow heir with Christ.

Jesus, You are my Living Bread. I live not only by the food I eat, but I mainly live out of the Word that comes from Your mouth. You are the Living Bread that came down from heaven. Jesus, I know You are the Gate and Door to a better life on this earth and beyond. You are the door through which I must enter for salvation and blessing. You give me a rich and satisfying life in You and through You.

You are the One who opens the windows of heaven for me and my family because I am faithful to You with my Finances. You are the God who pours out a great blessing over me in such a way that I don't have enough room to take it in because we have more than enough.

You are the manna from heaven that sustains me and my family. You rebuke the devourer and protect my finances as I am faithful to You. You prosper those who fear You because You are the Giver of good things. You are my inheritance and my cup of blessing. You are my supernatural Provider. You bring me to a good and spacious land in my city to prosper me. I know You will restore my fortunes and give me double for my trouble.

Father, You are my great Shepherd, my great Pastor. I shall not want because I have all I need. In You I found green pasture, so I will lack nothing, for You are my God, *Jehovah-Jireh*, the Lord, my Provider. You are my Abba Papa who cares tenderly for me. You honored me by anointing my head with oil and made my cup overflow with blessings. Lord, You are my exceeding joy. You give me all the things abundantly for my enjoyment. You are not a stingy or penny-pinching God. You are the great divine Giver of all time.

Lord, You are the One who changed my name and nature because You call me to a higher and superior purpose.

You possess the power to make me extremely fruitful. You grant me the ability to create riches and wealth, becoming a conduit of blessings to others. Father, you bestow honor upon those who honor you. Lord, You are the source of renewal, You make all things new. You are the divine Creator of the twelve pearly gates in heaven and the originator of every Kind of precious stones. You are the Creator of diamonds and gems. Father, you are the ultimate owner and

Giver of all wealth and power on this earth. You are the rightful Owner of silver and gold.

Lord, You are the God of success. You give me success by revealing to me Your divine secrets and strategies. You are not just the Inventor of the highest intelligence; You are the Source of Supreme Intelligence. Lord, empower me with Your intelligence and discernment on this day. Lord, give me the anointing and the supernatural empowerment to successfully dominate over every challenge through You the power of your Holy Spirit. You are my Everything in everything, my eternal Source. You are the Solution to everything. You solve every issue in my family, business, and ministry.

You are the God who overflows with richness wherever You are. You empower the godly to possess the land of blessings and opportunities. Lord, I know You are the Source of honor and wealth. You always make way for my financial needs. You make a way where there is no possible way.

Holy Spirit, You are my best Teammate. You are the Champion of all time. You give me creativity and reveal secrets to me from Your eternal throne. You declare new things before they happen. Lord, I know You plan with the heavenly hosts to bless and prosper me and my family. You supply all my needs out of Your riches in glory.

You satisfy the thirst and fill the hungry with good things; You are the Provider and Giver of blessings. You bring prosperity to my life. You are the ultimate Blessing, the source of all my blessings. You are my primary and eternal Blessing: God, the Almighty who showers me with blessings from the heavens above.

You extend your hand to satisfy the hunger and thirst of every living thing. Father, you are mighty. You water the mountains from your upper chambers. You send rain to water the earth and bless its abundant grain harvest. You are the Lord and Possessor of heaven and earth. You give me a land to possess. You create open spaces (Rehoboth) for me to prosper in my city. You are the God who accomplishes all things on my behalf and fulfills your divine purpose in my life. You have granted me an eternal inheritance. Lord, you are the Builder and Owner of my home, business, ministry, and city, and you are the wall of protection around it. Lord, you are the one who blesses my city. You bless not only my home but also the homes of my neighbors and every home in this city. You are the sustainer of all living beings. You empower me to live a sustainable life on this earth. Father, I acknowledge that the earth and everything in it belongs to you. Lord, you fill my life with good things and sustain me so that I may lack nothing.

Lord, bless my business and my ministry. May You always bless the work of my hands, for these hands honor Your Name. Lord, You are the One who gives and takes away in due time; I bless Your Name. Lord, You are the One who restores my fortunes and never abandons me or my family, especially when I need You more. You are the One who always takes care of the godly.

Lord, You make me live safely in this city and prosper me. Father, I know that as I delight myself in You, You give me the desires of my heart. I will not let my needs dominate my thoughts, for You know my needs better than I do. Instead, I will seek Your will above all other things and live righteously on this day, and I know You will give me everything I need. You fill my life with blessings and rejuvenate me like an eagle.

Lord, You will transfer the wealth of the wicked to me and my family because we fear and Honor Your Name. Lord, You are the Owner of all land, the Landlord of the earth. You give land to Your people to possess it as You please. Remember me and my family on this day, Lord. You are the One who holds success in store for the upright. You are the God of riches and honor as well as enduring wealth and true justice.

Your gifts are better than the purest gold; Your wages are better than sterling silver. You are the Father of good and perfect gifts. Your blessing makes me rich, and it does not come with sorrow. You know I love You, God, and You promised to reward those who love You with wealth. You say in Your Word that You will not let the godly go hungry.

You are the One who grants me hope. You protect the property of Your servants. Father, You work in me to give me the desire and the power to do what pleases You. Lord, fill me with the strength that spills over into joy.

Lord, You are my divine Insurance and Assurance of safety and prosperity. You are my Peace of Mind. Lord, stamp me with Your approval, helping me in every endeavor on this day. May Your divine providence spill over my life today in ways above my wildest imagination. May Your goodness, kindness, and mercy pour out today over my life, family, health, strength, business, and ministry. May You open my eyes to see a sign of Your love and mercy on this day. May You let me see Your loving, glorious signature of love and blessing throughout this day over my life, family, ministry, and business.

Oh, Abba Papa, I am grateful to You because I am aware that You always listen to my prayers and answer them at the right time according to Your will, as I have surrendered my will to You eternally. Now, may Your kingdom come and Your will be done over my life as it is in heaven today, tomorrow and always.

In Jesus' mighty Name, amen and amen!

15

HIS MERCY AND COMPASSION

The faithful love of the LORD never ends! His mercies never cease. Great is his faithfulness; his mercies begin afresh each morning. I say to myself, "The LORD is my inheritance; therefore, I will hope in him!" The LORD is good to those who depend on him, to those who search for him. So it is good to wait quietly for salvation from the LORD.

Lamentations 3:22–26

Surely goodness and mercy shall follow me All the days of my life; And I will dwell in the house of the Lord Forever.

Psalm 23:6 NKJV

You are:

1. The God who does not reject the broken and contrite of the heart (Psalm 51:17)
2. Jesus, my Advocate before the Father (1 John 2:1)

3. The gracious merciful God (Psalm 124:8; Hebrews 4:16; James 5:11)
4. The One who sits on heaven's mercy seat (Hebrews 9:5–12; Romans 3:25)
5. My heaven's Mercy Seat (Exodus 25:10–22; Hebrews 9:5)
6. The Lord, full of compassion and mercy (James 5:11)
7. The Lord who is full of tenderness (James 5:11)
8. The One who weeps with those who weep (Romans 12:15)
9. The God who keeps covenant and mercy forever (Psalm 105:8; Deuteronomy 7:9)
10. Yahweh, a God compassionate and gracious (Exodus 34:6)
11. The Lord who showers compassion on all Your creation (Psalm 145:9)
12. The God who answers my prayer in the day of anguish (Psalm 91; 118:5; Jeremiah 33:3)
13. The God who comforts my heart on the day of tribulation (2 Corinthians 1:4)
14. The God who carries me in Your arms each day (Psalm 68:19)
15. The God who gives to all men liberally (James 1:5)
16. The God who protects the foreigner (Psalm 146:9)
17. The God who extends Your hands to me (Psalm 90:17)
18. The God who gives heed to my prayer (Psalm 61:1; 86:6)
19. The Lord who takes care of the godly and innocent (Psalm 37:17–18)
20. The God who never gives up on me (Psalm 136)
21. A witness in my favor (John 5:32)
22. The merciful Father (Psalm 145:8; 2 Samuel 24:14; Luke 6:36)
23. The Father of great mercy (1 Peter 1:3; 2 Samuel 24:14)
24. The God who gives me more and more grace and peace (1 Peter 1:2)
25. My everlasting Mercy (Luke 1:54)
26. The God with mercy higher than the heavens (Psalm 108:3)
27. The God who forgives all my sins (Psalm 103:3)
28. The God who crowns me with love and tender mercies (Psalm 103:4)

29. The Lord, tender and compassionate, Father to those who fear You (Psalm 103:13)
30. The God who crowns me with lovingkindness and compassion (Psalm 103:4)
31. The Lord who is merciful and gracious to me (Psalm 103:8)
32. The Lord who is slow to anger and abounding in lovingkindness (Psalm 103:8)
33. The Lord who has compassion on those who fear You (Psalm 103:13)
34. The God who works with my shortcomings and weaknesses patiently (Proverbs 24:16; Exodus 4:1–8; 4:10–14)
35. The God who hears my groaning and remembers Your covenant and promises (Exodus 2:24)
36. The God who lets Yourself be found to those who search for You (Proverbs 8:17)
37. The merciful God who will not destroy a city on account of ten righteous (Genesis 18:32)
38. Jesus Christ, my Advocate who plead my case before the Father (1 John 2:1)
39. The Lord with a throne of grace and mercy (Hebrews 4:16)
40. My peace, mercy, and grace in time of need (Hebrews 4:16)
41. The God who causes everything to work together for my good (Romans 8:28; 2 Corinthians 4:8-9)
42. The Lord whose mercy triumphs over judgment (James 2:13; Psalm 118:29)
43. The Father, You are so good to me (Psalm 86:5)
44. The God who is always ready and willing to forgive generously (Psalm 86:5; Isaiah 55:7)
45. The Lord, full of unfailing love for those who call upon You (Psalm 86:5)
46. Jesus, who set me free from all condemnation (Romans 8:1–2)
47. The Lord who set me free from the law of sin and death (Romans 8:1–2)
48. The Lord who requires me to do what is right (Micah 6:8)
49. The Lord who requires me to love mercy (Micah 6:8)
50. The Lord who requires me to walk humbly with You (Micah 6:8)

51. The God who is rich in mercy and love for me (Ephesians 2:4)
52. The Lord with a mercy that never comes to an end (Lamentations 3:22)
53. The Lord with great faithfulness (Lamentations 3:23)
54. The God who is full of new mercies every morning (Lamentations 3:23)
55. The God with tender mercy (Luke 1:78)
56. The Lord, my sunrise from on high (Luke 1:78)
57. The One who gives light to those in darkness (Luke 1:79)
58. The God who guides me to the path of peace (Luke 1:79)
59. The Father who delights in steadfast love (Micah 7:18)
60. The Father of forgiveness (Luke 23:34; Matthew 6:14–15; Micah 7:18)
61. The Lord who shows mercy from generation to generation to all who fear You (Luke 1:50)
62. The God who wipes out my bad record (Psalm 51)
63. The God who Scrubs away my guilt (Psalm 51)
64. The God that washes me from my iniquity and cleanse me from my sin (Psalm 51:2)
65. The God of mercy (Ephesians 2:4–5)
66. The Lord whose anger lasts only a moment, but Your favor lasts a lifetime (Psalm 30:5)
67. The merciful Healer of the blind (Matthew 20:34)
68. The One who is merciful to thousands of generations (Deuteronomy 7:9)
69. The One who cares for people and animals alike (Psalm 36:6)
70. The One who gave me confidence that I will inherit eternal life (Titus 3:7)
71. The One who saved me by Your mercy (Titus 3:4–5)
72. The One who generously poured out the Spirit upon me through Christ (Titus 3:6)
73. The One with mercies that never cease (Lamentations 3:22)
74. The Lord who is good to all (Psalm 145:9; 86:5)
75. The Lord who has mercy over all Your works (Psalm 145:9)
76. The compassionate Father (Luke 6:36)]

77. The one that wants us to show mercy, rather than offer sacrifices (Matthew 12:7)

A PRAYER DECLARING HIS MERCY AND COMPASSION

My Father God, in Jesus' mighty Name, I come boldly before Your throne of grace and mercy. I praise You, Lord, for Your great divine mercy and compassion toward me and my family. You are great in faithfulness, and Your mercies are new every morning. You are merciful to thousands of generations. You show mercy from generation to generation to all who fear Your Name.

You are a God of mercy. Your anger lasts only for a moment, but Your favor lasts a lifetime. You fill my heart with Your compassion. You are the merciful Healer of the sick and heartbroken.

To the One who sits on heaven's mercy seat, I implore Your mercy over me and my family on this day. Cover me with Your compassion and mercy.

I know You weep with those who weep because You are *Yahweh*, a compassionate and gracious God. You always remember Your covenant and promises. You keep Your covenant and mercy forever over my life. You are the merciful God who will not destroy a city on account of ten righteous.

Father, You always pay attention to my prayers and show me Your compassion. Lord, You know my anguish and answer me when I need You. You comfort me on the day of tribulation. Lord, I know You carry me in Your arms each day, and You extend Your hand to me when I need You most. I know You care for the godly and innocent, and You give generously to those who fear Your Name.

Lord, I know You are always willing and ready to forgive all my sins because of Your great mercy and compassion. Jesus, You are a witness and an advocate in my favor. You are a gracious God. I know You never give up on me because of your love.

Lord, You are so good to me always. You are slow to anger and abounding in lovingkindness toward me. You are full of unfailing love for those who call upon Your Name. Lord, You work with my shortcomings and weaknesses with divine patience. You are my merciful Father, the Father of forgiveness. You say that the godly may trip seven times but that they will get up again and not stay down. You have declared in your word that although we are troubled in everything, we will not be distressed; even if we are in trouble, we will not be desperate; even if we are persecuted, we will not be forsaken; and even if we are struck down, we will not be destroyed.

Jesus Christ, You are my Advocate who pleads my case before the Father. Lord, You set me free from the law of sin and death by the law of the Spirit of life. You wiped out my bad record, my past, and Scrubbed away my guilt. Lord You washed me from my iniquity and cleansed me from my sin. Christ Jesus, it was You who set me free from all condemnation, so now I do not have to worry about Your final judgment day.

Lord, Your throne is filled with grace and mercy eternally. You are the Father who delights in steadfast love. Lord, You are my place of mercy and grace, where I find help in times of need. You cause everything to work together for my good. I know You are rich in mercy and love for me. Your compassion never comes to an end. You are a God with tender mercy.

Lord, fill me with Your mercy, for Your mercy triumphs over judgment. Thank You, Lord, for You are good and always forgiving. You abound in steadfast love for all those who ask for Your help. Father, You are tender and merciful toward me. I want to be like You. Lord, help me always do what is right, help me love mercy, and walk humbly before You as You require it. O Holy Spirit, guide me to the path of peace.

Lord, You are my Sunrise and Joy from on high. You give light to those in darkness. You crown me with Your lovingkindness, mercies, and compassion. You are a tender, loving, and compassionate Father to those who fear You. You hear my groanings and remember Your covenant and promises over my life. You have given me confidence that I will inherit eternal life. You saved me by Your mercy. You generously poured out Your Spirit upon me through Christ. Your mercy is higher than the heavens; it never ends. You are the Lord who is so good to all and has mercy over all You have made.

You give me more and more grace, and You flood me with Your peace. Your loyal love and mercies are everlasting over me. Where would I be today if it were not for Your mercy and compassion? My help is found in Your Name, O Lord, You who made heaven and earth. I will always trust in Your great Name, my Lord, my Origin. Thank You, Lord, when I seek Your Presence, You allow me to find You. Thank You for Your sweet mercy, O Father God.

I love You so much because You first loved me. Amen and Amen!

16

HIS PROTECTION AND SECURITY

"Because he loves me," says the LORD, *"I will rescue him; I will protect him, for he acknowledges my name."*

Psalm 91:14

This I declare about the LORD: *He alone is my refuge, my place of safety; he is my God, and I trust him. For he will rescue you from every trap and protect you from deadly disease. He will cover you with his feathers. He will shelter you with his wings. His faithful promises are your armor and protection.*

Psalm 91:2–4

You are:

1. God, a Rewarder of those who sincerely and diligently seek You (Hebrews 11:6)
2. The Lord who watches over me and my family (Psalm 121:3, 5)
3. The God who makes me dwell in safety (Psalm 4:8)

4. The God who keeps me (Psalm 121:5; 91:7)
5. God, my total confidence (Hebrews 4:16)
6. God, who watches over me closely (1 Peter 3:12)
7. God, my Protector (Psalm 18:2; Isaiah 54:17)
8. The Lord, my Defender (Isaiah 54:17; Romans 8:31)
9. The Lord my Vindicator (Isaiah 54:17)
10. God, the Rod that protects me and brings me comfort (Psalm 23:4)
11. God, the One who can be trusted blindly (1 Corinthians 1:9–11)
12. The Lord my Shield (Genesis 15:1; Deuteronomy 33:29; Psalm 18:2)
13. God, my Shadow from the heat (Isaiah 4:6)
14. The God who affirms me and guards me against all evil (Isaiah 41:10; Psalm 91:7)
15. God, my Ever-Present Help in trouble (Isaiah 41:4)
16. God, the Protective Wall of Fire around me (Zechariah 2:5; Psalm 3:5)
17. The God who answers by fire (1 Kings 18:24)
18. The God of the fire (1 Kings 18:24)
19. God, the confidence of all the ends of the earth (Proverbs 3:26)
20. The Lord who is in my midst (Deuteronomy 7:21)
21. The Lord my God who goes before me (Deuteronomy 31:8)
22. God, my Covering (Psalm 32:1–2; 3:5)
23. The Lord who will keep me safe forever (Psalm 37:28)
24. The Dwelling Place in all generations (Psalm 90:1)
25. My Shelter, the Most High (Psalm 91:1)
26. The Shadow of the Almighty over me (Psalm 91:1)
27. My Keeper, and my *Protective Shade* (Psalm 121:5)
28. The One who keeps watch over my going and coming now and forever (Psalm 121:7–8)
29. Jesus, the power that saves me (Psalm 18:2)
30. God, my Place of Safety (Psalm 18:2; Psalm 91:2)
31. God, the Shield for those who live with integrity (Proverbs 2:7)
32. The Lord whose Name is a fortified tower where I find safety (Proverbs 18:10)
33. The God who inspires in me confidence (Psalm 3:5; Hebrews 11)
34. The God who has not given me a spirit of fear (2 Timothy 1:7)

35. The God who gave me the spirit of power (2 Timothy 1:7)
36. The God who gave me the spirit of love (2 Timothy 1:7)
37. The God who gave me the spirit of self-discipline (2 Timothy 1:7)
38. God, *Jehovah-Nissi*—the Lord my Victorious Banner (Exodus 17:15)
39. Jesus, the One who overcomes the world (1 John 5:5)
40. The God who calls me to fear nothing (Isaiah 41:10; Psalm 27:1)
41. The Lord who goes out like a mighty man of war (Isaiah 42:12)
42. The God who surrounds me with songs of victory and deliverance (Psalm 32:7; 42:8; 40:3; 118:14–21)
43. The One who protects me and surrounds me with songs of deliverance (Psalm 32:7)
44. God, the Victor—You always win, You never lose a battle (2 Chronicles 20:15; John 16:33)
45. God, the Avenger—vengeance is Yours (Hebrews 10:30)
46. The God who saves me from my enemies (Psalm 18:3; 91:7)
47. The God who prepares a table for me in the presence of my enemies (Psalm 23:2–5)
48. The God who delivers the righteous from all their afflictions (Psalm 34:19)
49. God, the One who rescued me from every trap (Psalm 91:3)
50. God, the One who protects me from deadly diseases (Psalm 91:3)
51. God, the One who covers me with Your feathers and shelters me with Your wings (Psalm 91:4)
52. God, my Shelter in the storm where no evil can conquer me (Psalm 91:9)
53. God, the mighty Shield around me, my Glory (Psalm 3:3)
54. God, the One who trains my arms for war (Psalm 144:1–2)
55. The God who annihilated satan's plans (Hebrews 2:14)
56. The one before whom even the demons believe and tremble in fear (James 2:19)
57. The God who cast out the nations before me (Deuteronomy 9:4)
58. God, the Great Commander of the armies of heaven (Psalm 24:10)
59. *Jehovah-Tsebaoth*, the Lord of heaven's armies (Zechariah 1:3)
60. God, *El Gibbor*, the great Mighty Warrior and Champion (Jeremiah 32:17–18)

61. God, the Buckler and Shield to all those who trust in You (2 Samuel 22:31)
62. The One who makes me confident and bold as a lion (Proverbs 28:1)
63. The God who keeps my feet from stumbling (Psalm 66:9)
64. God, the One who orders Your angels to protect me wherever I go (Psalm 91:11)
65. The God who holds the key to life and death in Your hand (Revelation 1:18)
66. The God who trains and strengthens my hands and arms for battle (Psalm 18:34)
67. The Lord who watches over me and keep me from all harm (Psalm 121)
68. The God who holds me by Your hand so if I stumble, I will never fall (Psalm 37:22–24)
69. The Lord, the Pillar of Fire at night (Exodus 13:21–22)
70. The Lord, the Pillar of Cloud in the day (Exodus 13:21–22)
71. The One who frees me from all my fears (Psalm 34:4)
72. The Lord who surrounds me and defends me (Psalm 34:7)
73. The God who puts a hedge of protection on every side over me, my house, and all I have (Job 1:10)
74. The One who sends the angels to care for me (Hebrews 1:14)
75. The Lord who protects all those who love You (Psalm 145:20)
76. The God who speaks tenderly to me in my desert moments (Hosea 2:14)
77. The God of Peace who calms me in the storms (Matthew 8:23)
78. God, *Jehovah-Shalom*—the Lord my peace (Judges 6:24)
79. The Lord who gives a peace that guards my heart and mind (Philippians 4:7)
80. God, my Security and Assurance in everything (Hebrews 11:1; Romans 5:5; Psalm 23:4)
81. The God who leads me beside peaceful streams (Psalm 23)
82. God, my peaceful Place of Security (Isaiah 32:18)
83. The God who anoints my head with oil until my cup overflows with blessings (Psalm 23:5)
84. God, the One who holds my head up high (Psalm 3:3)

85. The God who protects the foreigners (Psalm 146:9; Ruth 1:16)
86. The God who cares for the orphans and widows (Psalm 146:9)
87. Jesus, the Defender of women (Luke 13:16; John 8:10–11; Psalm 68:5)
88. Jesus, the Defender of children (Mark 10:13–16; Matthew 18:10)
89. The Lord, the Refuge for my children (Proverbs 14:26)
90. The One who builds and protects my home, my business, my ministry, and my city (Psalm 127:1)
91. The One who blesses my city (Psalm 127:1)
92. The One who blesses my home (Psalm 127:1)
93. The Lord who rescues the godly from the wicked (Psalm 37:39–40)
94. The God who will not let the godly be condemned when put on trial (Psalm 37:33)
95. The God who protects those who are faithful to You (Proverbs 2:7–8)
96. The God who prolongs my life because I fear You (Proverbs 10:27)
97. The God who gives me true rest (Psalm 127:2)
98. The God who gives me a sweet sleep so I may have a good night (Proverbs 3:24; 3:5)
99. My peace when I lay down to sleep, for You keep me safe (Psalm 4:8) The
100. The God who gives rest to Your loved ones (Psalm 127:2)
101. The God who enables me to go to bed without fear (Proverbs 3:24)
102. My Shield and my great Reward (Genesis 15:1)
103. The God who is close beside me through the darkest valley (Psalm 23:4)
104. The God whose rod and staff protect and comfort me (Psalm 23:4)
105. The God who rescues me from my enemies (Psalm 30:1)
106. The God who refused to let my enemies triumph over me (Psalm 30:1)
107. The Lord who protects and rescues me (Psalm 97:10)
108. The God in whom all humanity finds shelter (Psalm 36:7)
109. The God who protects all that belongs to me (Psalm 16:5)

110. The God who keeps me safe from the evil one (John 17:15; Matthew 6:13)
111. The One I start my prayer my morning (Psalm 5:3)
112. The One I wait for in expectancy each morning (Psalm 5:3)
113. The Lord who hides me in the shelter of Your Presence (Psalm 31:20)
114. Jesus, my secure place (Psalm 46:1)
115. God, my only Safe Haven (Psalm 43:2)
116. My Hiding Place where the enemy cannot see me (Psalm 32:7)
117. God, a Hiding Place and refuge from the wind (Isaiah 32:2)
118. God, my Highest Place of safety (Habakkuk 3:19)
119. God, my High Tower (Psalm 144:2)
120. The Strong Tower that protects me from the enemy (Proverbs 18:10)
121. Jesus, my Secure and Firm Foundation (Isaiah 28:16; 1 Corinthians 3:11)
122. My Rock of Safety where I can always hide and be saved (Psalm 71:3: 62:2)
123. God my Refuge, a Rock where no enemy can reach me (Psalm 62:7)
124. God, my Strong Fortress where I will not be shaken (Psalm 18:2; 62:6)
125. The Lord, my Rock, my Fortress, and my Savior (Psalm 18:2; Psalm 71:3)
126. My Strong Rock in whom I find protection (Psalm 18:2; Psalm 31:2)
127. God, the Rock of Salvation (Psalm 62:6)
128. God, my Mighty Rock of Refuge (Psalm 62:7)
129. The God who set my feet upon a Rock, making my steps secure (Psalm 40:2)
130. The God who drew me up from the pit of destruction (Psalm 40:2)
131. God, my Victory and Honor (Psalm 62:7; 118:14–21)
132. God, the Wall of Fire of protection around me (Zechariah 2:5)
133. The Lord who takes my burdens, and takes care of me (Psalm 55:22)

134. The Lord who will not permit the godly to slip and fail (Psalm 55:22)
135. The God who is kind to me; to you I sing each night (Psalm 42:8)
136. The One who gives victory to kings (Psalm 144:10)
137. The One who is with me when I go through deep waters (Isaiah 43:2)
138. The One who saves me when I go through rivers of difficulty (Isaiah 43:2)
139. The One who is with me when I go through the fire of oppression (Isaiah 43:2)
140. The Fourth man in the furnace who is also with me (Daniel 3:16-28)
141. The God who shut the lions' mouths (Daniel 6:22)
142. The one that will not let the flames consume me (Isaiah 43:2)
143. The LORD who fights for me while I just stay calm (Exodus 14:14)

A PRAYER DECLARING HIS PROTECTION AND SECURITY

Father God, I come before Your mighty Presence in Jesus' Name. I want to thank You for this new day You have created for me; thank You in advance for Your protection over my life, my family, finances, health, business, and/or ministry. Lord, I seek You on this day with sincerity and diligence, for I know that You are my Reward. I know You are the Shield and great Reward for those who live with integrity. I know You always listen to my cry for help because I pray to no one but You, my King and my God. You listen to my voice in the morning. Every morning I lay out the pieces of my life on Your altar and wait in expectancy for Your fire to descend on it. You are the confidence of all the ends of the earth, and You are my confidence. I worship Your great Name above all names.

Lord, on this new day, I present my life and my family's life to You; watch over me and my family on this day. Jesus, You are my secret Refuge; my Secured Place. You are my Hiding Place. My Safe Haven from my spiritual enemies. You hide me so they cannot find me. You are my Highest Place, my High Tower of Protection. My Rock of Safety. My Rock of Fortress where I can always hide. Lord, You make me dwell in safety, and You are the One who keeps me and my family from the evil one. You protect and surround me with songs of deliverance; You hide me in the shelter of Your Presence. You always protect me and rescue me. O Lord, You are the God in whom all humanity finds refuge. You care for the foreigner, the orphans, and the widows. Jesus, You are the Defender and Refuge for women and children, the Defender of widows and orphans.

Lord God, You are my strong Rock where I can stand in total confidence. You watch over me closely because You care for me. God, You are my Protector, my Defender, and my Vindicator. You are the Rod that protects me. You protect all that belongs to me. Lord, You always bring me comfort. You can be trusted blindly, for You are good and faithful, and Your love endures forever over me and my family.

O Father, You are my Shield and my strong Fortress from the storms of life. You are my Hiding Place from the wind and my Shadow from the heat. You are my ever-present Help in trouble. You are the God who affirms and guards me against evil. You are the Strong Tower that protects me from the enemy. You are the LORD who fights for me while I just stay calm trusting in You.

Lord God, You are my firm and Secure Foundation; I feel safe in You. You are a mighty protective Wall of Fire around me. You are the God of fire who answers by fire. You are the Lord who dwells in me always. You are my God, my mighty Rock of Refuge. You always go before and after me like a mighty warrior and bodyguard covering me with Your mantle of protection. Thank You, Lord, for You keep me safe forever.

Father, You have been our Home, our Dwelling Place through all generations. You are my Home; I feel at home in Your sweet Presence. You are my Shelter and Most High, the Mighty Shadow over me. You are my Keeper and my Protective Shade.

You keep watch over my going and coming now and forever. You are the Lord who protects me. You go out like a mighty man of war to protect me, Lord. Oh, Jesus, thank You because You are the Power that saves me. You are my Place of Safety. Jesus, Your Name is a fortified tower where I find security.

You inspire in me a firm confidence towards you. You are the One who gives me sweet and peaceful sleep. You have not given me a spirit of fear, but You gave me the spirit of power, love, and self-discipline. God, You are my *Jehovah-Nissi*—the Lord, my Victorious Banner. Jesus, You are the One who overcomes the world, and You have given me the power to overcome all fear and challenges. I know You do not want me to fear anything. You surround me with songs of victory and deliverance. You are my Victor; You always win and never lose a battle. You are my Avenger; vengeance belongs to You.

Lord, You save me from danger. You are the One who prepares a table for me in the presence of my enemies. You rescue me from my enemies, and You refuse to let them triumph over me. Father, You deliver the righteous from all their afflictions. You rescue me from every trap set before me. You protect me from deadly diseases every day of my life. Thank You because You cover me with Your feathers and shelter me with Your wings. You are my Shelter in the storm where no evil can conquer me. O Lord, You are the mighty Shield around me, my Glory. You train and strengthen my arms for battle and war so I can fight the enemy. You make me confident and bold as a lion.

You are the One who annihilates satan's plans. Even the demons believe and tremble with fear because You are the maximum Authority.

You are the God who cast out the nations before me because You are the Great Commander of the armies of heaven. You are the Lord *Jehovah* of the armies. God, the Buckler and Shield to all those who trust in You. You order Your angels to protect me wherever I go. I will never fall because You hold me by my hand so my feet won't stumble.

You always watch over me and my family to keep us from all harm.

Jesus, I know You hold the key of life and death in Your hands. You are the Lord, the Pillar of Fire at night and the Pillar of Cloud in the day over Your people. You free me from all my fears. You surround me and defend me by putting a hedge of protection on every side of me, over me, my house, my family, my business, and all I have. You send the angels to care for me, and You protect me because I love You.

Lord, You speak tenderly to me in my desert moments. You are the God of Peace who calms me in the storms. You are *Jehovah-Shalom*—the Lord, my Peace. Lord, Your peace guards my heart and mind. You are my Security and Assurance in everything. You hold my head up high. Lord, my mind and heart will be still for I know that You are God, and You alone control every event in my life.

O Lord, You lead me beside peaceful streams. You are my peaceful Place of Safety. The God who anoints my head with oil until my cup overflows with blessings.

Lord, You are the One who builds, prospers, and protects my home, business, ministry, city, and nation. Thank You, Lord, because You protect all that You have given me, all blessings that belong to me. You are the One who blesses my home, my city, and my nation. You rescue the godly from the wicked. You are the God who will not let the godly be condemned when put on trial.

O Lord, You are my Rock, Fortress, and Savior. You always protect those who are faithful to You. You prolong my life because I fear and revere Your Name. You are the One who gives me true rest. I can rest in You today and forever. I can feel safe and secure in You. I blindly trust in Your great Name. I trust that my spouse, children, and family are in Your caring hands today and always until we meet You in heaven.

Father, thank You for giving me a sweet sleep so I may have a good night's rest, for You give rest to Your loved ones. You enable me to go to bed without fear. I can rest in total peace by Your grace while You watch over me and my home. Lord, You are my peace when I lay down to sleep, for You alone keep me safe all night. Lord, thank You because You are with and beside me through the darkest valleys. Your rod and Your staff protect and comforts me. You are such a good Father to me.

Father, my heart rests in Your faithfulness today and forever. Thank You for Your divine protection over my life, health, mind, heart, and over marriage, spouse, children, family, business, and/or ministry today and until we meet in heaven in Jesus' mighty and powerful Name. Amen and amen!

17

HIS DOMINION AND POWER OVER ALL

*Now he is far above any ruler or authority or power or leader or anything else—
not only in this world but also in the world to come. God has put all things
under the authority of Christ and has made him head over all things for the
benefit of the church. And the church is his body; it is made full and complete by
Christ, who fills all things everywhere with himself.*

Ephesians 1:21–23

*In order that in everything God may be glorified through Jesus Christ. To him
belong glory and dominion forever and ever. Amen.*

1 Peter 4:11 ESV

You are:

1. God, the Mighty of the mighty (Jeremiah 9:3; Psalm 93:4)
2. The God with all dominion forever and ever (Job 25:2; 1 Peter
   4:11; 5:11; Job 25:2)

3. The God of eternal power (Romans 1:20–21)
4. God the Creator of the visible and invisible (Colossians 1:15–18)
5. God the Creator and Owner of thrones, powers, rulers, and authorities (Colossians 1:15–18)
6. The God who stretched out the heavens (Isaiah 44:24)
7. The God who holds the sun, moon, and stars in their place (Psalm 8:3; Isaiah 40:26)
8. The God who calls for the waters of the sea to pour them out upon the face of the earth (Amos 9:6)
9. The Lord God of the mountains and hills (1 Kings 20:28; Psalm 36:6)
10. The God who melts the mountains beneath Your feet (Micah 1:4)
11. The God who strides across the alpine ridges (Amos 4:13)
12. God, the Mountain-Shaper (Amos 4:13)
13. God, the Wind-Maker (Amos 4:13)
14. The One who reveals Your thoughts to humans (Amos 4:13)
15. The God who turns the dawn into darkness (Amos 4:13)
16. The Lord; God of the Armies is Your Name (Amos 4:13)
17. The God who gives the wild donkey its freedom (Job 39:5)
18. God, the Fountain of Living Waters (Revelation 21:6)
19. The One who gives me of the fountain of the water of life freely (Revelation 21:6)
20. The God and Creator of the great ocean (Proverbs 8:29; Genesis 1:9–10; 21)
21. God, the Way Maker, who makes a way where there is no way (Exodus 14:16, 21)
22. The God who gathers and controls the winds in Your fists (Proverbs 30:4; Genesis 8:1–2)
23. The God who wrapped the oceans in Your garment (Proverbs 30:4)
24. The God who established all the ends of the earth (Proverbs 30:4)
25. The God of the islands (Genesis 1:9-10; 2 Peter 3:5; Ezekiel 26:18; Psalm 97:1)
26. The Lord, the God of all flesh (Jeremiah 32:27)
27. God; no one can be rescued from Your powerful hand (Deuteronomy 32:39)

28. The God who kills and gives life (Deuteronomy 32:39)
29. Jesus, Appointed Heir and Lawful Owner of all things (Hebrews 1:2)
30. Jesus, the One sitting at the right hand of the Father (Mark 16:19)
31. Jesus, the One who ascended to the Father (John 20:17)
32. Jesus, the God who holds the key of David (Revelation 3:7)
33. Jesus, whose power works best in my weakness (2 Corinthians 12:8–9)
34. Jesus Christ, the Sustainer of the galaxies of the universe (Hebrews 1:2)
35. The Lord who commands the winds and they obey You (Luke 8:25)
36. The Maker of all the galaxies and planet earth (2 Peter 3:5)
37. The Lord who created all that exists by the word of Your command (2 Peter 3:5)
38. The God who fills all in all (Ephesians 1:23)
39. The God who holds the seven stars in Your right hand (Revelation 1:16)
40. The God who can do exceedingly, abundantly above all that we can ask or think (Ephesians 3:20–21)
41. The God who keeps me from falling (Jude 24)
42. The God who is higher than the highest (Ecclesiastes 5:8)
43. The One with dazzling power who destroys the strong, crushing their defenses (Amos 5:9)
44. The God who works miracles among us (Galatians 3:5)
45. Jesus Christ, the One who lives forever eternally (Psalm 90:2; Isaiah 57:15)
46. The God who walks in the midst of the seven churches (Revelation 1:12–13)
47. The Lord, strong and mighty in battle (Psalm 24:8)
48. The Most High over all the earth (Psalm 83:18)
49. The Lord who possesses honor and eternal dominion (1 Timothy 6:16)
50. The One with authority, honor, and sovereignty over all nations (Daniel 7:14)

51. The maximum and highest Authority over all and in all things (John 17:2; Matthew 28:18)
52. Jesus, the Teacher with real authority (Matthew 7:28)
53. Jesus, the Giver of all authority (Matthew 10:1)
54. Jesus, the One who gave me the authority to change atmospheres and circumstances by faith (Matthew 21:21–22)
55. God, the One who gives me authority over all the nations (Revelation 2:26-28)
56. God, the One who gives me the authority to overcome all the power of the enemy (Luke 10:19)
57. The God who commands submission to His authorized delegated authority (Hebrews 13:17; 1 Peter 2:17–18)
58. The God who established submission to authority (Genesis 16:9)
59. The One who is above any ruler, authority, power, leader, or anything else (Ephesians 1:21–22)
60. Father, the One who put all things under the authority of Christ for my benefit (Ephesians 1:21–22)
61. The Owner of all authority (Ephesians 1:21–23; Matthew 10:1; John 14:12)
62. The One who put all creation under my authority through Jesus Christ (Genesis 1:28; Romans 16:20; Matthew 16:13–20; 21:21–22; Luke 10:19; John 14:12; Psalm 8:4–8; 91:13; Hebrews 2:8)
63. God, who makes the clouds Your chariots (Psalm 104:3)
64. The God who rides on the wings of the wind (Psalm 104:3; 18:10)
65. God, the immortal One (1 Timothy 6:16)
66. God, the One who lives forever eternally (Daniel 12:7; Hebrews 7:24)
67. God, the One who dwells in unapproachable light (1 Timothy 6:16)
68. The Lord who is robed in majesty and armed with strength (Psalm 93:1)
69. The God who is greater than we can understand (Job 36:26)
70. The Father God whose years cannot be counted (Job 36:26)
71. The Unseen/invisible God who never dies (1 Timothy 1:17; Colossians 1:15)
72. The immortal God forever (1 Timothy 1:17)

73. The God whose throne stands from time immemorial permanently forever (Psalm 45:6; 93:2)
74. The Father who exists from the everlasting past (Psalm 93:2)
75. The One who is mightier than the roar of raging seas (Psalm 93:4)
76. The One who is mightier than the breakers on the shore (Psalm 93:4)
77. The Father whose royal laws cannot be changed (Psalm 93:5)
78. The holy God who reigns forever and ever (Psalm 93:5)
79. The Lord whose Presence gives Your temple unparalleled beauty (Psalm 27:4; 93:5)
80. The One who deserves honor and glory to Your Name eternally (1 Timothy 1:17)
81. The Lord whose voice strikes with bolts of lightning (Psalm 29:7)
82. The Lord whose voice is powerful and majestic (Psalm 29:4)
83. The Lord whose voice echoes above the sea (Psalm 29:3)
84. The Lord whose voice thunders like the mighty ocean (Job 40:9)
85. The God of glory thunders, who thunders over the mighty sea (Psalm 29:3)
86. The Lord King over the floodwaters (Psalm 29:10)
87. The Lord who reigns as King forever and ever (Psalm 29:10; Exodus 15:18)
88. Lord, the King of all time (1 Timothy 1:17)
89. The God who commanded the morning to appear (Job 38:12)
90. The God who commands the sun to start a new day from the beginning (Job 38:12)
91. The God who caused the dawn to rise in the east (Job 38:12)
92. The God who counts the stars and calls them by name (Psalm 147:4–5; Isaiah 40:26)
93. God, the One with absolute Power (Psalm 147:5)
94. The God whose understanding is infinite (beyond measure) (Psalm 147:4–5)
95. The God who kept the sea inside its boundaries as it burst from the womb (Job 38:8–9)
96. The God who clothed the sea with clouds and wrapped it in thick darkness (Job 38:8–9)

97. The God who has no competition and absolutely no rival (Philippians 2:9–11; 1 Timothy 1:17)
98. The God who breaks the pride of princes (Psalm 76:12)
99. The God who rules with an iron scepter (Revelation 2:27)
100. The One who rules with a scepter of justice (Psalm 45:6)
101. The God who establishes law and order (Exodus 2)
102. The God who owns the mountain peaks (Psalm 95:4)
103. The Lord who owns greatness (1 Chronicles 29:11)
104. The Lord who owns the power (1 Chronicles 29:11 Psalm 62:11; Proverbs 8:14)
105. The Lord who owns the victory (1 Chronicles 29:11)
106. The Giver of victory (Psalm 44:3–8; 62:1; 62:7; 118:14)
107. The Lord who owns the majesty (1 Chronicles 29:11)
108. The Lord who owns the riches (1 Chronicles 29:12)
109. The God with no limitations or boundaries in Your greatness (Psalm 145:3–12)
110. The God whose voice is like a trumpet blast (Revelation 1:10)
111. The One who holds the seven stars in Your right hand (Revelation 2:1)
112. Jesus, the One who overcomes the world (1 John 5:5; John 16:33)
113. God, *Jehovah-Nissi*—the Lord my Victorious Banner (Exodus 17:15)
114. The One who upholds me with a victorious Right Hand (Isaiah 41:10)
115. The limitless and endless One (Matthew 19:26)
116. The God of the immense ocean (Psalm 93:4)
117. The God of the storms and whirlwinds (Job 38:1)
118. The God whose workmanship is marvelous (Psalm 139:14)
119. God, the all-sufficient One (Colossians 1:13–20)
120. The God who rules over all things (1 Chronicles 29:12)
121. The God who rules all the nations (Psalm 22:28)
122. The Lord in whose hands are power and mighty strength (1 Chronicles 29:12)
123. The God who controls the course of world events (Daniel 2:21)
124. Christ, the One who holds the jurisdiction over all present and future generations (Ephesians 1:21–22)

125. Jesus, Your Name is power and hope for all (Acts 3:6; Mark 16:17-18)
126. The Most Famous God eternally (John 3:16; Philippians 2:9; 1 Kings 8:41–42; Nehemiah 9:10)
127. The Lord who made the earth with great power and with outstretched arm (Jeremiah 32:17)
128. The God of powerful decrees (Exodus 18:20; 2 Chronicles 34:31; Matthew 21:18–22)
129. The God of maximum power (Revelation 15:8; Psalm 147:4–5)
130. God, the Rock of my strength and my glory (Psalm 62:7)
131. God, almighty in strength (Job 9:4)
132. The God with incredible greatness in power (Ephesians 1:19)
133. Jesus, the One that sustains all things by Your mighty powerful word (Hebrews 1:3)
134. God, nobody can revoke Your deeds or plans (Romans 11:29; Galatians 3:17)
135. God, higher and greater than I can feel, think, or see (1 Corinthians 2:9; Isaiah 55:8–9)
136. The God who has possession of me (1 Peter 2:9)
137. The God who comes from above and is above all (John 3:31; Psalm 97:9)
138. The God of gods (Daniel 2:47)
139. The God of heights (Micah 6:6)
140. The Lord who owns the entire earth and everything in it (Psalm 24:1)
141. God, *Jehovah-Elohim*—the all-powerful Creator of the universe (Genesis 1:1–3; Deuteronomy 10:17; Psalm 68, Mark 13:19)
142. God, the Most High (Hebrews 7:1, Psalm 87:5)
143. The God with majestic power (Isaiah 63:12 NET)
144. The God with mighty divine power (1 Peter 5:6; 2 Peter 1:3; Ephesians 1:19)
145. The Lord who is in full control of my life (Romans 8:28)
146. The God of the impossible, nothing is too difficult for You (Luke 18:27)

147. Christ, the One who existed from the beginning before anything was created (1 John 1:1; 1 John 2:13; Colossians 1:15–17; Proverbs 8:22)
148. Christ, supreme over all creation (Colossians 1:15)
149. The Lord who is supreme over all gods and all powers (Deuteronomy 10:17)
150. The Lord who is supreme over all the earth (Psalm 97:9)
151. Christ, through You, God created everything in the heavenly realms and on earth (Colossians 1:16)
152. Christ, the Maker of things we can and cannot see (Colossians 1:16)
153. Christ the Creator or thrones, kingdoms, rulers, and authorities in the unseen world (Colossians 1:16)
154. Christ, the one who defeated death and sin (Luke 24:6–7; Romans 10:9)
155. Jesus Christ, the Resurrection and Life (John 11:25–26; Romans 6:9)
156. The One who raised me from the dead along with Christ (Ephesians 2:6)
157. Jesus, the One who gave me the keys to the kingdom of heaven (Matthew 16:16–19)
158. God, the Lord with world dominion (Psalm 22:28)
159. The God with dominion over the universe (Genesis 1:26; Colossians 1:15–18)
160. You are the Spirit of self-control (Galatians 522–23)
161. The God of limitless power (Matthew 19:26; Ephesians 3:20–21)
162. The Owner of the earth and all that it contains (1 Corinthians 10:18–26)
163. The Lord who has made the heavens Your throne, from which You rule (Psalm 103:19)
164. The Lord who remains forever with those who fear You (Psalm 103:17)
165. The God in whose hands is the life of every living thing (Job 12:10)
166. The God in whose hands is the breath of every human being (Job 12:10)

167. The One who whatever You destroy cannot be rebuilt (Job 12:14)
168. The One who imprisons a man, and there is no escape (Job 12:14)
169. The One who holds back the rain, and the earth becomes a desert (Job 12:15)
170. The One who releases the waters, and they flood the earth (Job 12:15)
171. The God whose Word is a two-edged sword (Hebrews 4:12)
172. He who uncovers mysteries hidden in darkness (Job 12:22)
173. He who brings to light the thick darkness (Job 12:22)
174. The One who builds up nations and destroys them (Job 12:23)
175. God, my Owner (Psalm 16:2)
176. The Lord who made the earth with Your great power (Jeremiah 10:12)
177. The LORD God of heaven's armies (Hosea 12:5)
178. The Mighty Warrior (Psalm 45:3)
179. God, Yours is the power (Proverbs 8:14)
180. The God of Consuming Fire (1 Kings 18:38, 2 Kings 1:10; Exodus 3:2; Hebrews 12:25-29)
181. The One who seated me in the heavenly realms with Christ Jesus (Ephesians 2:6)
182. The Everlasting God who never grows tired or weary (Isaiah 40:28)
183. The *El Shaddai*—Almighty, Omnipotent God (Genesis 17:1; Psalm 49:24; 91:1; 132:2, 5)
184. The One who removes the royal robe of kings (Job 12:18)
185. He who silences the trusted adviser and removes the insight of the elders (Job 12:20)
186. The One who pours disgrace upon princes and disarms the strong (Job 12:21)
187. The God who sees everything and nothing is hidden from Your eyes (Hebrews 4:13)
188. The God whose Word is a two-edged sword that cuts between my soul and spirit (Hebrews 4:12)
189. The God whose two-edged sword exposes my innermost thoughts and desires (Hebrews 4:12)
190. The God whose Word is alive and powerful (Hebrews 4:12)

191. The God who breaks the aging laws and transforms human limitations into strengths (Genesis 18:11–14; Genesis 21:1–3; Psalm 92:12–14; Joshua 14:10–11; Isaiah 46:4)
192. The God who decides how hard the winds should blow (Job 28:25)
193. The God who decided how much rain should fall (Job 28:25)
194. The One who reserves the storehouses of the snow and hail as weapons of war (Job 38:22–23)
195. The God who makes the rain fall on barren land, in a desert where no one lives (Job 38:26)
196. The God who sends rain to satisfy the parched ground and make the tender grass spring up (Job 38:26)
197. The One who can tilt the water jars of heaven (Job 38:37)
198. The God who gives the horse its strength (Job 39:19)
199. The God who clothed the horse's neck with a flowing mane (Job 39:19)
200. The One who provides the horse with the ability to leap like a locust (Job 39:20)
201. The One who taught the falcon to fly and head south (Job 39:26)
202. The One who commands that the eagle mounts up and makes his nest on high (Job 39:27)
203. The God who answers me from the whirlwind (Job 40:6)
204. The God who can do anything and no one can stop You (Job 42:2)
205. Jesus, the Alpha and the Omega (Revelation 22:13)
206. Jesus, the First and the Last (Revelation 1:17; Revelation 22:13)
207. Jesus, the Beginning and the End (Revelation 22:13)
208. Jesus, the One who holds the keys of death and the grave (Revelation 1:18)
209. God with a perpetual everlasting dominion (Daniel 4:34)
210. God, Your rule is everlasting (Daniel 4:34)
211. The God who speaks and silences the whole earth (Habakkuk 2:20)
212. The One who made first heroic warrior on earth (Genesis 10:8–9)
213. The One who makes me a strong and heroic warrior (Philippians 4:13; Genesis 10:8–9)

214. Lord, the One with an unshakable, indestructible, invincible kingdom (Daniel 7:14; Hebrews 12:28)
215. God, a Devouring Fire (Hebrews 12:28)
216. The Lord God Almighty (1 Kings 19:10)
217. The Lord God, a victorious mighty Warrior (Zephaniah 3:17)
218. The Giver of victory (Psalm 44:3–8; 62:1; 62:7; 1 Corinthians 15:57)
219. The God with invisible qualities, eternal power, and divine nature (Romans 1:20)
220. The One who holds all the power in His hands (Psalm 22:28; 62:11)
221. The God who told Peter "Kill and eat!" (Acts 10:13-15)
222. The One who is even greater than the Temple! (Matthew 12:6)

A PRAYER DECLARING HIS DOMINION AND POWER OVER ALL

Father, I come before You in Jesus' Name and through Your Holy Spirit's help. I thank You because I know You hear my prayers even before I utter them. You are just waiting for me to connect with You so that I may always learn to depend on You. I know I can't do anything without You or apart from You. You are the ONLY essential One in everything each day of my life.

Father, You are the One who holds the sun, moon, and stars in their place. You are the Lord of the mountains and hills. You are the One who melts the mountains beneath Your feet as lava into the valleys. You stride across the alpine ridges of the earth. Lord God, You are the Mountain-Shaper and the Wind-Maker. You are the One who grabs and controls the winds in Your fists. You command the winds, and they obey You because You are their Master.

You give the wild donkey its freedom. Lord, with wisdom, You make the hawk soar and spread its wings toward the south. By Your command, the eagle mounts up and makes his nest on high. You gave the horse his strength and clothed the horse's neck with a flowing mane. You give the horse the ability to leap like a locust.

Lord, You are the Creator of the great ocean. You kept the sea inside its boundaries as it burst from the womb. You call for the waters of the sea to pour out upon the face of the earth. You wrapped the waters in Your garment. You clothed the sea with clouds and wrapped it in thick darkness. You are the God who answers me from the whirlwind. Lord, Your voice is over the waters. You are the God of glory thunders over the many waters. You are the God of the immense ocean.

You are the One who decides how hard the winds should blow. The God who decides how much rain should fall. The One who reserves the storehouses of the snow and hail as weapons of war. Lord, it is You who makes the rain fall on barren land in a desert where no one lives. The God who sends rain to satisfy the parched ground and make the tender grass spring up. You are the One who can tilt the water jars of heaven.

You are the God of the storms and whirlwinds. Lord, You are mightier than the violent raging of the seas and the mighty breakers of the sea. You are *Jehovah-Elohim*—God is the all-powerful Creator of the universe. You are the Sustainer of the galaxies of the universe. Lord, help me not forget that by the very word of Your command, You created all these galaxies and this planet Earth.

You are the God with majestic and mighty divine power. The God of the heights. The One who holds back the rain, and the earth becomes a desert. The One who releases the waters, and they flood the earth. The Lord who made the heavens and the earth with great power and outstretched arm. Nothing is too hard for You, my Lord.

You are the God of powerful decrees. Whatever You say goes, for You are the God of maximum power and glory. Lord, nobody can revoke Your deeds or your plans. No one can give You advice because you own the knowledge. You own the entire earth and everything in it. You make the clouds Your chariots and ride on the wings of the wind. You are the immortal God who lives forever and eternally. You dwell in unapproachable light.

You are the Lord who is robed in majesty and armed with strength. O Lord, You are greater than we can understand. Lord, I know a day is like a thousand years to You, and a thousand years like a day. Father, Your years cannot be counted. You are the unseen One who never dies—the immortal One. Your throne stands from time immemorial permanently. You are from the eternal past. Oh, great Majestic King, glory to Your Name forever and ever!

No matter how the floods of life come, You are mightier than the violent raging of the seas, stronger than the breakers on the shore. I know when I go through deep waters, You will be with me. I know when I go through rivers of difficulty, I will not drown. I know when I walk through the fire of oppression,

I will not be burned up; and the flames will not consume me. You are more powerful than all these combined. Father God, Your royal laws cannot be changed, for You reign eternally. O Lord, You are holy forever and ever.

Father, You bring everything out of nothing. You command the sun to start a new day and the morning to appear from the beginning of creation. You caused the dawn to rise in the east. I know that you created this day out of love for me.

You are the Fountain of Living Waters. You give me this water of life freely on this day. Lord, You are the One who established all the ends of the earth and designed all the islands. You are the Supreme Master over all the masters and powers of the earth. There is no limitations or boundaries in Your greatness.

Jesus, You are the Appointed Heir and Lawful Owner of all things. You sit at the right hand of the Father, and You ascended to the Father because You were raised from the dead. You are the resurrected One! Yes! You are alive. Jesus, You own and you hold the key of David in Your hands. You open and no one can close, you close and no one can open.

Lord, You hold the seven stars in Your right hand. You walk in the midst of the seven churches and reveal Your thoughts to Your people. Jesus, you are even greater than the Temple. Your Presence gives Your temple unparalleled beauty. Father God, You are the One who fills all in all. You are the One who uncovers mysteries hidden in darkness; You bring light to the deepest gloom. Lord, You see everything, and nothing is hidden from Your eyes.

Father, You are the God who tenderly tells me not to be afraid because You are with me. You give me strength and uphold me with your victorious Right Hand. Lord, You can do exceedingly, abundantly above all that I can ask or think. You are the Source of my exceeding joy and great happiness. Lord, You alone can keep me from falling away. You will bring me with great joy into Your glorious Presence without a fault.

You are the Lord who works miracles among us. Jesus, You sustain everything by the mighty power of Your word. You are the Way Maker, You make a way where there is no way.

Jesus Christ, You live forever and eternally. Lord, no matter what happens, You are always strong and mighty in battle, fighting for me and my family.

You are the everlasting God who never grows weak or weary. You are the mighty of the mighty, for You are the God of perpetual everlasting dominion and power over all that exists. Lord, You created the visible and invisible, the seen and unseen. Your power is eternal with no end. You own all thrones, powers, rulers, and authorities. God, when You speak, the whole earth is silenced.

Jesus, You possess honor and eternal dominion. You are a Supreme God. You are the Lord God Almighty with dominion over the entire universe, the galaxies and the earth. You are the God of eternal power. You are the only One with authority, honor, and sovereignty over all nations. The maximum authority over all and over everything. You are the giver of all authority.

Jesus, You gave me the authority to change atmospheres and circumstances by faith. And You give me authority over all the nations. Lord, You give me the authority to overcome all the powers of the enemy. You are the only great Teacher with true authority. Jesus, Your Name is power and hope for all the world.

Lord, Your voice is powerful and majestic; it strikes with bolts of lightning. You are the God of glory thunders whose voice echoes and thunders over the mighty sea. You are the One who rules over the floodwaters. Oh, my Lord, You reign as King forever. Lord, Your kingdom is an unshakable, indestructible, and invincible kingdom.

Lord, You are the One who has absolute, unlimited and endless power. Your understanding is infinite. There is no limit to what You know. Father, You own the mountain peaks. You own greatness. You count the stars and call them by name.

You own the power, the victory, the majesty, and the riches. Lord, there are no limitations or boundaries to Your greatness.

Father, Your voice is like a trumpet blast. You hold the seven stars in Your right hand. Lord, You are the One who has overcome the world. Therefore, I will overcome trials and tribulations with Your power. Lord, You are the limitless and endless One. Your workmanship is marvelous. The God who is the all-sufficient One. The God who rules over all things and all the nations. Lord, in Your hands, are power and mighty strength. You own the Power.

God, it is You who controls the course of world events. Jesus Christ, everything is under Your jurisdiction. You have power over all generations—past, present, and future. You are greater than any ruler, authority, power, or leader. Father, You are the One who put all things under the authority of Christ and made Him the head of the church for my benefit. Jesus, Your Name is power and a source of strength and hope for me and my family. Lord, You are and will always be the Most Famous One for all generations.

Lord, You have possession of my life. Lord, You are higher and greater than I can feel, think, or see. You are the great God Most High. Lord, You are in full control of my life today and forever. You are my Rock, my strength, and my glory. God, You are almighty in strength with incredible greatness in power. Jesus, You uphold all things by the power of Your Word.

Father, You are the God above all. The God of gods and Lord of lords, King of kings. When something seems difficult for me, I remember that You are the God of the impossible; nothing is too difficult for You.

Christ, You are the One who existed before anything was created. You are the Supreme Ruler of all creation, the earth, all gods, and all forces. Lord, You created everything in the heavenly realms and on earth. Jesus Christ, You are the Originator of both visible and invisible things. Christ, You are the Creator of thrones, kingdoms, rulers, and authorities in the unseen world.

Jesus, You are the Christ who has risen from the dead. You are not dead; You are alive! You are the Power of resurrection and life. You have overcome the world and I can now be an overcomer through Your victory. You are *Jehovah-Nissi*—my Victorious Banner. You give me life abundantly. Your Spirit of resurrection lives in me and through me. You give me the power to live on this earth and through eternity.

Father, You have raised me from the dead along with Christ, and You have given me the keys to the kingdom of heaven. Now I can overcome through Your resurrection power. You have seated me in the heavenly realms with Jesus, where I can make my prayer declarations and decrees in Your mighty Name.

Lord, You are my Master. You are the Spirit of self-control. You give me self-control so I can manage my emotions and actions, synchronizing them to Your will and Divine Nature.

Lord, the earth and all it contains belong to You. Lord, You made the heavens Your throne from where You rule. You are the Lord who remains forever with those who fear You; I know You are with me today. Lord, I know that the life of every living thing is in Your hands. The air in my lungs and my breath are in Your hands. I will praise and worship You until my last breath and then in heaven eternally.

You are the Lord God of heaven's armies. The mighty warrior, Yours is the power. You have the power to make me a strong heroic warrior. You are the God of consuming fire. *El Shaddai*—the Lord God Almighty, Omnipotent God.

My beloved Lord, You have no competition or rival, because you have no equal. Father God, Your throne is permanent forever and ever. You break the pride of princes. You rule with an iron scepter filled with justice. You established law and order and commanded submission to delegated authorities that are authorized by You.

Father, You are the God of all flesh. No one can be rescued from Your powerful hand. You are the One who kills and gives life. The Most High over all the earth. Lord, God of the Armies is Your Name.

You are the One who removes the royal robe of kings, for You are the King of all time. Lord You are the dazzling power that destroys the strong, crushing their defenses. When You destroy, it cannot be rebuilt. You build up nations and destroy them. You imprison a man, and there can be no release.

You pour disgrace upon princes and disarm the strong. You are the God who can do anything, and no one can stop You. Your rule, power, and kingdom are eternal; they will never end.

God, Your Word is a two-edged sword that cuts between my soul and spirit. It is Your Word that exposes my innermost thoughts and desires. God, Your Word is alive and powerful. I can live a victorious life through the power of Your Word. You are the God who can break or interrupt the aging laws and transforms human limitations into strengths. Jesus, Your power works best in my weakness.

Jesus, You are the Alpha and the Omega, the First and the Last, the Beginning and the End. You hold the keys and have control over death and the grave. You are the All-Powerful God.

You are my Rock, my Hero, my Support, and my everything. I came from You, and I shall go back to you. Oh, mighty God I am a fragment of Your glory, I was created to worship You eternally. It brings me a sense of security and trust to know all of these great truths. Lord, I trust and I believe in you. Almighty God, You have complete sovereignty over my life today and forever.

Thank You for revealing to me Your Mighty Dominion and Power, You are an amazing God!

In Jesus' Name, amen.

18

HIS HELP IN TROUBLED TIMES

For he delivers the needy when he calls, the poor and him who has no helper. He has pity on the weak and the needy, and saves the lives of the needy. From oppression and violence he redeems their life, and precious is their blood in his sight.

Psalm 72:12–14 ESV

"Thus says the LORD who made the earth, the LORD who formed it to establish it —the LORD is his name: Call to me and I will answer you, and will tell you great and hidden things that you have not known."

Jeremiah 33:2–3 ESV

You are:

1. The God who cares for me and my family (1 Peter 5:7)
2. The Lord who is with me in troubled times (Psalm 91:15)

3. The One who places Your hand of blessing on my head (Psalm 139:5)
4. The Lord who blesses me with peace (Psalm 29:10)
5. The One who examines my heart (Psalm 139:1; Psalm 7:9)
6. The One who knows everything about me (Psalm 139:1)
7. The God who knows everything I do (Psalm 139:3)
8. The God who knows what I'm about to say even before I say it (Psalm 139:4)
9. The One who knows when I sit down and stand up (Psalm 139:2)
10. The One who knows my thoughts even when I'm far away (Psalm 139:2)
11. The God who sees me when I travel and when I rest at home (Psalm 139:3)
12. The God who goes before me and behind me (Psalm 139:5)
13. The Holy Presence I can never escape from (Psalm 139:7)
14. The Lord whose anger lasts only a moment, but Your favor lasts a lifetime (Psalm 30:5)
15. The Spirit who gives me power, love, and self-discipline (1 Timothy 1:7)
16. God, the Father to the fatherless and orphans (Psalm 68:5)
17. God, the Revealer of mysteries (Daniel 2:47)
18. Jesus, a Man of sorrows and acquainted with grief (Isaiah 53:3)
19. Jesus, my Rock of offense (1 Peter 2:8)
20. Jesus, the Advocate who pleads my case before the Father (1 John 2:1)
21. Jesus, my Sunrise and Joy from on high (Luke 1:78; Psalm 30:5)
22. The God with world dominion (Psalm 22:28)
23. Jesus, who delivered us from the wrath to come (1 Thessalonians 1:10)
24. The Lord whose eyes are on the righteous (Psalm 34:15)
25. The God who is mighty to save (Isaiah 63:1)
26. God, the Holy Spirit and my Intercessor (Romans 8:34)
27. God, the Holy Spirit and my Counselor (John 14:26)
28. The Holy Spirit, my Comforter (John 14:26)
29. The God of generosity (Psalm 145:6; 19)
30. The Father who honors me (Psalm 91:15; John 12:26)

31. The God of all-sufficiency who makes me sufficient (2 Corinthians 3:5)
32. The God of favor (Psalm 5:12)
33. The God of Peace (Romans 15:3)
34. The Lord who gives me strength (Psalm 29:11)
35. The God of patience (Exodus 34:6)
36. The God of my heart's mercy (Psalm 51)
37. The God of mercy (Ephesians 2:4–5)
38. God, the All-Knowing One (John 18:4)
39. God, the Shelter and Refuge of the poor (Psalm 9:9)
40. God, the All-Seeing (Genesis 16:13)
41. God, who will hold me up wherever I go (Psalm 91)
42. God, the Refuge of Salvation for Your anointed ones (Psalm 28:8)
43. God, my Rock, my Tower of Refuge (Psalm 18:2)
44. God, my Refuge and Strength from the storm (Psalm 46:1)
45. The God of promise (Hebrews 6:13)
46. The God of happiness (Matthew 25:21; Psalm 146:5)
47. The God of contentment (Song of Solomon 8:10)
48. The God whose faithful promises are my armor and protection (Psalm 91:4)
49. The God who makes me lie down in green pastures (Psalm 23)
50. The God who leads me beside quiet waters (Psalm 23)
51. The God who blesses the humble (Matthew 5:5–15)
52. The Lord who blesses Your people with peace (Psalm 29:11)
53. The Lord who blesses me with true peace (Psalm 29:11)
54. God, the Tower of Salvation (2 Samuel 22:51)
55. God, the Defender of Your people Israel (Isaiah 49:7)
56. God, my Best Friend (John 15:15)
57. The Lord who cares for those who trust in You (1 Peter 5:7; Nahum 1:7)
58. The God who speaks and silences the whole earth (Habakkuk 2:20)
59. The only God; there is no other God but You (Deuteronomy 32:39)
60. The Almighty God who wants me to walk before You and be perfect (Genesis 17:1)

61. The God who erases all my transgressions for love of You (Isaiah 43:25)
62. The God that forgives and forgets by Your own choice (Isaiah 43:25; Numbers 14:18; Jeremiah 33:8)
63. The God who will not remember my sins (Hebrews 8:12)
64. God, the Forgiver of all iniquity past, present, and future generations (1 John 1:9)
65. The Lord God who is present in our midst (Matthew 18:20; Zephaniah 3:17)
66. God, my Deliverer (Psalm 32:7; Colossians 1:13; Micah 2:13)
67. God, the Altar of Peace for my fears (Judges 6:24)
68. God, the One who comforts me (Isaiah 51:12)
69. God the Lord, *Yeshua*, the God of compassion and lovingkindness (Psalm 25:6)
70. Jesus, the Consolation of Israel (Luke 2:25)
71. The God who extends Your hands to me (Psalm 90:17)
72. My eternal God (Psalm 90:1–4; Genesis 21:33)
73. The God who gives justice to the oppressed (Psalm 146:7; 82:3)
74. God, the One who gives me joy and peace amid my trials (Psalm 94:19; 30:5)
75. The Lord my Shield (Genesis 15:1; Deuteronomy 33:29; Psalm 18:2)
76. God, who commands me to be still and know that You are God (Psalm 46:10)
77. The God who vindicates me (Psalm 135:14)
78. God, my strong Fortress (Psalm 18:2)
79. God, a Hiding Place from the wind (Isaiah 32:2)
80. God, a Rewarder of those who sincerely and diligently seek You (Hebrews 11:6)
81. God, my Shadow from the heat (Isaiah 4:6)
82. God, my Strong Tower that protects me from the enemy (Proverbs 18:10)
83. God, my Secure Foundation (Isaiah 28:16)
84. God, my ever-present help in trouble (Isaiah 41:4)
85. God, the Wall of Fire around me (Zechariah 2:5)
86. The God who answers by fire (1 Kings 18:24)

87. The God of the fire (1 Kings 18:38–39; Exodus 3:1–4:17; Exodus 24:17)
88. The God who is attentive to my prayer (Psalm 61:1; 86:6)
89. The God who answers prayers (John 15:7)
90. The God who is with those whose spirits are contrite and humble (Isaiah 57:15)
91. The God who restores the crushed spirit of the humble (Isaiah 57:15)
92. The God who revives the courage of the repentant heart (Isaiah 57:15)
93. God, the One who gives me laughter (Psalm 126:2)
94. The God who wipes every tear from my eyes (Revelation 21:4)
95. The God who is always by my side and never leaves me (Isaiah 41:10)
96. The God who leads me beside peaceful streams (Psalm 23)
97. God, my peaceful Place of Security (Isaiah 32:18)
98. The Lord who prepares a feast for me in the presence of my enemies (Psalm 23:5)
99. The God who anoints my head with oil until my cup overflows with blessings (Psalm 23:5)
100. The God who calls things that are not as if they were (Romans 4:17)
101. God, the Master over the threshing floor (Matthew 3:12)
102. The Father who knows all my needs always (Matthew 6:32)
103. The God who tests me and refines me as silver is refined (Psalm 66:10)
104. The Way-Maker, who always makes a way (Isaiah 43:16)
105. The God who arms me with strength and power (Psalm 18:32)
106. The Lord who gives strength to Your people (Psalm 29:11)
107. God, the Strength of the poor needy in distress (Isaiah 25:4)
108. God, the One who renews my strength (Psalm 103:5–7)
109. The God who is near (Jeremiah 23:23)
110. *El Roi*—the God who sees me (Proverbs 24:12; Genesis 16:13)
111. God, the air and breath in my lungs (Genesis 2:7; Job 27:3; Ezekiel 37:9; Psalm 150:6)

112. The Lord who rejoices over me with joyful and loud singing (Zephaniah 3:17)
113. The God who intercedes for me always (Romans 8:26–27, 33–34)
114. The God who knows what's in my heart (Psalm 7:9; 139:2–23)
115. God the Source of my strength (Psalm 18:1)
116. The Lord my Defender (Psalm 89:18; Exodus 15–2–3)
117. The Lord my Protector (Psalm 18:2)
118. The Lord my Covering (Psalm 105:39)
119. The Lord my High Place of serenity (Habakkuk 3:19)
120. The Lord, the Giver of wisdom, knowledge, and intelligence (James 1:5; Proverbs 2:6; Ephesians 1:17; Colossians 2:2–3)
121. The God who comforts those who are cast down (2 Corinthians 7:6)
122. God, my Helper (Psalm 54:4)
123. The Upholder of my life (Psalm 54:4)
124. God, the Solution to all my challenges (John 15:5)
125. The God who is greater than my emotions (1 John 3:20)
126. Lord, my Light at the end of the tunnel (John 8:12)
127. God, the Defender of widows (Isaiah 54:4; Psalm 68:5)
128. The God who never criticizes me (John 8:11)
129. The God who overlooks my weaknesses (2 Corinthians 12:8–11)
130. The God of second and multiple chances (John 8:1–11; 1 John 2:1–2; Lamentations 3:21–23)
131. The God who comforts me with Your unfailing love (Psalm 119:76)
132. The God who restores my soul (Psalm 23:3)
133. The God who strengthens me to do all things through Christ (Philippians 4:13)
134. The God of peace that surpasses all comprehension (Philippians 4:7)
135. The God who guards my heart and mind with Your peace in Christ Jesus (Philippians 4:7)
136. The God who is where my help comes from (Psalm 121:2; 124:8)
137. Lord, my Hope (Romans 15:3: Psalm 62:5)
138. The God who has good plans for me (Jeremiah 29:11)
139. The God who gives me a future and hope (Jeremiah 29:11)

140. The God who comforts me on the day of tribulation (2 Corinthians 1:4; Psalm 55:22)
141. The Lord God, my Sustainer (Psalm 54:4)
142. The God who I trust with all my heart (Proverb 3:5; Psalm 56:4)
143. The God who tells me to fear not for You are with me (Isaiah 41:10)
144. The One who tells me not to be discouraged for You are my God (Isaiah 41:10)
145. The God who strengthens me and helps me (Isaiah 41:10)
146. The God who upholds me with Your victorious hand (Isaiah 41:10)
147. The Lord who knows how weak we are, like dust (Psalm 103:14)
148. The God who renews my youth like the eagle's (Psalm 103:5)
149. The One who helps me when I commit all to You and trust You blindly (Psalm 37:5)
150. The loving God who keeps track of all my sorrows (Psalm 56:8)
151. The God who has collected all my tears in Your bottle (Psalm 56:8)
152. The God who has registered all my tears in Your book (Psalm 56:8)
153. The God who is for me and on my side (Psalm 56:9)
154. The God who will not let me be shaken for You are always with me, right beside me (Psalm 16:8)
155. The Lord who performs righteous deeds (Psalm 103:6)
156. The Lord who performs righteous judgments for all who are oppressed (Psalm103:6)
157. The God who sees my troubles and takes notice of me (Exodus 2:25; 3:8–10)
158. The God who sees my afflictions and gives heed to my cry (Exodus 3:7)
159. The God who is aware of my sufferings (Exodus 3:7
160. The God who hears my groaning and remembers Your covenant/promises (Exodus 2:24)
161. The Lord who hears the prayers of the righteous (Proverbs 15:29)
162. The God who promises to protect and prosper my life (Psalm 37:3)

163. The God who helps me when I trust in You (Psalm 37:5)
164. The One who edifies me (Psalm 127:1; 1 Corinthians 14:4)
165. God, my Helper and Sustainer (Psalm 54:4)
166. Holy Spirit, my Helper (John 14:26)
167. The Lord who resurrects and brings back to life my dead dreams (Genesis 18:14)
168. The God who always plans ahead to rescue Your children from trouble (Genesis 42:8–9)
169. The Lord of my joy who is my Strength (Nehemiah 8:10)
170. The God whose anger lasts only a moment, but Your favor lasts a lifetime (Psalm 30:5)
171. The Lord whose favor makes me secure as a mountain (Psalm 30:7)
172. The God who turns my mourning into joyful dancing (Psalm 30:11)
173. The One who clothes me with joy instead of mourning (Psalm 30:11)
174. The God who never despises a broken and contrite heart (Psalm 51:17)
175. The God who transforms me into a new person (Romans 12:2)
176. The God who changes my paradigms (Romans 12:2)
177. The God whose will for my life is good, pleasing, and perfect (Romans 12:2)
178. The God who causes everything to work together for my good (Romans 8:28)
179. The One who will wipe every tear from my eyes (Revelation 21:4–7)
180. The Trustworthy and True One (Revelation 21:4–7)
181. The One who changes my name to align to Your eternal purposes (Genesis 17:4–6; John 1:42; Genesis 32:22–28; 17:15–16)
182. The God in whose Presence I walk, in Your life-giving light (Psalm 56:13)
183. The God who will not ignore the cries of those who suffer (Psalm 9:12)
184. The Lord who gives me strength (Psalm 29:11)
185. The Lord blesses me with peace (Psalm 29:11)

186. The God who places the lonely in families (Psalm 68:6)
187. The God who sets the prisoners free and gives them joy (Psalm 68:6)
188. The God who will wipe away every tear from my eyes (Revelation 21:4)
189. The God who will cancel death forever (Revelation 21:4)
190. The God who will take away all mourning, crying, and pain (Revelation 21:4)
191. The God who will not abandon me (Psalm 27:10)
192. The God who holds me close (Psalm 27:10)
193. My Crown of everlasting joy (Isaiah 35:10)
194. The Lord who will return for me (Isaiah 35:10)
195. My Joy and Gladness (Isaiah 35:10)
196. The One who has gone through suffering and testing (Hebrews 2:18)
197. The One who understands me and helps me through my trials and temptations (Hebrews 2:18)
198. The God who won't abandon me (Psalm 27:10)
199. The God who holds me close (Psalm 27:10)
200. The Lord who gives me victory (1 Corinthians 15:56–57; Psalm 35:3; 62:1–2)
201. The God who won't abandon me (Psalm 27:10)
202. The God who holds me close (Psalm 27:10)
203. The God who is with me and no one can stand against me (Romans 8:31; Isaiah 54:16–17; Joshua 1:5)
204. The One who will not allow any weapon formed against me to prosper (Isaiah 54:16–17)
205. My Vindicator (Isaiah 54:16–17)
206. My safe Refuge (Psalm 61:3)
207. A Fortress where my enemies cannot reach me (Psalm 61:3)
208. The Lord who redeemed me from the depths of the pit (Lamentations 3:55–58)
209. The God who will neither fail me nor abandon me (Deuteronomy 31:8)
210. The God who delivers me when I cry out for Your help (Psalm 72:12)

211. The One who pities the weak and needy (Psalm 72:12–13)
212. The One who redeems my life from oppression and violence (Psalm 72:14)
213. The One who makes everything all right (Deuteronomy 32:4; Psalm 103:10–18)
214. The One who gives me wisdom generously and without reproach (James 1:5; Proverbs 2:6; Ephesians 1:17; Isaiah 33:6)
215. The God who speaks and creates something new out of nothing (Genesis 1:3)
216. The One true God who is my mighty Refuge (2 Samuel 22:33)
217. The One who removes the obstacles out of my way (2 Samuel 22:33)
218. The LORD who lifts up those who are weighed down (Psalm 146:8)
219. The God who shut the lions' mouths (Daniel 6:22)
220. The God who saved Daniel from the power of the lions (Daniel 6:27)
221. The God who delivers and rescues me (Daniel 6:27)
222. The Lord who fights for me while I just stay calm (Exodus 14:14)
223. He who cares for me like the apple of his eye (Psalms 17:8; Zechariah 2:8)

A PRAYER DECLARING HIS HELP IN TROUBLE TIMES

Abba Papa, I come before Your mighty Presence in Jesus' Name and through the guidance of Your Holy Spirit. I thank You for all Your goodness and mercy on this day. Thank You for Your protection and providence. Thank You for Your unfailing and unending eternal love toward me.

I know you care for my troubles, and you are tender with me, especially when I most need it.

Thank You for taking care of me and my family. You are always there for me during difficult moments. You are the Lord who bestows blessings on the humble. Lord, I humble myself before Your throne of grace. Place Your hand of blessing on my head today. You are the Lord who gives me Your divine peace. You comfort and show me that everything will be well since everything is perfect and pleasing in You. You always make everything all right. You are the God who speaks and creates something new out of nothing. I believe Your Word.

Father, You examine my heart. You know everything about me and everything I do every day. You know what I'm about to say even before I say it. You know when I sit down and stand up. You know all my thoughts even when I'm far away.

You are the God who sees me when I travel and when I rest at home, for You watch over me like the apple of Your eye.

Lord, You go before me and behind me, guarding me always. I know I can never escape from Your Presence. You are the Spirit who gives me power, love, and self-discipline.

Lord, You have gone through suffering and testing. You alone understand me and help me through my trials and temptations. You are the Lord who gives me strength; You are the One who gives me victory. You lift me up when I am weighed down. You bless me with peace. Lord, I thank You for not ignoring the cries of the suffering. You are the Lord who provides me with strength. You are the One who gives me victory and helps me win. You bestow peace on me and my family. You are my mighty Refuge.

You are the One who sets the prisoners free and gives them joy. You place the lonely in families. You are the God who will wipe away every tear from my eyes. You will cancel death forever. The God who will take away all mourning, crying, and pain. You are the Lord who will return for me. You are my Crown of everlasting joy. You are my exceeding Joy and Gladness.

You are the Revealer of mysteries, Lord, and You love those who seek You. You let yourself be found by those who seek you with all their hearts and you make yourself known to them. You are near to and have a special love for the humble and contrite in heart, and You will never reject them. You always reward those who believe in You and truly seek You.

Jesus, You were a Man of sorrows and acquainted with grief. Human beings disliked and rejected You. You understand what it means to be broken and know what it's like to be unappreciated and abandoned by Your friends. You are familiar with pain and understand when we face difficulties. Lord Jesus, You are the solid Rock. A Living Stone chosen and precious in the eyes of God.

Now You are the Advocate who pleads my case before the Father. Jesus, You are my Morning Sunrise and Joy from on high. No matter my challenge, I know You are the God with world dominion who has the control and the rudder of my life.

Lord, I know Your eyes are on the righteous always. You are the Refuge of Salvation for Your anointed ones. You are a God of promise and will achieve Your promises over my life and family. You, Lord Jesus, will deliver me from the wrath to come. Thank You, Lord, for You are mighty to save me and my family.

You are a generous God. You, Father, honor me because I honor Your Name. You are all-sufficient for me O Lord. You are a God of grace and favor who gives me Your divine peace. You give me strength in the middle of my trials. Lord, my victory comes from You, You will uphold me everywhere I go.

You are the God of patience. You are the merciful God who fills my heart with mercy. Father, You are the All-Seeing One and I know You can see my situation today.

Lord, You are the Mighty Shelter and Refuge to the poor; and You bring justice to the oppressed. You are the Father of orphans and fatherless children. You are with the contrite and humble in spirit. You will not ignore my cries of pain. You restore the crushed spirit of the humble. The God who revives the courage of the repentant heart.

Lord, help me to always be still in the midst of difficulty and to know that You are God, the one who controls everything. I only must trust that you know what you are doing and that you are fighting for me. Jesus, You are my Tower of Salvation and my Defender. Lord, You are my Deliverer from the enemy's schemes and traps. Lord God, You are a Victorious Warrior who goes into battle for me and my family. You are in our midst when we gather in Your Name. You are the Altar of Peace for my fears, You always comfort me. *Yeshua*, You are the God of compassion and lovingkindness. You are the God who extends Your hands to me to rescue me from the pit. You are my eternal God and Savior. You are my Shield of Protection from the enemy. Lord, I trust You, I know You care for me. You are eager to give me wisdom with generosity and without reproach. You give me wisdom generously and without reproach.

In the midst of life's storms, You are the One true God, my Mighty Refuge. Lord, You remove the obstacles in my way with Your mighty strength. In the midst of my hardships, You offer me joy and tranquility. Your steadfast promises are my armor and shield. You make me lie down in green pastures, Lord. You take me along calm waters. You are the Source of all my triumphs.

Because You are the God of happiness, I find happiness and pleasure in You. You are my Best Buddy, Lord. You are the Almighty God, and it is You who inspires me to walk perfectly before You.

Thank You, Lord, for erasing my iniquity and transgressions for Your Name's sake and not remembering my sins. Abba Papa, You are a forgiving God. Father, You are the forgiver of all iniquity of past, present, and future generations because of Your blood shed on Calvary.

Lord, You are my vindicator. O Lord, You are my strong Fortress, Tower, and Hiding Place that protects me from the enemy. You are my Secure Foundation. With You, I feel secure and protected.

Lord, I know You are the Rewarder of those who diligently seek You. I commit myself before You to seek You every day of my life. Lord, empower me with the strength to be consistent and determined to seek You day and night.

Lord, You are my Shadow from the heat, my ever-present Help in trouble. Thank You, Lord, for You are the Wall of Fire around me and you protect me. Lord, You answer with fire because You are the God of fire. Lord, I know You are always attentive to my prayers and always respond to them. Lord, You wipe every tear from my eyes and give me laughter. You are always by my side. You lead me beside peaceful streams.

Lord, You are my peaceful Place of Security. You prepare a feast for me in the presence of my enemies. You anoint my head with oil until my cup overflows with blessings. Father God, You call things that are not as if they were. Father, You know all my needs; I can trust You will always take care of me and my family.

Lord, You are the Master over the threshing floor. You have control over my threshing floor, for Your plans are good and pleasing over my life. You test me and refine me as silver is refined.

You cause everything to work together for my good because I love You and you have called me for Your Purposes. You are the One who changes my name to align me with Your divine plans. You are the One who transforms me into a new person, changing my paradigms and aligning me with Your perfect will. Lord, Thank You because I know Your will for my life is good, pleasing, and perfect, even if I don't understand it right now.

Father, Your mighty voice silences the whole earth. There is no other God but You. Father, You always make a way where there is no way. You are the God who arms me with strength and power to overcome and triumph. O, Lord

God, You are the Source of my strength. You are the air and breath in my lungs, my Hope.

Father, You exult over me with loud singing when I suffer for Your cause and obey You.

You are the Strength of the poor and needy in distress. You are a God who is always near to me and my family. You are *El Roi*—the God who sees me.

Lord, You are my Helper, my Protector, my Covering, my shelter, and my Highest Place of Serenity. Lord, You are the Giver of wisdom, knowledge, and intelligence. You always comfort me when I am cast down. You are the Solution and the answer to all my challenges. Lord, no matter what I feel, I recognize that You are greater and superior than my emotions or feelings because you know everything. You are my Light at the end of the tunnel in every hardship. You are the Defender of the defenseless.

Lord, I know You always intercede for me. You know what's in my heart even better than I can know. Lord, You know that humans are weak as dust but I know that Your love remains forever with those who fear You. Your salvation extends to my children and my children's children because of my faithfulness and obedience to you.

You comfort me with Your unfailing love. You restore my soul and strengthen me to do all things through Christ. O Lord, Your peace surpasses all human comprehension. You guard my heart and mind with Your peace in Christ Jesus.

My help comes from You in every difficult and challenging situation. You never criticize me and you always overlook my weaknesses. Because when I am weak, then Your power is perfected in me and you make me strong. You are a loving God of second and multiple chances. Jesus, You are my Hope. I know you have good plans for me. I know you plan to give me a future and a living hope.

Father, You always comfort me on the day of tribulation. You sustain me when I trust You with all my heart. Lord, You command me not to fear or get discouraged, for You are always with me. You strengthen, help, and uphold me with Your victorious hand.

You, my Lord God, renew my youth like the eagle. Lord, when I commit everything to You and trust You radically, You always help me. You are the loving God who keeps track of all my sorrows. You collect all my tears in Your bottle and register them in Your book. Lord, I know Your Presence is with me, taking care of me because of your profound love for me.

You are the Lord who performs righteous deeds and judgments for oppressed. You see my troubles and take notice of me. You see my afflictions and heed my cry, for You are aware of my sufferings, oh my Lord Jesus. You always hear my groaning and remember Your covenant promises over my life. Lord, I know You hear all the prayers of the righteous.

You are the God who promises to protect and prosper my life. You help me in every situation because I trust in You.

Lord, You are the One who builds me up and edify me. Holy Spirit, I know You are my Intercessor, Counselor, and Comforter. You are my very present Help in trouble and I will not fear no matter what my eyes may see because You Jehovah, Lord of Hosts are with me. You are my Sustainer eternally.

You are the One who resurrects and brings back to life my seemingly dead dreams. I love that You always plan ahead to rescue Your children from trouble. Lord, this gives me joy, and Your joy is my strength.

I know You are the One who will wipe every tear from my eyes. You are the Trustworthy and True One; I can blindly trust in You eternally. I sing to You, my Lord; I praise Your holy Name because Your anger lasts only a moment, but Your favor lasts a lifetime. Lord, Your favor has made me secure and firm as a mountain.

You turn my mourning into joyful dancing. You clothed me with joy instead of mourning. I will not stay silent Oh Lord. I will sing praises to your Name and I will thank your for the rest of my life. I will walk in Your Presence, in Your life-giving light on this day and eternally.

In Jesus' Name, amen and amen.

19

HIS APPROACHABLE GOODNESS

FEATURED SCRIPTURES TO PONDER

Surely your goodness and unfailing love will pursue me all the days of my life, and I will live in the house of the LORD forever.

Psalm 23:6 NLT

For the LORD is good. His unfailing love continues forever, and his faithfulness continues to each generation.

Psalm 100:5

You are:

1. God, You are good (Psalm 100:5; 86:5)
2. You are the very definition of goodness (Exodus 34:6; Psalm 145:9; 1 Chronicles 16:34)
3. The Good Father (Luke 11:11–13)
4. The Generous and Gracious Father (Psalm 126:2–3)
5. The God who is good and upright (Psalm 25:8; Jeremiah 33:11)

6. The One who grants me Your precious and great promises (2 Peter 1:3–4)
7. The One who grants me all things that pertain to life and godliness (2 Peter 1:3–4)
8. The God who gives me good and perfect gifts (James 1:17)
9. The God of all grace (1 Peter 5:10; Ephesians 2:8–9)
10. The God of Grace who will restore, confirm, strengthen, and establish me (1 Peter 5:10)
11. The God of favor (Psalm 5:12)
12. The God who gives favor to those whom You choose (Exodus 33:18)
13. The God who favors Zion with Your goodness (Psalm 51:18)
14. God, the good Master and Lord of my life (Matthew 23:8–10)
15. The God who crowns the year with goodness (Psalm 65:11)
16. The goodness and mercy that will follow me all the days of my life (Nehemiah 9:25; Psalm 23:6)
17. The God who gives greater grace (James 4:6)
18. The God who gives me all things abundantly for my enjoyment (1 Timothy 6:17)
19. The God who is coming soon to reward me according to my work (Revelation 22:12)
20. The God who chose me and called by Your marvelous grace (Galatians 1:15)
21. The God of amazing grace and divine peace (Nehemiah 9:31; Judges 6:24)
22. The God who is pleased with sacrifices offered in the right spirit (Psalm 51:19)
23. The God who gives me the desires of my heart when I delight in You (Psalm 37:4)
24. *Yahweh*, a God compassionate and gracious (Exodus 34:6; Matthew 9:36)
25. The very definition of perfect peace (John 14:27)
26. The One who will crown me with never-ending glory and honor (1 Peter 5:4)
27. The God who lifts me in honor by Your gracious hand, as I humble myself to You (1 Peter 5:6)

28. The God who gives grace to the humble (James 4:6)
29. The God who will lift me in honor at the proper time (1 Peter 5:6)
30. The God who has granted me everything pertaining to life and godliness (2 Peter 1:3)
31. The God who called me by Your marvelous glory and excellence (2 Peter 1:3)
32. The God who gives me more and more grace and peace (1 Peter 1:2)
33. The Lord who blesses me with peace (Psalm 29:11)
34. The Lord who gives me strength (Psalm 29:11)
35. The Lord whose smile brings forth life into my soul (Proverbs 16:15)
36. The Lord whose favor refreshes like a spring rain (Proverbs 16:15)
37. The Lord who delights in me (Psalm 18:19)
38. The Lord who rejoices over me with gladness (Zephaniah 3:17)
39. The Spirit who produces all kinds of good fruit in my life (Gal 5:22–23; Colossians 1:9–10)
40. The Spirit of joy and happiness (Galatians 5:22–23)
41. The Spirit of patience (Galatians 5:22–23)
42. The Spirit of kindness (Galatians 5:22–23)
43. The Spirit of infinite goodness (Galatians 5:22–23)
44. The Spirit of gentleness (Galatians 5:22–23)
45. The God who saved me by Your grace (Romans 11:6; Ephesians 2:8)
46. The God who has blessed me with all spiritual blessings (Ephesians 1:3)
47. The God who filled me with laughter and joy (Psalm 126:2–3)
48. The God who has done amazing things for me, what a joy (Psalm 126:2–3)
49. The God who gives me rest because You love me (Psalm 127:2)
50. The Spirit who sanctifies me by Your grace (2 Thessalonians 2:13)
51. The God of sufficient and sustaining grace (2 Corinthians 12:9–10)
52. The Lord, my Sabbath (Matthew 12:8)
53. The God who made the seventh day holy (Genesis 2:3)
54. Jesus, my place of broad rivers and streams (Isaiah 33:21)

55. The Lord, my only inheritance (Psalm 16:5)
56. The Lord, my Cup of Blessing (Psalm 16:5)
57. The Lord, my Springs of joy (Psalm 87:7)
58. The God whose favor lasts a lifetime (Psalm 30:5)
59. The joy of the morning (Psalm 30:5)
60. The One whose face shines upon me (Psalm 80:19)
61. The God of grace and peace (Nehemiah 9:31; Judges 6:24; Philippians 1:2)
62. The God who turns all evil against me toward the good for me and others (Genesis 50:20; Romans 8:28)
63. The God who gives me dignity (Job 40:10)
64. Lord, the Grace that gives me strength (Hebrews 13:9)
65. The Lord my help (Psalm 124:8)
66. The great grace that empowers me (Acts 4:33–34)
67. Lord, Your grace is all I need (2 Corinthians 12:8–9)
68. The God with the incredible wealth of grace and kindness toward me (Ephesians 2:7)
69. The gracious God who has given me gifts according to the grace given to me (Romans 12:6)
70. The God who gives me the ability to prophesy (Romans 12:6)
71. The God who gives me the faith to speak out as I should (Romans 12:6)
72. The God of Peace (Romans 15:33)
73. The great Peacemaker (Colossians 1:20; Matthew 5:9)
74. The God who reveals to me an abundance of peace and truth (Jeremiah 33:6)
75. The Lord of favor who makes me as secure as a mountain (Psalm 30:7)
76. The One who made partaker of Your divine nature (2 Peter 1:3–4)
77. The God who opposes the proud (James 4:6)
78. The One who gives grace generously to the humble (James 4:6)
79. The Lord with a favor that lasts a lifetime (Psalm 30:5)
80. The God who restores my fortunes and gives me double for my trouble (Job 42:10–11; Jeremiah 33:11)
81. The Lord who is patient toward all, wishing that all should reach repentance (2 Peter 3:9)

82. The Lord whose face smiles with favor on me (Psalm 67:1)
83. The good Lord, filled with kindness (Psalm 145:17b)
84. The Lord who is close to all who call on You in truth (Psalm 145:18)
85. The Lord who hears my cry for help and rescues me (Psalm 145:19b)

A PRAYER DECLARING HIS APPROACHABLE GOODNESS

Father, in Jesus' Name, I approach your throne of grace, knowing that You listen to all my prayers. Thank You for Your love, favor, grace, and goodness. You are a God of incredible wealth in grace and kindness toward me.

I know You are the God of all grace; You give Your favor and compassion to those You choose. You are the One who favors Zion, Your people, with Your goodness. Lord, You are always good and upright for eternity. You are the good Master and Lord of my life. You are the very definition of goodness.

Father, You crown my year with your goods because you are a great God of love and goodness. Truly, your kindness and your inexhaustible love will follow me all the days of my life and I will live with you forever. You give me grace and abundantly provide for me all things for my enjoyment on this earth. Lord, You are the God who gives me the desires of my heart as I delight in You. You are the God of Peace, the great Peacemaker. Thank You, Lord, for blessing me with Your supernatural unequaled peace.

You are the God who is pleased with sacrifices offered in the right spirit. You are the God who is coming soon to reward me according to my works.

You are the God who chose me and called me by Your marvelous glory and excellent grace before I was born. You are the God who pours amazing grace and divine peace on my life. Lord, You are the One who edifies me. You are *Yahweh*, a compassionate and gracious God. You are the very definition of perfect peace. When I am worried, You are my perfect Place of Peace. You are the God of favor, The One who will crown me with unending glory and honor because I love and obey you. Lord, when I humble myself before You, You lift me in honor at the proper time by Your gracious hand. This is because You give grace to the humble and contrite of heart.

I know that by Your divine power, You have given me everything I need so I can live a godly life. Thank You as I have come to know You, I've been granted all of these blessings. Thank You for calling me to Yourself through Your marvelous glory and excellence. Thank You for Your great and precious promises over my life because they enable me to share Your Divine Nature. Thank You for enabling me to escape the world's corruption.

You are a gracious God who has given me gifts according to Your grace and love. You are the God who gives good and perfect gifts to enjoy. You want me to enjoy life with You O, Lord.

You give me the ability to prophesy and faith to speak out fearless with boldness and power. You are the God who gives me more and more grace and peace as I remain in You. The Lord who gives me strength. The good Lord and the good Father. Lord, Your smile brings forth life into my soul.

Lord, Your favor refreshes like spring rain. You are the Lord who delights in me. You are the Lord who rejoices over me with gladness. You are the Spirit who produces all kinds of good fruit in my life. You are the Spirit of joy and happiness. You are the Spirit of patience. You are the Spirit of kindness. You are the Spirit of goodness. You are the Spirit of gentleness.

You are The Lord who saved me by Your grace. The God who has blessed me with all spiritual blessings. Thank You, Lord, because You bless me with peace and fill me with laughter and joy. You, O Lord, have done amazing things for me; You are my joy. You are the God who gives me rest because You love me. You are the Spirit who sanctifies me by Your grace. The God of sufficient and sustaining grace, my Sabbath. You are the God who made the seventh day holy.

Jesus, my Place of broad rivers and streams. You are the Lord, my only eternal inheritance. You, Lord, are my Cup of Blessing, my Source of joy. Lord, You take pleasure in the prayers of the upright. Your kindness lasts a lifetime. You are my Morning Joy every day.

Lord, Your face shines upon me. You turn everything evil against me into good for me and others. Lord, You give me grace, peace, and dignity on this day. You are the One who empowers me by Your amazing grace. Your grace is my strength.

Thank You, Jesus, for Your grace is all I need in this life; I worship You for Your great favor, amazing grace, and awesome goodness today and forever. I am Yours, and You are mine!

In Your sweet Name Jesus, Amen!

20

HIS POWERFUL DELIVERANCE

FEATURED SCRIPTURES TO PONDER

The LORD sets the prisoners free; the LORD opens the eyes of the blind. The LORD lifts up those who are bowed down; the LORD loves the righteous. The LORD watches over the sojourners; he upholds the widow and the fatherless, but the way of the wicked he brings to ruin.

Psalm 146:7–9 ESV

The LORD is my strength and my song; he has given me victory. Songs of joy and victory are sung in the camp of the godly. The strong right arm of the LORD has done glorious things! The strong right arm of the LORD is raised in triumph. The strong right arm of the LORD has done glorious things!

Psalm 118:14–16

You are:

1. The God who sets me free (Romans 8:2, 6, 13)
2. The God who delivers me form the enemy (Psalm 34:4; 40:13)

3. The God who has rescued me from the depths of death (Psalm 86:13)
4. God, the Holder of the keys and Great Conqueror of death, hell, and the grave (Revelation 1:18)
5. Jesus, the One who gave me the keys to the kingdom of heaven (Matthew 16:19)
6. Jesus, the One who has authorized me to forbid or to permit on earth (Matthew 16:19)
7. The God who is with me in the valley of the shadow of death (Psalm 23)
8. The God who rescues me from death (Psalm 68:19)
9. Jesus Christ, who gives us victory over sin and death by Your power (1 Corinthians 15:56)
10. God, the One who resurrects the dead (John 11:25; Matthew 27:52; Daniel 12:2)
11. Jesus Christ, the One who died and rose again (2 Corinthians 5:15)
12. Jesus, the One who died for my sins (Romans 5:8)
13. Jesus, the Resurrection, and the Life (John 11:25)
14. Jesus, the Good News of great joy (Luke 2:10)
15. The Lord whose Presence delivers me and gives me freedom (Romans 8:2)
16. The God who performs all things for me (Psalm 57:2)
17. The God of *Dunamis* power (Matthew 22:29; Acts 1:8)
18. God, my Superpower (Acts 1:8; 2 Chronicles 20:6; Psalm 71:18)
19. The Lord who is supreme over all gods and all powers (Deuteronomy 10:17)
20. The burning Flame of Fire that shines with glorious splendor and radiance (Ezekiel 1:27)
21. Father, the Supreme One (Deuteronomy 10:17–22)
22. The God of revival (2 Chronicles 7:14; Psalm 119:50; Psalm 119:25)
23. God, the Christ in me (Galatians 2:20, 27; John 14:20; Romans 8:10)
24. The God who makes the winds Your messengers and the flames Your ministers (Psalm 104:4; Hebrews 1:7)

25. God, the Almighty One (Revelation 11:17)
26. Jesus, the One who bruised the enemy's head (Genesis 3:15)
27. Jesus Christ, Your blood is precious and powerful (1 Peter 1:19)
28. Christ, the God of triumph and victory (2 Corinthians 2:14)
29. God, the Spirit of freedom who frees me (2 Corinthians 3:17; Romans 8:2)
30. The God of the brave and courageous (2 Samuel 10:12)
31. God, my Great Warrior (Jeremiah 20:11)
32. God, the Banner of War (Isaiah 59:19; Psalm 20:5; 60:4)
33. The God whose Word is as powerful as a two-edged sword (Hebrews 4:12)
34. God, the Victor—You always win, You never lose a battle (2 Chronicles 20:15; John 16:33)
35. The God who fights the battles, for the battle is Yours (2 Chronicles 20:15)
36. God, my Security and Assurance in everything (Hebrews 11:1; Romans 5:5; Psalm 23:4)
37. The God who annihilated satan's plans (Hebrews 2:14)
38. The God who prepares a table for me in the presence of my enemies (Psalm 23:2–5)
39. The Lord who even demons believe and tremble with fear before You (James 2:19)
40. The God who cast out the wicked nations before me (Deuteronomy 9:4)
41. God, the Great Commander of the armies of heaven (Psalm 24:10)
42. The Lord who is a great and awesome God (Daniel 9:4)
43. The Lord *Jehovah* of the armies (Zechariah 1:3)
44. God, the Shield to all those who trust in You (2 Samuel 22:31)
45. God, the One who holds my head high (Psalm 3:3)
46. The God who fills me with great victories (Psalm 18:50)
47. The Defender of those who believe in You (Psalm 68:5)
48. The Lord who is glorious and strong (Psalm 96:7)
49. *El Nekamoth*—the avenger God (Psalm 18:47)
50. God, *Jehovah-Sabot*—*Jehovah* of armies (1 Samuel 1:3; Isaiah 6:1–3)
51. The God of powerful declarations (Psalm 2:7–12)

52. The God who makes the clouds Your chariots of war and rides on the wings of the wind (Psalm 104:3)
53. The God who takes revenge (Romans 12:19)
54. The God who keeps my feet from stumbling (Psalm 66:9)
55. The God who vindicates (Psalm 135:14)
56. The God who commands the winds and they obey You (Luke 8:25)
57. Christ, the Power of God (1 Corinthians 1:24)
58. The God who can do exceedingly, abundantly above all that we can ask or think (Ephesians 3:20–21)
59. The God who can keep me from falling (Jude 24)
60. The God with dazzling power who destroys the strong, crushing their defenses (Amos 5:9)
61. The God who made the daylight spread to the ends of the earth to bring an end to the night's wickedness (Job 38:12–13)
62. God, the One who gives me authority over all the nations (Revelation 2.26)
63. The One who gives me the authority to overcome all the power of the enemy (Luke 10:19)
64. Jesus Christ, the One who gave me power over the enemy (Matthew 16:16–19)
65. Jesus Christ, the One who made me a conqueror over all the powers of hell (Matthew 16:16–19; Romans 8:37)
66. Jesus, whose Name is Power and Hope (Acts 3:6)
67. The God who is never late (2 Peter 3:9; 1 Peter 5:7; Habakkuk 2:3)
68. The God of the impossible, nothing is too difficult for You (Luke 18:27)
69. Jesus, in Your Name, there is freedom (Isaiah 61; Mark 16:17–18)
70. Lord, the Spirit of my freedom (2 Corinthians 3:17)
71. The God of deliverance (Psalm 37:39–40)
72. The God who fights my battles (Chronicles 20:17; Exodus 14:14)
73. The God of great power (2 Corinthians 4:7)
74. The God who delivers and rescues me from the power of my enemies (Exodus 3:8–10; Psalm 30:1)
75. The God who delivered Israel from slavery (Exodus 6:6–9)

76. The God who delivers me from my oppressors (Exodus 6:6–9)
77. The One who revives me (Psalm 80:18; 119:25)
78. The one who makes me a strong and heroic warrior (Philippians 4:13; Genesis 10:8–9)
79. The God who rescued me from the place of my slavery (Exodus 20:2)
80. The God who refuses to let my enemies triumph over me (Psalm 30:1)
81. The God who is for me, and no one can ever be against me (Romans 8:31)
82. The One who rescued me from the kingdom of darkness (Colossians 1:13)
83. The One who transferred me into the kingdom of Jesus Christ (Colossians 1:13)
84. The Lord my Rock and my Fortress, my Deliverer (2 Samuel 22:2)
85. The Victorious Lord, victory belongs to You (Proverbs 21:31; Colossians 2:14–15)
86. The Lord who answers my prayer and delivers me from all my fears (Psalm 34:4)
87. The Lord who hears my cry and delivers me out of all my troubles (Psalm 34:17)
88. God, the One who surrounds me with songs of victory and deliverance (Psalm 32:7)
89. The God who sets the prisoners free and gives them joy (Psalm 68:6)
90. The Designer of the ark who saved Noah and his family from the flood (Genesis 6:14–18)
91. The God of the armies of Israel (1 Samuel 17:45)
92. The All-Powerful God (Revelation 19:15)
93. The Lord who crowns the humble with victory (Psalm 149:4)
94. The Lion who roars in victory (Amos 3:8; Isaiah 31:4; Ezekiel 1:10)
95. The One who sets my heart free (John 8:36; Galatians 4:4–7)
96. My Strength and my Song (Exodus 15:2; Isaiah 12:2)
97. The Lord, the Great Warrior; *Yahweh* is Your Name (Exodus 15:3)

98. The One who gave me power and authority to cast out demons (Luke 9:1)

99. The Healer of all demon-possessed, epileptic, or paralyzed (Matthew 4:23–25)

100. The God who casts out evil spirits with a simple command (Matthew 8:16)

101. The God who delivers the demon-possessed and oppressed (Matthew 8:16)

102. The God of powerful decrees (Exodus 18:20; 2 Chronicles 34:31)

103. The Lord who fights for me while I just stay calm (Exodus 14:14)

104. The One who gave me power and authority to heal all diseases (Luke 9:1)

105. The God who helps me do mighty things (Psalm 60:12)

106. God, my strong Tower of Power (Psalm 61:2–4)

107. The One with unquestioned and immeasurable power (Ephesians 1:19; Hebrews 1:3; Romans 1:20)

108. The One who crushed the heads of Leviathan and gave him as food for the creatures of the wilderness (Psalm 74:14)

109. The LORD who will punish Leviathan, the fleeing, twisting serpent, and will slay the dragon that is in the sea (Isaiah 27:1)

110. The God who broke the heads of the sea monsters on the waters (Psalm 74:13)

111. The One who calms the raging seas and roaring waves (Psalm 65:7)

112. God who divided the sea by might (Nehemiah 9:11; Psalm 78:13; 136:13; Isaiah 63:12)

113. The One in whose strength I can crush an army and scale any wall (Psalm 18:29)

114. The God who crushes satan under my feet (Romans 16:20)

115. The only Name that holds every victory guaranteed (2 Chronicles 20:15; John 16:33; 1 John 4:4)

116. The God who power and dominion belong to (Psalm 62:11–12)

117. The God with divine power (2 Peter 1:3)

118. The God who shall arise, and Your enemies shall be scattered (Psalm 68:1)

119. The Lord with a great Name, a strong hand, and a powerful arm (1 Kings 8:41–42)
120. The One who gives victory to kings (Psalm 144:10)
121. The Lord, a jealous and avenging God (Nahum 1:2)
122. The Lord who is slow to anger and great in power (Nahum 1:3)
123. The Lord who displays Your power in the whirlwind and storm (Nahum 1:3)
124. The Lord the clouds are the dust of Your feet (Nahum 1:3)
125. The God who rebukes the sea and makes it dry (Nahum 1:4)
126. God, in Your Presence the mountains quake, and the hills melt away (Nahum 1:5)
127. God, in Your Presence the earth trembles and its people are destroyed (Nahum 1:5)
128. The Lord God, no one can stand before Your indignation (Nahum 1:6)
129. The Lord God, no one can endure the heat of Your anger (Nahum 1:6)
130. The Lord whose wrath is poured out like fire (Nahum 1:6)
131. The good Lord, a stronghold in the day of trouble (Nahum 1:7)
132. The One who knows those who take refuge in You (Nahum 1:7)
133. The God who with an overflowing flood will make a complete end of Your adversaries (Nahum 1:8)
134. The God who will pursue Your enemies into darkness (Nahum 1:8)
135. The slavery abolisher (Luke 4:18; Acts 16:16–18; Philemon 1:80–21)
136. The God who will not allow any weapon formed against me to prosper (Isaiah 54:17; Romans 8:31)
137. The One who empowers me to silence every accusing voice (Isaiah 54:17)
138. God, my Armor, and Ammunition against the enemy (Ephesians 6:11)

A PRAYER DECLARING HIS POWERFUL DELIVERANCE

Father God, I come before You in the Name of Jesus Christ, my powerful Deliverer, and through the Holy Spirit of freedom. I want to thank You on this day for the powerful deliverance and freedom You have given me. Thank You for setting my heart free. You are my powerful Deliverer who sets me free and delivers me from the enemy. You have seated me in the heavenly places with Jesus Christ, and from this position, I stand and declare Your powerful words. Father, You are the God of powerful decrees and declarations. I unite my declarations with Your declarations and synchronize my decrees with Your decrees on this day. I invite your powerful spirit of deliverance over my life and I call on the holy angels of the Lord to surround this place as I make the following declarations and decrees about the Almighty I AM.

Jesus, You are the holder of the keys and the great Conqueror of death, hell, and the grave. You rescued me from the depths of death. You are with me when I go through the valley of the shadow of death. Jesus Christ, You give me victory over sin and death by Your power. You are the Power of resurrection and life.

Lord Jesus Christ, You died and rose again by the power of the Holy Spirit who also lives in me. Thank You, for I know You died for my sins so that the law of sin and death would no longer conquer me. You are the Good News of great joy, and I rejoice in You. Lord, Your powerful Presence is my deliverance and my freedom. You are the God who performs all things for my benefit. The God of *Dunamis* power. God, You are my Superpower and my Superhero. You are the Lord who is supreme over all gods and all powers. You are the burning Flame of Fire that shines with glorious splendor and radiance. You make the winds Your messengers and the flames of fire Your ministers.

Father, You are the Supreme One forever. You are the God of revival; having Your Holy Presence is having revival. God, You are the Christ in me; I am clothed in You. Lord, You are the Almighty One. Jesus, You bruised the enemy's head and You crushed satan under my feet. Your blood is so precious and powerful. Christ, You are the God of triumph and the Lion that roars in victory. You are the Spirit of freedom who frees me. You are the God of the brave and courageous. My Great Warrior and War Banner.

Father, You are the God who is always on my side, and no one can ever be against me. You rescued me from the kingdom of darkness and transferred me into the kingdom of Your beloved Son, Jesus Christ. You are my Rock and my Fortress, my Deliverer. You are the Victorious Lord; victory belongs to You. You always answer my cry and deliver me from all my fears and all my troubles.

Oh, good Lord, You are a stronghold in the day of trouble and You are never late. You know those who take refuge in You.

Lord, You are the only Name that holds every victory guaranteed. You dominate, O God, because power belongs to You. Lord, You are my Security and Assurance in everything. You annihilated satan's plans over me and my family. You are the One who crushed satan under my feet. You are the God of great power who fights all my battles. You are the All-Powerful God who delivers me from the power of my enemies and my oppressors. You revive my soul and transform me into a fierce warrior. You are the God who is always on my side protecting me. You have declared that no weapon turned against me will ever succeed. You have empowered me to silence every voice raised up to accuse me. You have declared that these benefits are enjoyed by Your servants Oh, Lord; for Your vindication will come from You Oh Father.

You prepare a table for me in the presence of my enemies. You always rescue me from evil-doers. You will never let my enemies triumph over me because I am the apple of Your eye. My soul is solely Yours, I belong to You oh, Lord.

You are God, the Victor—You always win, You never lose a battle. You are the Victor in me; with You and through You, I can always win all my battles, for the battle is all Yours. You fight for me while I just stay calm.

Lord, even the demons believe and tremble with fear before Your mighty Presence.

You have given me power and authority to cast out demons and heal all diseases in your Name for Your Name is Greater and All-Powerful.

You are the deliverer of all demon-possessed and oppressed and You cast out evil spirits with a simple command.

You cast out the nations before me. God, You are the Great Commander of the armies of heaven. Lord, You are a great and awesome God. The Lord, *Jehovah-Sabot—Jehovah* of the armies. No army general can ever compete with You for You have no equal.

Father, You are the Shield to all those who trust in You. God, You hold my head up high. You keep my feet from stumbling. You are the God who surrounds me with great victories. You are the Defender of those who believe in You. You are the glorious and strong Lord. You are *El Nekamoth*—the God who avenges, the God who takes revenge and vindicates me.

You are the Lord, a jealous and avenging holy God, slow to anger and great in power. You never let the guilty go unpunished. You display Your power in the whirlwind and the storm. The billowing clouds are the dust beneath Your feet. At Your command, O Lord, the oceans dry up and the rivers disappear. In Your Presence the mountains quake and the hills melt away. God, in Your Presence the earth trembles, and its people are destroyed. No one can stand before Your indignation, and no one can endure the heat of Your anger. Your wrath is poured out like fire, and the rocks are broken into pieces. You will come with an overflowing flood that will make a complete end of Your adversaries. You will pursue Your enemies into darkness. You are the God with blinding speed and power that destroys the strong, crushing all their defenses. No one can be delivered from Your hand. You are the God who spreads the daylight to the ends of the earth to end the night's wickedness.

You make the clouds Your chariots of war and You ride on the wings of the wind. Your works are mighty over the seas of the earth. You crushed the heads of Leviathan; and gave him as food for the creatures of the wilderness. O Lord, You are the punisher of the Leviathan, the fleeing twisting serpent, and You are the One who slayed the dragon in the sea. You are the God who broke the heads of the sea monsters on the waters. You are the God who divided the sea by Your might. You command the winds, and they obey You. Lord, You are the only One who has the power to calm the raging seas and roaring waves. You are the One with unquestionable and uncontainable power. O Lord, I can crush an army in Your strength, and confidently scale any wall with You by my side.

You are Christ, the Power of God. You are the God who is able to do exceedingly, abundantly above all that we can ask or think. You are the God who can keep me from falling.

God, You give me authority over all the nations. You give me the authority to overcome all the power of the enemy. God, You are my strong Tower of Power. You are the God who helps me do mighty things. You are the God of the impossible, and nothing is too difficult for You. Jesus, in Your Name, there is freedom. You set the prisoners free and give them joy. Jesus Christ, You are the One who gave me power over the enemy. You made me a conqueror over all the powers of hell. You gave me the keys to the kingdom of heaven. You gave me the power and authority to forbid or to permit on earth, and it will be authorized in heaven, for You have promised that the Father will do it for us. Jesus, Your Name is my power and eternal hope. You are the God of the armies of Israel. You are the One who liberated Israel from slavery. You rescued me and delivered me from the place of slavery for you are the eternal slavery abolisher.

Father, You surround me with songs of victory and deliverance. You crown the humble with victory. You are the Spirit of my freedom, the God of deliverance. How exciting!

Your Word is as sharp as a two-edged sword, piercing between my soul and spirit and judging my thoughts and heart attitudes. Your Word is alive and active in me, bringing me salvation and regeneration. Thank You because I am strong in You, Lord, and in Your mighty power. You are my Armor and Ammunition against the enemy of my soul. I put on Your whole armor so I can stand firm against all the strategies of the devil. I know my fight is not against flesh-and-blood enemies, but against the evil rulers and authorities of the unseen world, against mighty powers in the dark world, and against evil spirits in the heavenly places. Because of this, I put on every piece of God's armor so I can resist the enemy in the time of evil.

In this way, after the battle, I will be standing firm. In Jesus' Name, I will stand my ground by putting on the belt of Truth and the body armor of God's righteousness. I will put on the peace that comes from the Good News as my shoes so I may be fully prepared. I will also hold up the Shield (my protective cover) of faith to stop the fiery arrows of the devil. I will put on salvation as my helmet (my protective head covering) and take the Sword of the Spirit (the Word of God). I will also pray in the Spirit at all times and on every occasion. And finally, I will stay alert and be persistent in my prayers for me, my family, and all believers as directed by Your Spirit.

Thank You, Lord, for Your powerful deliverance over my life and my family today and into eternity. I love You eternally, my Lord, and I worship Your mighty powerful Name forever and ever. I declare all this in Jesus' Almighty Name, amen and amen!

21

HIS ETERNAL KINGDOM

FEATURED SCRIPTURES TO PONDER

He was given authority, honor, and sovereignty over all the nations of the world so that people of every race, nation, and language would obey him. His rule is eternal—it will never end. His kingdom will never be destroyed.

Daniel 7:14

All honor and glory to God forever and ever! He is the eternal King, the unseen one who never dies; he alone is God. Amen.

1 Timothy 1:17

You are:

1. God, the Blessed and Only Sovereign of the kings (1 Timothy 6:11–19)
2. God, the King of kings and Lord of lords (Revelation 19:16; 1 Timothy 6:15)
3. The God who owns the kingdom (1 Chronicles 29:11–13)

4. The *El Olam*—the everlasting God (Isaiah 40:28; Psalm 90:2)[1]
5. The Lord who will reign forever (Psalm 146:12)
6. The great King of all kingdoms (2 Kings 19:15; Psalm 68:32)
7. The God who owns all the kingdoms (1 Chronicles 29:11)
8. The God enthroned between the mighty cherubim; God over all kingdoms (2 Kings 19:15)
9. The God of the kingdom of priests (Revelation 1:6)
10. The God whose kingdom is eternal, unmovable, and indestructible (Daniel 4:4; 34–37)
11. Jesus, the One who made us a kingdom of priests for God, our Father (Revelation 1:6)
12. The King of Glory who shall enter the ancient gates and doors (Psalm 24:7)
13. The Invincible in battle (Psalm 24:8)
14. The Lord, strong and mighty (Psalm 24:8)
15. The Lord of the heaven's armies (Psalm 24:10)
16. God, the King of heaven (Daniel 4:34–37)
17. The God who is feared by the kings of the earth (Psalm 76:12)
18. The God who removes kings and sets up other kings (Daniel 2:21)
19. The Supreme King seated on a great white throne (Revelation 20:11–15)
20. The Lord and King of the twenty-four elders and four living creatures (Revelation 19:4)
21. The loving King who takes me into Your inner chambers (Song of Solomon 1:4)
22. My Invincible One and only great King (1 Timothy 1:17)
23. Lord, the Everlasting King (Jeremiah 10:10; Romans 16:23)
24. The Lord and King of the universe (Hebrews 11:3)
25. Jesus, the Ruler of all the kings of the world (Revelation 1:5)
26. The Lord who rules over the floodwaters (Psalm 29:10)
27. The God who rules over all things (1 Chronicles 29:12)
28. The God whose kingdom will last forever; You rule through all generations (Daniel 4:3)
29. The Lord of the kingdom, who rules over the nations (Psalm 22:28)
30. The God who rules with an iron scepter (Revelation 2:27)

31. The God who rules from heaven (Daniel 4:26)
32. The God whose rule is everlasting (Daniel 4:34–37)
33. Jesus, the Prince and Ruler of the kings of the earth (Revelation 1:5)
34. God, the Most High and honored One (Daniel 4:34–37)
35. God, the Lord over kings (Daniel 2:47)
36. The God who struck down mighty kings (Psalm 136:17)
37. The Most High, worthy of being feared, the great King over all the earth (Psalm 47:2)
38. The great King and Lord of hosts; Your Name is feared among the nations (Malachi 1:14)
39. The One dressed in splendor and majesty (Isaiah 63:1)
40. The One who marches in the greatness of Your strength ready to save me (Isaiah 63:1)
41. God, the King of glory (Psalm 24:8)
42. God, Yours is the kingdom, the power, and the glory (1 Chronicles 29:11; Psalm 62:11)
43. The Lord who owns the glory (1 Chronicles 29:11)
44. The Lord, worthy to receive glory, honor, and power (Revelation 4:11)
45. *Jehovah*, the God of the twelve tribes of Israel (Acts 7:8)
46. God, the great Governor of the world (Isaiah 33:22; Psalm 67:4)
47. God, the most essential One (Matthew 6:33; Colossians 3:10)
48. The God whose throne is in heaven (Psalm 11:4; Isaiah 66:1)
49. The God whose government and its peace will never end (Isaiah 9:7)
50. The Lord who is surrounded by honor and majesty (Psalm 96:6)
51. God, the Master Planner of all nations and kingdoms (Isaiah 14:26; Jeremiah 10:7)
52. Jesus, King of the Jews (Matthew 27:37; John 19:21)
53. Jesus, the King of Zion (Matthew 21:5)
54. Jesus Christ, the eternal King of the nations forever and ever (Psalm 10:6; 1 Timothy 1:17)
55. The King who never dies (1 Timothy 1:17)
56. God, the great King over of all ages (1 Timothy 1:17)
57. God, the King of all heaven and earth (Psalm 146:6; Daniel 4:37)

58. God, the King of the saints (Revelation 6)
59. Jesus, the Head of every man (1 Corinthians 11:3)
60. The God who is enthroned from ages past (Psalm 90:2; 93:2)
61. The God who is enthroned upon my praises (Psalm 22:3)
62. The Lord God, the One who lives forever eternally (Daniel 12:7; Hebrews 7:24)
63. The One who dwells in unapproachable light (1 Timothy 6:16)
64. The Lord who is robed in majesty and armed with strength (Psalm 93:1)
65. The God who is greater than I can understand; Your years cannot be counted (Job 36:26)
66. The King of Creation (Genesis 1; Psalm 8)
67. The Lord who reigns for eternity (Psalm 146:10; Psalm 96:10)
68. The God who breaks the pride of princes (Psalm 76:12)
69. The God whose throne endures forever and ever (Psalm 45:6)
70. Jesus, the Victorious, who sat with the Father on His throne (Revelation 3:21; Hebrews 8:1)
71. God, the One who sits on the throne (Revelation 5:13)
72. The Lord whose throne is circled with the glow of an emerald-like rainbow (Revelation 4:3)
73. The Lord God who lives from eternity to eternity (1 Chronicles 16:36)
74. The One who removes the royal robe of kings (Job 12:18)
75. The One who owns the royal power; it belongs to You (Psalm 22:28)
76. The One who overthrows those with long years in power (Job 12:19)
77. The One who silences the trusted adviser and removes the insight of the elders (Job 12:20)
78. The One who pours disgrace upon princes and disarms the strong (Job 12:21)
79. The One who builds up nations and destroys them (Job 12:23)
80. The God whose throne endures forever and ever (Psalm 45:6)
81. You are the Lord, the everlasting God, and Creator of all the earth (Isaiah 40:28)
82. The God with a kingdom of joy and peace (Romans 14:17)

83. The One who deserves honor and glory to Your Name eternally (1 Timothy 1:17)
84. Lord, the King of all time (1 Timothy 1:17)
85. The Father whose royal laws cannot be changed (Psalm 93:5)
86. The holy God who reigns over me forever and ever (Psalm 93:5)
87. The Lord who reigns as King forever and ever (Psalm 29:10; Exodus 15:18)
88. The Lord and King of peace (Hebrews 7:2)
89. The God who affirms Your upper rooms on the waters (Psalm 104:3)
90. The Lord King (Psalm 97:1)
91. The King who sits enthroned between the cherubim (Psalm 99:1)
92. The Lord whose decrees are very trustworthy (Psalm 93:5)
93. The Lord who reigns forever; Your throne endures to all generations (Lamentations 5:19)
94. The Lord with an everlasting kingdom (Psalm 145:13)
95. The Lord whose dominion endures throughout all generations (Psalm 145:13)
96. The Lord who is faithful in all Your words and kind in all Your works (Psalm 145:13)
97. The God with a glorious splendor and powerful kingdom (Psalm 145:10–13)
98. The One who inhabits eternity (Isaiah 57:15)
99. The One who gives victory to kings (Psalm 144:10)
100. The King with an unshakable, indestructible, invincible kingdom (Daniel 7:14; Hebrews 12:28)

A PRAYER DECLARING HIS ETERNAL KINGDOM

Father, I come before You with thanksgiving in my heart, in the Name of Jesus, and through Your Holy Spirit. Lord, You are the Blessed and Only Sovereign of the kings, King of Kings, and Lord of Lords. The kingdom is Yours, and You will reign forever. You are the Supreme Ruler of all kingdoms; You control all the kingdoms of the world. You own greatness and power eternally. You alone are God over all kingdoms. You are *El Olam*—the everlasting God. You are the Lord of the kingdom; You rule over the nations. Lord, Your decrees are very trustworthy. The Lord who reigns forever. Your throne and dominion endures throughout all generations. You are the Lord with an everlasting kingdom. Lord You are faithful in all Your words, and You are kind in all Your works. Your kingdom is glorious and powerful in splendor.

You are enthroned among the cherubim. You are the God of the priestly kingdom. Your kingdom is indestructible, unmovable, and eternal. You reign above all generations, and Your kingdom will last perpetually. Jesus, You made us a kingdom of priests for God our Father. You are the King of heaven who the kings of the earth fear. You are the One who removes kings and sets up other kings as chess pieces.

You are the Supreme King seated on a great white throne. You are the Lord and King of the twenty-four elders and four living creatures around the throne.

You are the loving King in the inner chamber of Songs of Solomon, my beloved. My Everlasting King. The Invincible One. The One and only great King of my heart. The King of kings, Lord of lords, and the Lord over kings. You are the Lord and King of the universe. Jesus, You are the Ruler of all the kings of the world; Your rule is everlasting. Lord, You are the Most High and honored of all. Father, You are the One who struck down mighty kings. You are the Lord, strong and mighty, invincible in battle for You are the Lord of heaven's armies.

Oh, great King, You are the Most High, worthy of being feared over all the earth. You are the great King and Lord of hosts—Your Name is feared among the nations. You are dressed in splendor and majesty. You march in the greatness of Your strength ready to save me. Lord, You rule from heaven. You are the King of glory; Yours is the kingdom, power, and glory. You are worthy to receive glory, honor, power, and adoration.

Jehovah, You are the God of the twelve tribes of Israel. Lord, You are the great Governor of the world. You are the most Essential. Your throne is in the heavens; Your government and its peace will last forever. You are surrounded with honor, dignity, and majesty, Lord. You are the Master Planner of all nations and kingdoms. Jesus, You are the King of the Jews, the King of Zion. You are the Ruler of the kings of the earth. Jesus Christ, You are the eternal King of all nations, forever and ever. You are the King who never dies.

You are God, the great King of all ages. The King of all heaven and earth. The King of the saints. The Head of every man. Lord God, You live from eternity to eternity. You are enthroned from ages past. You are enthroned upon my praises.

You are the King of Creation who reigns for eternity. You are the God who lives forever eternally and dwells in unapproachable light. You are the Lord who is robed in majesty and armed with strength.

Lord, You are greater than I can understand; Your years cannot be counted.

You are the God who breaks the pride of princes. Your throne endures forever and ever. You rule over all things with an iron scepter—Jesus, the victorious One who sat on the throne at the right hand of the Father. You are seated on the throne, dazzling as gemstones like jasper and carnelian. Lord, Your throne is surrounded by the radiance of an emerald-like rainbow. You are the Lord God who exists from all eternity.

Lord, You own the royal power; it belongs to You. You remove the royal robes of kings; they are taken away with ropes around their waists. You overthrow people who have been in power for a long time. You silence the trusted adviser and remove the insight of the elders. You pour disgrace upon princes and disarm the strong. You uncover mysteries hidden in the dark; You bring light to the deepest secret. You build up nations and destroy them, but Your throne endures forever and ever. Father, Your royal laws cannot be changed.

You are the Lord, the everlasting God and Creator of all the earth. You are who rules over the floodwaters. You are the God who affirms Your upper rooms on the waters. The One who deserves eternal honor and glory for Your Name.

Lord, You are the King of all time. You are the holy God who reigns over me forever and ever. God, You are the Lord and King of justice and peace who has an eternally unshakable kingdom. Your kingdom is a kingdom of joy and peace. Lord, You will always reign as King for all eternity. Amen and amen!

---

1. Stelman Smith and Judson Cornwall, *The Exhaustive Dictionary of Bible Names* (North Brunswick, NJ: Bridge-Logos, 1998), 82.

22

HIS SOVEREIGNTY

His rule is everlasting, and his kingdom is eternal. All the people of the earth are nothing compared to him. He does as he pleases among the angels of heaven and among the people of the earth. No one can stop him or say to him, "What do you mean by doing these things?

Daniel 4:34–35

For my thoughts are not your thoughts, neither are your ways my ways, declares the LORD. *For as the heavens are higher than the earth, so are my ways higher than your ways and my thoughts than your thoughts.*

Isaiah 55:8–9 ESV

You are:

1. The One with authority, honor, and sovereignty over all nations (Daniel 7:14)
2. God, and there is no other like You (Isaiah 46:9–10)

3. The Lord—apart from You, there is no other God (Isaiah 44:6)
4. The One who alone possesses immortality and will never die (1 Timothy 6:16)
5. The unseen One who never dies; You alone are God (1 Timothy 1:17)
6. The Lord my God (Exodus 6:7)
7. The Lord God; You are One (John 10:30)
8. God, the great Lord (Psalm 147:5)
9. God, the Ancient of Days (Daniel 7:9)
10. Lord, the Everlasting King (Jeremiah 10:10)
11. *El Olam*, the God of eternity; the everlasting God (Genesis 20:13)[1]
12. The Highest of the kings of the earth (Psalm 89:27)
13. The One who declares the end from the beginning (Isaiah 46:10)
14. The God who can see the beginning and the end simultaneously (Isaiah 46:10)
15. The only One that can tell me the future before it happens (Isaiah 46:10)
16. The most and highest Sovereign of the kings (1 Timothy 6:11–19)
17. The Blessed and Almighty God (1 Timothy 6:15)
18. The King of kings and Lord of lords (1 Timothy 6:15; Deuteronomy 10:17)
19. The One who dwells in unapproachable light (1 Timothy 6:16)
20. The One with all honor and power forever (1 Timothy 6:16)
21. The blessed and only Sovereign God (1 Timothy 6:15)
22. The Sovereign God of eternity (Psalm 135:6)
23. The God whose eyes contemplate everything (Psalm 11:4)
24. The God of details (Proverbs 16:33)
25. God of supremacy (Colossians 1:18)
26. The God that is not of this world (John 17:16)
27. The Lord God, Omnipresent, present in all places at the same time (Jeremiah 23:23–24; Psalm 139:7–13; Acts 17:27–28)
28. The Lord God, Omnipotent, with unlimited authority and power to do what You will (Revelation 4:8; 11:17; 2 Corinthians 4:7; Mark 10:27)

29. The Lord God, Omniscient, infinite in knowledge and understanding of things past, present, and future[2] (Psalm 44:21; Psalm 147:5)

30. The Lord God, Omnificent, with unlimited power to create all things (Colossians 1:15–17; Psalm 40:5; Genesis 1:1)

31. The Lord God, Omnibenevolent, supremely good (Mark 10:18; Psalm 106:1; Genesis 1:31)

32. The God who is supreme over everything everywhere (Ephesians 4:6; 1 Corinthians 15:28)

33. Christ, the only thing that matters because You fill everything in all (Colossians 3:11; Ephesians 1:23)

34. God, *Jehovah-Shammah*—the Lord who is here, present (Ezekiel 48:35)

35. Lord, the eternal All-Sufficient God (Exodus 3:14)

36. The God of time and eternity (Ecclesiastes 3:11)

37. The God that never change Your mind (Hebrews 6:17)

38. The God who never lies, it is impossible for You to lie (Hebrews 6:18)

39. God, the Immutable, Your Word remains forever (Malachi 3:6; 1 Peter 1:25)

40. The God who is, who was, and who is to come, the Almighty (Revelation 1:8)

41. The God whose Spirit moves on the surface of the sea (Genesis 1:2)

42. The God of the universe (Psalm 8:3–4)

43. God, the Lord of lords (1 Timothy 6:15; Psalm 136:3)

44. God, *El Roi*—the God who sees me (Genesis 16:11–14; Psalm 139:7–12)

45. *Yahweh (YHWH)*, the God of Israel for all generations (Exodus 3:15)

46. The God who laid the foundations of the earth, and they will never be removed (Psalm 104:5)

47. The I Am from Eternity (Isaiah 43:13)

48. The God of the day and night (Psalm 42:8)

49. The Lord with an infinite understanding (Psalm 147:5)

50. God, the Governor of the universe (Psalm 147:4)

51. Jesus Christ, the first who rose from the dead (Colossians 1:18)
52. The God who turns dawn to darkness (Amos 4:13)
53. The God who treads on the heights of the earth (Amos 4:13)
54. God, the One with endless names and attributes (Romans 1:20)
55. The God who is way more than we know of (John 21:25)
56. The God with sovereign power (Job 37:7)
57. The One who is always the same and lives forever (Hebrews 1:12)
58. The Lord whose sovereignty rules over all (Psalm 103:19)
59. The One who performs awe-inspiring deeds (Psalm 45:4)
60. The God of the bush's blazing fire that does not consume (Exodus 3:2)
61. The great Lord who is to be feared above all gods (Psalm 96:4)
62. The Sovereign Lord who is my strength (Habakkuk 3:19)
63. God, the All-Knowing One who knows it all (John 18:4; Matthew 10:29–30; Hebrews 4:13)
64. The God who is perfect in knowledge (Job 36:4)
65. The God who is greater than we can understand (Job 36:26)
66. The God whose years cannot be counted (Job 36:26)
67. The One with an understanding beyond human comprehension (Psalm 147:5)
68. The God who possesses supreme power in authority (Ephesians 1:10)
69. The Lord, no one can interrupt Your work or call Your rule into question (Daniel 4:35)
70. God, the All-Seeing (Genesis 16:13; Ezekiel 1:18–21)
71. The Lord who rules over the floodwaters (Psalm 29:10)
72. The Lord who reigns as King forever (Psalm 29:10)
73. The Lord, the mighty God who spoke and summoned all humanity (Psalm 50:1)
74. The God with supreme rulership (Psalm 66:7)
75. The God who is mighty in both power and understanding (Job 36:5)
76. The God who causes everything to work together for my good (Romans 8:28)
77. The Creator of thrones, kingdoms, rulers, and authorities in the unseen world (Colossians 1:16)

78. The God of great riches, wisdom, and knowledge (Romans 11:33)
79. The God with decisions and ways hard to understand (Romans 11:33)
80. The God with no advisers, for no one can know Your thoughts or give You advice (Romans 11:34)
81. The God who owes nothing to anyone (Romans 11:35)
82. The Source from where everything comes (Romans 11:36)
83. The One who chose me before the creation of the world (Ephesians 1:4–6)
84. 96.The God who chose me through Jesus Christ (Ephesians 1:4)
85. The One who predestined me for adoption to sonship through Christ (Ephesians 1:4–6)
86. The one who will devour and destroy death forever (Isaiah 25:8–9)
87. The Sovereign Lord who will wipe away all my tears (Isaiah 25:8–9)
88. The Lord who reign over the heavens and the earth (1 Chronicles 16:31)
89. The faithful God who won't allow my temptation to be more I can stand (1 Corinthians 10:13)
90. The God who will show me a way out of temptation so I can endure it (1 Corinthians 10:13)
91. The patient Lord who waits for everyone to repent so they won't be destroyed (2 Peter 3:9)
92. The God who counts the number of the stars and names them all (Psalm 147:4)
93. The God who has a count of all my hairs (Luke 12:7)
94. The God who does all that You please and want (Psalm 115:3)
95. The God whose counsel shall stand and accomplish Your purpose (Isaiah 46:10)
96. The God who changes times and seasons (Daniel 2:21)
97. The God who removes kings and sets up kings (Daniel 2:21)
98. The God who gives wisdom to the wise (Daniel 2:21)
99. The God who gives knowledge to those with understanding (Daniel 2:21)
100. The Lord on whose shoulders rests the government (Isaiah 9:6)

101. The Lord whose government and peace will never end (Isaiah 9:7)
102. The Eternal Father (Isaiah 9:6)
103. The One who is the LORD (Exodus 6:29)
104. The Mighty God (Isaiah 9:6)
105. The God who made the seven stars and Orion (Amos 5:8)
106. The God of the cherubim and archangels (Jude 9; Genesis 3:24)
107. The God and Designer of the ark of the covenant (Exodus 25:10–22)
108. God, the Architect of Noah's ark (Genesis 7)
109. The God who hides Yourself (Isaiah 45:15)
110. The Sovereign Lord who rescues me from death (Psalm 68:20)
111. The All-Powerful God (Revelation 19:15-16)
112. The One who possesses universal and eternal authority (John 17:2; Matthew 28:18; Ephesians 1:21; Colossians 2:10)
113. The One who will fulfill the number of my days (Exodus 23:25–26)
114. The God who is no respecter of persons (Acts 10:34; Galatians 2:6; Deuteronomy 10:17; 1 Peter 1:17)
115. The Lord, who sees a day like a thousand years, and a thousand years like a day (2 Peter 3:8)
116. The One who will come as a thief in the night (2 Peter 3:10)
117. The God who whatever You destroy cannot be rebuilt (Job 12:14)
118. The everlasting God; no one can measure the depths of Your understanding (Isaiah 40:28)
119. The One who inhabits eternity (Isaiah 57:15)
120. The Governor over all the nations (Psalm 22:28; Psalm 67:4)
121. The One who cannot be stopped or questioned (Daniel 4:34–35; Psalm 115:3)
122. The Awesome One I must bring tribute to (Psalm 76:11)
123. The One who breaks the pride of princes (Psalm 76:12)
124. The One is feared by the kings of the earth (Psalm 76:12)
125. The Potter over my life (Isaiah 64:8; Jeremiah 18:6)
126. The One who gives me power to get wealth (Deuteronomy 8:17–18)
127. The Christ with unsearchable riches (Ephesians 3:8)
128. The God who does great and unsearchable things (Job 5:9)

129. The One who does marvelous things without number (Job 5:9)
130. The Wonderful Counselor (Isaiah 9:6)

A PRAYER DECLARING HIS SOVEREIGNTY

Sovereign and All-Powerful God, in Jesus' mighty Name, I come before Your throne of majesty. Your sovereignty is irresistible and your supreme rulership is for eternity.

I recognize You are the One with authority, honor, and sovereignty over all the nations. Lord, no one can interrupt Your work or call Your rule into question, for You possess all universal and eternal authority and power. You are the Lord, the Mighty God, who spoke and summoned all humanity. The God with supreme rulership.

You are God, and there is no other like You. You are the Sovereign God of eternity.

You are the blessed and only Sovereign God. Lord, I know that outside from You, there is no other God; apart from You, I can do nothing. You are the Invisible One, the only one who possesses immortality and will never die; You alone are God, my God.

You are the only One who cannot be stopped or questioned. You are the God of supremacy. You are One, the great Lord, the Ancient of Days, the Everlasting King, and the highest of the earth's kings. Lord God, You are the most and highest Sovereign of the kings; You are not of this world.

Father, You declare the end from the beginning. You see the beginning and the end simultaneously. You declare things that are not yet done from ancient times; Your counsel shall stand. You always accomplish Your purpose. The God who causes everything to work together for my good, for You are the Potter over my life. You mold me as clay in Your hands into whatever You want me to be.

God, You are the One with endless names and attributes. The One who has all supreme and ultimate power. Father, I know You are Omnipresent, Omnipotent, Omniscient, Omnificent and Omnibenevolent. Lord, You have infinite understanding. You are the God who is way more than we know of and greater than we can understand. The God who is mighty in both power and understanding. The One with an understanding beyond human comprehension. The God whose eyes contemplate everything. Lord, I know You are the God of details.

You are supremely good to me. You are the God who is supreme over everything everywhere. You are Christ, You are all that matters for You fill everything in all with Your Presence. You are *Jehovah-Shammah*—You are here present with me. Lord, You are the eternal all-sufficient God, the God of time and eternity. You are the Immutable One who never changes Your mind. You are the God who was, who is, and who is to come, the Almighty. You are the Sovereign Lord who will wipe away the tears from all faces.

Lord God, You are the Spirit who moves on the surface of the sea, the God of the universe, the Lord of lords, King of kings, the God *El Roi*—who sees me. You are the God who has a count of all my hairs. Lord, You are the faithful God who won't allow temptation or trials to be more than I can stand. You will always show me a way out so I can endure it. Lord, You are a good God who waits patiently for everyone to repent so they won't be destroyed.

You are the God whose years are uncountable. Lord, You laid the earth's foundations, which will never be removed. The Lord who has authority over the floodwaters. The God who counts the stars and names all of them. The Lord, who rules over heaven and earth. You own the day and night, the God who turns dawn to darkness and sunset into the day. You are the One who walks on the heights of the earth.

Lord, You are the Creator of thrones, kingdoms, rulers, and authorities in the unseen world. You are God from eternity to eternity; You inhabit eternity. You are the Governor of the universe, and you rule over all nations. With the power of Your sovereignty You rule over all. You are the One who performs awe-inspiring deeds.

Jesus Christ, You are supreme over all who rose from the dead. God, the One who has the key of David. The One who is always the same and lives forever. Lord, You will reign as King in perpetuity. You will destroy death forever.

You are the God of the bush's blazing fire that does not consume. The great Lord who is to be feared above all gods. You are the Sovereign Lord who is my strength.

Lord, You are God, the One who knows it all, the All-Knowing One. Father, You are perfect in knowledge. You are God, the All-Seeing.

You are the God who does whatever pleases You or whatever You want.

The God who owes nothing to anyone. You are the God with decisions and ways hard to understand. You are the God with no advisers, for no one can know Your thoughts or advise You. You own great riches, wisdom, and knowledge. You are the Source from where everything comes.

You chose me before the creation of the world. You predestined me and chose me for adoption to sonship through Jesus Christ.

Lord, Your counsel shall stand and accomplish its purpose. You are the One who changes times and seasons. You remove kings and set up kings. You give wisdom to the wise and knowledge to those with understanding. Lord, the government rests on Your shoulders, and Your government and peace will never end. You are the Wonderful Counselor , Mighty God, Eternal Father, and Prince of Peace. *Yahweh*, the God of Israel for all generations.

You are the Blessed and Almighty God. The King of kings and Lord of lords. The One who can never die. The One who lives in light so brilliant that no one can approach You. The One with all honor and power forever and ever! Amen.

---

1. Stelman Smith and Judson Cornwall, *The Exhaustive Dictionary of Bible Names* (North Brunswick, NJ: Bridge-Logos, 1998), 82.
2. Walter A. Elwell and Barry J. Beitzel, "Omniscience," *Baker Encyclopedia of the Bible* (Grand Rapids, MI: Baker Book House, 1988), 1588.

23

HIS FAITHFULNESS

God is faithful [He is reliable, trustworthy and ever true to His promise—He can be depended on], and through Him you were called into fellowship with His Son, Jesus Christ our Lord.

1 Corinthians 1:9 AB

The faithful love of the LORD never ends! His mercies never cease. Great is his faithfulness; his mercies begin afresh each morning.

Lamentations 3:22–23 NLT

You are:

1. Lord, You are always faithful and keep Your promises (Psalm 145:13; 1 Corinthians 1:9)
2. The One who keeps every promise forever (Psalm 146:6; Daniel 9:4)

3. The One whose promises are always a yes and an amen (2 Corinthians 1:18–21)
4. The eternal Promise Keeper (Psalm 145:13; 146:6; Numbers 23:19; 2 Timothy 2:13; Daniel 9:4)
5. The One in whose promises I rest (Matthew 11:28; Psalm 23:1–2; 62:1; Matthew 11:28)
6. The One who builds the faith of men (1 Corinthians 3:10; Joshua 1:9)
7. Jesus, the merciful and faithful High Priest (Hebrews 2:17)
8. God, my perfect Eternal Spouse (Revelation 21:2–9; Isaiah 54:5; Ephesians 5:25–33)
9. The Lord whose Name is the Lord of the heaven's armies (Isaiah 54:5)
10. My Redeemer (Isaiah 54:5)
11. The Holy One of Israel (Isaiah 54:5)
12. The God of all the earth (Isaiah 54:5)
13. The Groom who will marry Your bride, the church (Revelation 19:7–9)
14. God; those united with You are One with You (1 Corinthians 6:17)
15. The Lord who is among any two or three who gather in Your Name (Matthew 18:20)
16. The God who answers prayers (John 15:7)
17. The God who fulfills Your covenant (Daniel 9:4)
18. The God of loyalty (Deuteronomy 7:12)
19. The God who honors me when I put my hope in You (Psalm 37:34)
20. The Spirit of faithfulness (Galatians 5.22–23)
21. God, the faithful Creator (1 Peter 4:19)
22. The God with a faithful love that endures forever (Psalm 138:8)
23. The Lord who will work out Your plans for my life (Psalm 138:8)
24. Jesus, You are called faithful and true (Revelation 19:11)
25. God, the Faithful One forever (2 Chronicles 5:13)
26. God, the true and faithful Witness of all things (Revelation 1:5; Jeremiah 42:5)

27. The God whose faithful promises are my armor and protection (Psalm 91:4)
28. God, the Faithful One who does no wrong (Deuteronomy 32:4)
29. God, the One who is just and upright (Deuteronomy 32:4)
30. God, my Rock (Deuteronomy 32:4)
31. The God of Covenants (Genesis 9:12; 17:2–5)
32. The Lord who will return soon for me (Revelation 22:20)
33. The God who gives me my heart's desires when I delight in You (Psalm 37:4)
34. Jesus Christ, who is the same yesterday, today, and forever (Hebrews 13:8)
35. The Lord with great faithfulness (Lamentations 3:23)
36. The God of lovingkindness and faithfulness (Psalm 92:2)
37. Lord, my Hallelujah (Revelation 19:1–6)
38. The Lord whose faithfulness continues to all generations (Psalm 100:5)
39. The Lord with a loving faithfulness that endures forever (Psalm 117:2)
40. The Faithful, Reliable, and Trustworthy One (1 Corinthians 1:9)
41. The God on whom I can always depend (1 Corinthians 1:9)
42. Lord, Your faithful love never ends (Lamentations 3:22–23)
43. The Lord, Your mercies never end (Lamentations 3:22–23)
44. The Lord, Great is Your faithfulness (Lamentations 3:22–23)
45. The One who has new mercies every morning (Lamentations 3:22–23)
46. The God that never change Your mind (Hebrews 6:17)
47. The God who never lies, it is impossible for You to lie (Hebrews 6:18)
48. God, the Immutable, Your Word remains forever (Malachi 3:6; 1 Peter 1:25)

A PRAYER DECLARING HIS FAITHFULNESS

Father, I come before Your throne of grace in Jesus' mighty Name. Thank You for keeping all of Your promises to me throughout my life. Your promises are always a yes and an amen over me. You are the eternal Promise Keeper; You are faithful to keep all Your promises forever. Your unfailing promises give me rest, comfort, and hope. My hallelujah belongs to You. You help me in establishing a firm and strong faith in You. Jesus, You are my gracious and loyal High Priest who intercedes for me before the Father.

Jesus, You are my perfect Eternal Spouse, You are the Bridegroom who will marry Your bride, the church. Your Name is the Lord of the heaven's armies, my Redeemer. The Holy One of Israel, the God of all the earth. God, those united with You are one with You. You are a God of covenants. I know You will return for me soon.

Lord, I know You are among any two or three who gather in Your Name, and You answer all our prayers. You are a God who fulfills Your covenant. Lord, You are a God of loyalty. You honor me when I put my hope in You. You are the Spirit of faithfulness, my faithful Creator. You are the Faithful, Reliable, and Trustworthy Lord of my life. I can always depend on You. Father, Your faithful love endures forever and your mercies never end. Oh Lord, great is Your faithfulness. Every morning when I wake up You are filled with new mercies over my life. Because of Your faithfulness, You give me my heart's desires when I delight in You. You are a God of lovingkindness and faithfulness.

Father, I know You will work out Your plans for my life. Jesus, You are called faithful and true. The trustworthy One who does no harm, You are unbiassed and upright. You are the everlasting trustworthy One, the real and faithful witness of all things. Your steadfast promises are my armor and shield. Lord, You are my Salvation, and I cling to You for my dear life. Jesus Christ, because You are the same yesterday, today, and forever, I know You will always be the Lord who is true to me and my family. You never change Your mind, You never lie because it is impossible for You to lie. You are the Immutable God and Your Word remains forever.

My Lord, You are so good. Your unfailing love continues forever, and Your faithfulness continues to each generation. Your unfailing love for me is so powerful; Your faithfulness endures forever. I Praise You oh, Lord!

Thank You, for Your unending love and faithfulness towards me, giving me hope, security, peace, and stability. I love You, Lord! In Jesus Name, amen!

24

HIS JUSTICE

The Lord is known for his justice.

Psalm 9:16

For the LORD loves justice, and he will never abandon the godly.

Psalm 37:28

You are:

1. My Mantle of Righteousness (Isaiah 61:10)
2. The God who is completely truthful (John 8:26)
3. The Lord my Righteousness (Jeremiah 23:6)
4. The righteous Reward of all who seek You (Hebrews 11:6)
5. The just God (2 Thessalonians 1:6)
6. The God who is good and upright (Psalm 25:8; Jeremiah 33:11)
7. The God of Jeshurun (upright) (Deuteronomy 33:26–29)

8. A faithful God who never does evil, nor is there iniquity in You (Deuteronomy 32:4)
9. Jesus Christ the righteous One (1 John 2:1)
10. Jesus, the Righteous Servant and Leader (Acts 24:7)
11. The Lord, the High Priest over the house of God (Hebrews 10:21)
12. Jesus, the Righteous Branch (Jeremiah 33:15; Zechariah 3:8)
13. Jesus, the Righteousness of our God and Savior (2 Peter 1:1)
14. Jesus, appointed as Judge of the living and the dead (1 Peter 4:4)
15. The God of justice (Psalm 7:11; 50:6; 1 Chronicles 16:14)
16. God, the Judge of judges (Genesis 18:25; 20:11–15; Psalm 94:2; 82:1; Job 12:17)
17. God, the righteous Judge of all creation (Psalm 67:4; Revelation 19:11)
18. God, the Justifier of those who have faith in Jesus (Romans 3:26)
19. God, the impartial and unbiased Judge; Your judgments are all fair (Romans 2:11; John 5:22; Deuteronomy 10:17)
20. The God who gives justice to the oppressed (Psalm 146:7; 82:3)
21. The God who weighs all actions (1 Samuel 2:3)
22. The Lord who searches the hearts and examines secret motives (Jeremiah 17:10; Psalm 7:9)
23. The Lord who gives all people their due rewards according to their actions (Revelation 22:12; Jeremiah 17:10; Hebrews 11:6)
24. The God who looks at those who tremble at Your Word and obey You (Isaiah 66:5; Psalm 119:120; Philippians 2:12)
25. God, the Buckler to them who walk uprightly (Proverbs 2:7)
26. God, the Habitation of justice (Jeremiah 50:7)
27. God, the most Upright (Micah 7:4)
28. The Lord God of truth (John 17:3; Isaiah 65:16)
29. God, the only true God (Jeremiah 10:10; John 17:3)
30. The God who is pleased with sacrifices offered in the right spirit (Psalm 51:19)
31. God, the definition of perfect, loving justice (Psalm 10:14–18; 2 Samuel 22:31; Matthew 5:47)
32. The God whose ways are perfect and loving (2 Samuel 22:31; Matthew 5:47; Psalm 10:14–18)
33. The One who is to be feared (Psalm 89:7)

34. The Lord who loves those who speak honestly and with righteous lips (Proverbs 16:13)
35. The God of order (1 Corinthians 14:33–40)
36. The Creator of law (Exodus 31:18)
37. The God who guides along right paths for Your Name's sake (Psalm 23:3)
38. God, the One who is holy and true (Revelation 3:7)
39. The Lord who gives righteousness and justice to those treated unfairly (Psalm 103:6)
40. The Lord who loves justice and hates evil (Hebrews 1:9; Psalm 11:7; 37:28; 45:7; 82:2)
41. The Lord who laughs at the wicked, for You see their day of judgment coming (Psalm 37:13)
42. The One who makes my innocence radiate like the dawn (Psalm 37:6)
43. The One who makes the justice of my cause shine like the noonday sun (Psalm 37:6)
44. The God who exercises and delights in righteousness and justice on earth (Jeremiah 9:24)
45. The God who defines what is a good thing and what is not good (Genesis 1)
46. The God who helps me do what is right, just, and fair (Proverbs 1:3–4)
47. The Lord who refuses to satisfy the craving of the wicked (Proverbs 10:3)
48. The Lord who detests people with crooked and perverted hearts (Proverbs 11:20)
49. The Lord who delights in those with integrity (Proverbs 11:20)
50. The Lord who approves of those who are good (Proverbs 12:2)
51. The Lord who detests lying lips (Proverbs 12:22)
52. The Lord who delights in those who tell the truth (Proverbs 12:22)
53. The Lord who delights in the prayers of the upright (Proverbs 15:9)
54. The Lord who detests evil plans (Proverbs 15:26)
55. The Lord who is far from the wicked (Proverbs 15:29; Isaiah 59:2; John 9:31)

56. The Lord who detests the proud (Proverbs 16:5)
57. The God who rules with a scepter of justice (Psalm 45:6; Hebrews 1:8)
58. God, the Judge of judges (Job 12:17)
59. God, You are with the generation of the righteous (Psalm 14:5)
60. The God who justifies me (Romans 5:1; 8:33; Galatians 2:16)
61. The One who does everything just and fair (Deuteronomy 32:4)
62. The Lord, God of vengeance (Psalm 94:1–2)
63. The One whose glorious justice shines forth (Psalm 94:1–2)
64. The Judge of the earth (Psalm 94:1–2)
65. The One who gives the proud what they deserve (Psalm 94:1–2)
66. The Lord who requires me to do what is right (Micah 6:8)
67. The Lord who delights in the prayers of the upright (Proverbs 15:9)
68. The One who pours disgrace upon princes and disarms the strong (Job 12:21)
69. God, the perfect Legislator (Psalm 119:138)
70. The Lord who demands accurate scales and balances (Proverbs 16:11)
71. The Lord who sets the standards for fairness (Proverbs 16:11)
72. The One who judges fairly and wages a righteous war (Revelation 19:11)
73. The God who is a devouring fire (Hebrews 12:29)
74. The God of the spotted and speckled lambs of Jacob (Genesis 30:39)
75. The God who judges all the earth (Psalm 58:11)
76. The God of unsearchable judgments and unfathomable ways (Romans 11:33)
77. The God who governs the nations with justice (Psalm 67:4)
78. The God who guides the people of the whole world (Psalm 67:4)
79. The One who judges the peoples with equity (Psalm 67:4)
80. The Lord who looks at the heart (1 Samuel 16:7)
81. The God who will repay all people according to what they have done (Psalm 62:12)
82. The LORD who loves the righteous (Psalm 146:8)
83. The LORD who opens the eyes of the blind (Psalm 146:8)

84. The LORD who lifts up those who are bowed down (Psalm 146:8)
85. The LORD who protects the foreigners among us (Psalm 146:9; Ruth 1:16)
86. The Lord who cares for the orphans and widows (Psalm 146:9)
87. The God who frustrates the plans of the wicked (Psalm 146:9)
88. The God with a kingdom of righteousness, peace and joy (Romans 14:17)
89. The LORD, righteous in everything You do (Psalm 145:17a)
90. The LORD who protects all those who love You, but You destroy the wicked (Psalm 145:20)
91. The King of the final Judgment Day (Matthew 25:31–46)
92. The One before whom all the nations will be gathered to be judged (Matthew 25:32)
93. The One who will separate people as a shepherd separates the sheep from the goats (Matthew 25:32)
94. The One that will place the sheep on his right, but the goats on the left (Matthew 25:33)
95. The Supreme Judge seated on the great white throne for the final Judgment Day (Revelation 20:11–15)
96. The One who was given authority to execute judgment (John 5:27)
97. Lord, the Righteous Judge (2 Timothy 4:6–8)
98. The Lord who will crown me with righteousness (2 Timothy 4:6–8)
99. The Prize that awaits me (2 Timothy 4:6–8)
100. The God who takes revenge (Romans 12:19; Isaiah 59:18)
101. The God who vindicates (Psalm 135:14)
102. The Lord who will bring our darkest secrets to light (1 Corinthians 4:5)
103. The Lord who reveals our private hidden motives (1 Corinthians 4:5)
104. The God that will give to each one whatever praise is due (1 Corinthians 4:5)
105. The LORD who will judge Your own people (Hebrews 10:30)
106. The Living God, a terrible thing is to fall into Your hands (Hebrews 10:31)

A PRAYER DECLARING HIS JUSTICE

Father God, I come before You in Jesus' mighty Name and through Your Spirit of grace. I acknowledge that you are the God of true justice and my Mantle of Justice. You are the Lord, my Righteousness. The God who guides me in the paths of righteousness and peace. Lord, You are the righteous Reward of all who seek You, my Reward. You delight in the prayers of the upright. You are the God of the spotted and speckled lambs of Jacob, for You are a good and just God.

Lord, You are completely truthful and a just God. You are good and upright all the time. You are a faithful God who never does evil, nor is there iniquity found in You. Jesus, You are the Righteous Servant and Leader. You are the Lord, the High Priest over the house of God. You are the righteous Branch. Jesus, You are the Righteousness of our God, and You are our Savior. Lord, Your kingdom is not a matter of eating and drinking but of righteousness and peace and joy in the Holy Spirit.

Jesus, You were appointed Judge of the living and the dead, for You are the God of justice. You are the Judge of judges, and the righteous Judge of all creation. You are the Justifier of those who have faith in Jesus. Lord, You love justice, and You are an impartial and unbiased Judge. Your judgments are all fair. You give justice to the oppressed. You are the One who weighs all actions. You search the hearts and examine the secret motives. You reveal our most private and hidden intentions.

You will bring to light our darkest secrets. On the day of Judgment, You will give the recognition and reward that corresponds to each one.

You look at those who tremble at Your Word and obey it, for You are the One who is to be feared and no one else.

Lord God, You are the Buckler to them that walk uprightly. You crown me with your righteousness. Lord, You are the Habitation of justice. You are the most upright and the God of truth, the only true God. You are pleased with sacrifices offered in the right spirit only. Lord, You laugh at the wicked, for You see their day of judgment coming. You are the One who pours disgrace upon princes and disarms the strong.

Lord, You detest lying lips, but You delight in those who tell the truth. You delight in the prayers of the upright. Lord, You detest evil plans and You are far from the wicked.

Lord, You detest the proud, and You give the proud what they deserve. You refuse to satisfy the craving of the wicked. You are the living God, a terrible and terrifying thing is to fall into your hands. You despise people with crooked and perverted hearts, but You delight in those who walk in integrity. Lord God, help me always do what is right, just, and fair through the help of Your Holy Spirit. You are the Lord who approves of those who are good. You are the God who defines what a good thing is and what it is not. You exercise and delight in righteousness and justice on earth.

You make my innocence radiate like the dawn. You make the justice of my cause shine like the noonday sun.

Lord, vengeance belongs to You, therefore I will never take revenge for You are my Vindicator. I will leave that to Your righteous anger oh Lord for you are the One who pays them back. Lord, You love those who speak honestly and with righteous lips. You are the Lord who gives righteousness and justice to those treated unfairly. Lord, You love justice and hate evil. You demand accurate scales and balances; You set the standards for fairness. You are the Creator of law and order, the perfect Legislator. You are the Lawgiver who judges fairly and wages a righteous war.

You are the Supreme King seated on a great white throne as the Judge ready for the final judgment day. You are the One before whom all the nations will be gathered to be judged according to what they have done, as recorded in the books. You will judge Your own people. You will separate people as a shepherd separates the sheep from the goats, and You will place the sheep on Your right but the goats on the left. You will say to those on Your right, "Come, you who are blessed by My Father, inherit the kingdom prepared for you from the foundation of the world." You are the prize that awaits me. Oh Lord, have mercy and teach me the path of righteousness so that I may always walk with integrity.

You are the definition of perfect, loving justice—the holy and true God and Judge of the universe. You are with the generation of the righteous. Let Your glorious justice shine forth. Jesus, You have the authority to execute judgment. You rule with a scepter of justice, for You are the Judge of judges, the Judge of all the earth. You are the Lord who justifies me. You do everything just and fair. You are the One who requires me to do what is right. You are a devouring fire. Save us Lord and Prepare us for the final judgment day. In Jesus' powerful Name, amen.

25

HIS MIGHTY AND GLORIOUS WORKS

All Your works shall praise You, O LORD, and Your saints shall bless You. They shall speak of the glory of Your kingdom, and talk of Your power, to make known to the sons of men His mighty acts, And the glorious majesty of His kingdom.

Psalm 145:10–12 NKJV

O LORD my God, you have performed many wonders for us. Your plans for us are too numerous to list. You have no equal. If I tried to recite all your wonderful deeds, I would never come to the end of them.

Psalm 40:5

You are:

1. The One whose works are proclaimed by the heavens (Psalm 19:1)
2. The God whose artistry is displayed by the heavens (Psalm 19:1)
3. The God who has done awesome miracles in my favor (Psalm 66:5)

4. The one who does the work of sanctification in my life (Exodus 31:13; Hebrews 10:10)
5. The Lord who has all my destiny and future planned out (Jeremiah 29:11)
6. The God of my victory and praise (Exodus 15:2; 1 Chronicles 16:25)
7. The God who killed the firstborn of Egypt (Psalm 135:8; 136:10)
8. Jesus, the God who has built Your house, the church (Matthew 7:24–27)
9. Jesus, the God who shall come soon on the clouds (Revelation 22:12)
10. The God who divided the Red Sea in two with Your mighty power (Psalm 136:13; 78:13; Exodus 14:21; Nehemiah 9:11; 136:13; Isaiah 63:12)
11. The God of the Scriptures (2 Timothy 3:16–17)
12. The God who has done awe-inspiring deeds for people (Psalm 66:5)
13. The God who can turn the sea into dry land (Psalm 66:6)
14. The Lord, Creator of everything, who made all things (Colossians 1:16)
15. The Lord who made the heavens skillfully by Your wisdom (Psalm 136:5)
16. The Lord who created the heavens by Your Word (Psalm 33:6)
17. The Lord who made Your army by the breath of Your mouth (Psalm 33:6)
18. The Lord, the One who formed in my mother's womb (Jeremiah 1:5; Isaiah 49:5)
19. The God who led Your people through the wilderness (Psalm 136:16)
20. The God who commanded that light shine out of darkness (2 Corinthians 4:6)
21. The God who works awesome, great wonders (Psalm 77:11–14)
22. The God who performs wonders that cannot be fathomed, miracles that cannot be counted (Job 5:9)
23. The God who did wonderful works to be remembered forever (Psalm 111:4)

24. God, the One who rescued me from the kingdom of darkness (Colossians 1:13–14)
25. God, the One who transferred me into the kingdom of Your dear Son (Colossians 1:13–14)
26. Jesus, the One who purchased my freedom and forgave my sins (Colossians 1:13–14)
27. The God who deserves to be praised for Your great love (Psalm 107:8)
28. The God who deserves to be worshiped for the wonderful things You have done for us (Psalm 107:8)
29. The God who satisfies the thirsty and fills the hungry with good things (Psalm 107:9)
30. God, the One who turns dessert land into springs of water (Psalm 107:35)
31. God, the Rock whose works are perfect; Your ways are just (Deuteronomy 32:4)
32. Jesus, who finished the work the Father gave You faithfully (John 17:4)
33. The Lord who has done many works in wisdom (Psalm 104:24)
34. The Lord who sets me apart, appoints me, and equips me for Your purposes (Exodus 3:10–12; Romans 8:28; Jeremiah 1:5; Hebrews 13:21)
35. The God who chooses the least likely and the most insignificant for Your plans (Exodus 3:10–12; 4:10–14; Judges 6:15; 1 Corinthians 1:27–29)
36. The God who controls the course of world events (Daniel 2:20–22)
37. The God who began and continues to work in me (Philippians 1:6)
38. The One whose deeds are perfect (Deuteronomy 32:4)
39. The God who works in me giving me the desire and the power to do what pleases You (Philippians 2:13)
40. The God who makes me sing with joy because of what you have done for me (Psalm 92:4)
41. The God of great works and very deep thoughts (Psalm 92:5)

42. The God who works in different ways through Your Spirit (1 Corinthians 12:6)
43. The God who empowers me (1 Corinthians 12:6–11)
44. The God of mighty works (Psalm 77:11–14)
45. The Lord, your work is done in faithfulness (Psalm 33:4)
46. My Creator, you made me fearfully and wonderfully (Psalm 139:14)
47. The Fourth Man in the furnace (Daniel 3:24–26)
48. The One who walks on water (Matthew 14:29; John 6:19)
49. The God who has performed many wonders in my favor (Psalm 40:5)
50. The God whose plans for me are too numerous to list (Psalm 40:5)
51. The God of endless wonderful deeds (Psalm 40:5)
52. The God of great wonders (Psalm 77:11–14)
53. The God without equal, nor rival, who always wins (Psalm 40:5)
54. The God who turned the rivers of Egypt into blood so that no one would drink from the streams (Psalm 78:44)
55. The One who makes a path that no one knew existed (Psalm 77:19)
56. The One who makes Jerusalem the pride of the earth (Isaiah 62:7)
57. The One who names Jerusalem "The City of His Delight" (Isaiah 62:4)
58. The One who calls Jerusalem "The Bride of God" (Isaiah 62:4)
59. The God of miraculous and great wonders (Psalm 77:14)
60. The God who demonstrates Your awesome power among the nations (Psalm 77:14)
61. The God who performs wondrous works and mighty awesome deeds (Psalm 145:5–6)
62. The God who shuts the Lion' mouths (Daniel 6:22)

A PRAYER DECLARING HIS GLORIOUS WORKS

Heavenly Father, I humbly approach Your throne of grace in the name of Jesus to acknowledge and honor Your glorious works. You are the God of mighty works, deserving of all praise. The heavens declare Your works, and the universe showcases Your artistry. You are the Creator of all things, skillfully crafting the heavens with wisdom and accomplishing countless incredible works. Your command brought light out of darkness, and Your word formed the heavens. By the breath of Your mouth, You created Your mighty army. You are the God of astounding wonders, performing miracles beyond comprehension.

You are the God of the Scriptures. You are the Fourth Man in the furnace, and the One who shuts the mouths of lions. You are the God who has done awe-inspiring deeds since the beginning. You displayed Your fearful power by striking down the firstborn of Egypt. Your mighty hand divided the Red Sea, leading Your people through the wilderness and transforming the sea into dry land. You are the Lord who walks on water, revealing Your unmatched authority. Your wonderful deeds have no end, for You are the God of great wonders, unmatched and victorious.

You are the God who performs works that leave a lasting impact, marvelous in craftsmanship. Jesus, You have built Your house, the Church, and You satisfy the thirsty and fill the hungry with good things. You have the power to turn barren deserts into springs of water, demonstrating Your life-giving nature.

O Lord, You are the Rock, whose every work is flawless, and Your ways are righteous. Your actions are always carried out with unwavering faithfulness. Jesus, You are the trustworthy Savior who completed the task entrusted to You by the Father. You are the Divine Sovereign God who controls the course of world events.

You have performed astounding miracles on my behalf. Thank you, Lord, for shaping me within my mother's womb. As a result, You are the Master of my destiny and future. Your plans for me are beyond measure. Jesus, You have paid for my freedom and forgiven my sins. God, You have rescued me from the domain of darkness and transferred me into the kingdom of Your beloved Son. You are the One who sanctifies me.

Lord, You are the One who sets me apart, appoints me, and equips me for Your divine purposes. Through Your Spirit, You work in various ways in my life. You empower me to operate in the gifts of the Spirit. I am grateful that You choose the unlikely and the seemingly insignificant for Your plans and purposes. Lord, You initiated Your work in me, and I trust that You will continue to mold me into the likeness of Jesus. It is You who instill in me both the desire and the ability to please You. You are the God of profound thoughts and remarkable deeds. Among the nations, You reveal Your awesome power through miraculous and extraordinary wonders.

Lord, Your actions are flawless, deserving of praise for Your immense love and the marvelous works You have accomplished. I sing with joy because of what You have done for me. My heart overflows with gratitude, oh Lord, for Your abundant acts of love upon me and my family. I will praise You eternally, for Your works are mighty and glorious!

In Jesus' Name, amen!

26

HIS SALVATION

Praise the Lord! Salvation and glory and power belong to our God.

Revelation 19:1

Everyone who calls on the Name of the Lord will be saved.

Romans 10:13

You are:

1. The Redeemer of my soul (Isaiah 47:4; 59:20; 54:5 Psalm 19:14)
2. The God of redemption (Genesis 3:15; Ephesians 1:7; Isaiah 44:22; Psalm 107:2; Psalm 111:9)
3. Jesus, my Prince and my Savior (1 Timothy 2:3)
4. Jesus, the Savior of Israel (Acts 13:23)
5. Jesus, my personal Savior, my Salvation (Romans 10:9–10)
6. The Name by which I am Saved (Acts 2:21; Romans 10:13)
7. The Lord, outside of You there is no other Savior (Isaiah 43:11)

8. Jesus, the Savior of the world (Matthew 1:21; 1 John 4:14; 42)
9. The God who redeems me from destruction (Psalm 103:4; Titus 2:14)
10. The God who rescued me from the domain of darkness (Colossians 1:13)
11. The God who transferred me to the kingdom of Your beloved Son (Colossians 1:13)
12. The God who gave Yourself as a ransom for everyone (1 Timothy 2:6)
13. The One with the last word (1 Peter 3:22)
14. The God who purchased me to be Your own (Ephesians 1:14)
15. The One who called me to Your eternal glorious kingdom through Jesus Christ (1 Peter 5:10; 1 Thessalonians 2:12)
16. The Lord, my *Agnus Dei*—Lamb of God (John 1:29)
17. The Father and Author of eternal life (John 3:16)
18. The Light of the nations (Isaiah 42:6)
19. God, the light that illuminates the gentiles (Isaiah 49:6; Acts 13:47)
20. God, the living Rock (1 Peter 2:4)
21. God, the Living Stone (1 Peter 2:4–8)
22. Jesus, the God of eternal salvation (Hebrews 5:9)
23. Jesus, my Passover (1 Corinthians 5:7)
24. Jesus, a precious Cornerstone for a sure foundation (Isaiah 28:16–17)
25. Jesus, the Mediator of a better covenant (Hebrews 8:6)
26. Jesus, the Mediator between God and humankind (1 Timothy 2:3–6)
27. The God of my salvation (Psalm 18:46; 62; 35:3; 25:5 Isaiah 12:2)
28. The One dressed in splendor and majesty ready to save me (Isaiah 63:1)
29. The God of consolation (Jeremiah 31:13)
30. God, the Giver of eternal life (John 10:28)
31. Jesus, the Friend of sinners (Matthew 11:19; Luke 7:34)
32. Jesus, Lord of total forgiveness (Romans 3:23; Psalm 130:3–4; 86:5)
33. God, a witness in my favor (John 5:32)

34. Jesus, the Door to salvation (John 10:9)
35. Jesus, the only Way, the Door to the Father (John 14:6)
36. Jesus the absolute Truth (John 14:6)
37. Jesus the Life (John 1:4; 6:48; 14:6)
38. Jesus, the Way; no one comes to the Father except through You (John 14:6; 1 Timothy 2:5)
39. Jesus, the Lamb of God who takes away the sin of the world (John 1:29)
40. Jesus, the One who sacrificed Your life for me (1 John 3:16; John 3:16)
41. Jesus, the Captain of our salvation (Hebrews 2:10–11)
42. The God who gives life unto the world (John 6:33)
43. God, the Anchor of my soul (Hebrews 6:19)
44. God, the Horn of my salvation (Psalm 18:2)
45. The Lord God, the Rock of my salvation (2 Samuel 22:47)
46. Lord, the Garment of Salvation (Isaiah 61:10)
47. Lord, the Joy of my Salvation (Psalm 51:12)
48. The God of hope (Romans 15:13; Romans 8:24)
49. The God who gave me the free loving gift of salvation (Ephesians 2:8)
50. The God who saved me by Your grace when I believed in You (Romans 11:6; Ephesians 2:8)
51. Jesus, the only Name by which we must be saved (Acts 4:12)
52. The One who bore my sins in Your body on the cross (1 Peter 2:24)
53. The God who redeems my life from the pit of death (Psalm 103:4)
54. The God who crowns me with love and tender mercies (Psalm 103:4)
55. The One who fills my life with good things (Psalm 103:4)
56. The One who renews my youth like the eagle's (Psalm 103:4)
57. The God who forgives all my sins (1 John 2:1–2, 12; Psalm 103:3)
58. The One who purchased the church with Your own blood (Acts 20:18–28)
59. The Lord who tells me not to be afraid for You have ransomed me (Isaiah 43:1)
60. Jesus, my Advocate and Lawyer before the Father (1 John 2:1–2)

61. Jesus, the Atoning Sacrifice for my sins (1 John 2:2)
62. The One who promised me the joy of eternal life (1 John 2:25)
63. The Preparer of my heavenly home (John 14:2)
64. The Salvation of my soul (Psalm 35:3)
65. The narrow Gateway to life (Matthew 7:14)
66. Jesus, the Savior of the world (Luke 2:11)
67. The God who is mighty to save (Isaiah 63:1)
68. Lord, the Stronghold of my life, of whom shall I be afraid? (Psalm 27:1)
69. Lord, my Light and my Salvation (Psalm 27:1; Exodus 15:2)
70. My kind, loving and merciful Savior (Titus 3:4–5)
71. The Savior who washed away my sins (Titus 3:4–5)
72. Jesus Christ, whose blood has cleansed me and washed me from all my sins (1 Peter 1:2; Psalm 51:2)
73. Christ, the Savior that was born in the City of David (Luke 2:11)
74. Jesus, God's anointed One (2 Corinthians 1:21; Luke 2:11; Daniel 9:26)
75. The Master and Possessor of heaven and earth (Genesis 14:19)
76. The Savior of all generations past and present (Psalm 100:5; Luke 1:50)
77. The Hope of the nations (Matthew 12:21)
78. The God who loved the world sacrificially, giving Your only Son (John 3:16)
79. The God who keeps me safe from the evil one (John 17:15)
80. The God who saves me (Psalm 68:20)
81. The Sovereign Lord who rescues me from death (Psalm 68:20)
82. The Rock of my salvation (Psalm 18:46; 78:35; 2 Samuel 22:32)
83. My Rock, my Redeemer (Psalm 19:14)
84. The Lord God, the everlasting Rock (Isaiah 26:4)
85. God, my heavenly Prize (Philippians 3:13–14)
86. The Lord; salvation belongs to You (Psalm 3:8; Jonah 2:9; Revelation 7:10)

A PRAYER DECLARING HIS SALVATION

Dear Father, I come before You in Jesus' Name and through Your gracious Holy Spirit, thanking You for my salvation. O Lord, thank You for redeeming me from eternal darkness and transferring me into Your eternal light. You rescued me from the domain of darkness and transferred me to the kingdom of Your beloved Son. You are the One with the last word.

Lord God, You are the God of redemption and the Redeemer of my soul. Lord you save me from destruction and eternal damnation. You bought me to be Yours.

Father, You loved the world sacrificially, giving Your only Son, Jesus, the Savior of the world. Jesus, You are the Savior of Israel, and You are the Prince of Peace. You are the Name by which I am Saved, my personal Savior. You are my Salvation. Outside of You, there is no other Savior. You gave Yourself as a ransom for everyone.

You called me to Your eternal glorious kingdom through Jesus Christ. Jesus, You are God's anointed One.

You are *Agnus Dei*—the Lamb of God and my Passover. Jesus, You are the Lamb of God who takes away the sin of the world. Father, You loved me so sacrificially by giving Your only Son in ransom for me. You are the Atoning Sacrifice for my sins. You bore my sins in Your body on the cross. Jesus Christ, Your blood has cleansed me and washed me from all my sins. Jesus, You are my kind, loving, and merciful Savior.

You redeem my life from the pit of death. You forgive all my sins. Father, by Your grace, You offered me the free loving gift of salvation, with which all I had to do was believe in You.

Jesus, thank You for sacrificing Your life for me. You are the Friend of sinners. You are the Door to Salvation. You are the way to salvation—the only way to the Father. Lord, You are the narrow gateway to life, the salvation of my soul. Lord, You are the Captain of my Salvation. Lord, You are the Giver of eternal life. You promised me the joy of eternal life. Jesus, You are God's eternal Salvation.

Lord, You are my heavenly Prize. You are the Preparer of my heavenly home.

You are the living Rock—the Rock of my salvation, my Rock and my Redeemer. You are the everlasting Rock. Jesus, You are a precious Cornerstone for a sure foundation. You are the Anchor of my soul—the Horn of my Salvation. You are the Garment and Joy of my Salvation. You are dressed in splendor and majesty ready to save me.

Jesus, You are the Way, the Truth and the Life; no one comes to the Father except through You. You are the Mediator of a better covenant based on better promises. The God of my salvation. The God of consolation. Jesus, the Lord of total forgiveness. You are a witness in my favor. The God who gives life unto the world.

Father, You are the Author of eternal life, the Light of the nations. You are the Light that illuminates the gentiles. You are the God of hope. The Hope of the nations. Jesus, the Savior of the world. You are the great Master Savior of all generations, past and present. The God who is mighty to save. Lord, my Light and my Salvation. Jesus, You are the only Name by which we must be saved. Jesus, You are the true Life.

You purchased the church with Your own blood. You are my Advocate and Lawyer before the Father. You crown me with love and tender mercies every day. You bring good things into my life. You renew my youth like that of the eagle's.

You command me not to be afraid, for You have ransomed me from the enemy and his evil plots. You keep me safe from the evil one. Lord, You are the stronghold of my life; of whom shall I be afraid? Thank You, my Lord, for You continue to save me every day from the enemy and even from myself. In Jesus' Name, Amen and Amen!

27

HIS HOLINESS

They were calling out to each other, "Holy, holy, holy is the LORD of Heaven's Armies! The whole earth is filled with his glory!"

Isaiah 6:3–4 NLT

Let them praise your great and awesome name. Your name is holy!

Psalm 99:3 NLT

You are:

1. God, the Way of Holiness (Isaiah 35:8)
2. *Elohim Kedoshim*—the Holy God (Joshua 24:19; Leviticus 19–20)
3. My God, the Holy One (Revelation 3:7; Habakkuk 1:12)
4. The True One (Revelation 3:7)
5. The Lord God, the Almighty (Revelation 4:8)
6. The God of the sacred and holy (Psalm 96:9; Isaiah 6:3)
7. The Lord whose Name is Holy (Isaiah 57:15; Psalm 99:3)

8. The Lord God of the holy prophets (Revelation 22:6)
9. The Holy One who anoints me to be part of Your royal priesthood (1 Peter 2:9)
10. God, the Holy of Holies (Hebrews 9:3; Exodus 26:34)
11. God, the holy, pure, immaculate One (1 Peter 1:16)
12. Jesus, the Holy One of God (John 6:69)
13. Lord, the Holy One of Israel (Isaiah 47:4)
14. The Most Holy God (Psalm 99:3; 1 Peter 1:16)
15. The Holy God, who is enthroned in the midst of Your people's praises (Psalm 22:3)
16. *Ruach Hakodesh*—God the Holy Spirit (Psalm 51:11)
17. God, the One who is holy and true (Revelation 3:7)
18. The God of holiness (Leviticus 19:2)
19. Jesus, the Lamb that was slain (Revelation 5:12)
20. Jesus, who is the sinless and spotless Lamb of God (1 Peter 1:19)
21. Lord, the incorruptible God (Romans 1:23)
22. The God of the pure in heart (Matthew 5:8)
23. The God of reverence and respect (1 Peter 1:15)
24. The God of the sacred altar (Matthew 23:19)
25. The Lord, glorious in holiness, awesome in splendor (Exodus 15:11)
26. The God who is to be feared, we tremble in Your Presence (Psalm 115:13; Deuteronomy 6:24; Jeremiah 5:22)
27. The Lord who grants the desires of those who fear You in reverence
28. The God who anoints my head with oil (Psalm 23:5)
29. The Spirit who makes me holy (1 Peter 1:1)
30. The God who says, "Be holy, for I am holy" (1 Peter 1:16)
31. The Lord who detests the proud (Proverbs 16:5)
32. The God who favors with grace the humble (James 4:6)
33. The Lord whose eyes are upon the faithful so they may dwell with You (Psalm 101:6)
34. The Lord who chooses those above reproach to serve You (Psalm 101:6)
35. The God who sanctifies me in Your Word and Truth (John 17:17)

36. *Yahweh* who sanctifies me (John 17:17; Hebrews 10:10; Leviticus 22:32)
37. The God of truth and without iniquity (Deuteronomy 32:4)
38. God, the One in whom there is no evil (Psalm 92:15, Matthew 5:48; Deuteronomy 32:4)
39. God, the Rock whose work is perfect; Your ways are just (Deuteronomy 32:4)
40. The One who makes me perfect and complete, needing nothing (James 1:4)
41. A Faithful God who does no wrong, who is righteous, upright, and just (Deuteronomy 32:4)
42. God the Father who made me holy by Your truth (John 17.17)
43. The God who is jealous for Your holy Name (Ezekiel 39:25)
44. The Lord who hates abomination (Proverbs 6:16–19)
45. The Lord who hates haughty eyes (Proverbs 6:17)
46. The Lord who hates a lying tongue (Proverbs 6:17)
47. The Lord who hates hands that shed innocent blood (Proverbs 6:17)
48. The Lord who hates a heart that devises wicked plans (Proverbs 6:18)
49. The Lord who hates the feet that make haste to run to evil (Proverbs 6:18)
50. The Lord who hates a false witness who breathes out lies (Proverbs 6:19)
51. The Lord who hates one who sows discord among brothers (Proverbs 6:19)
52. The God whose utterances are in righteousness (Proverbs 8:8)
53. The Lord who delights in pure words (Proverbs 15:26)
54. The One with a holy Name (Psalm 30:4)
55. My Refiner Fire, who purifies me like gold and silver (Malachi 3:3; Zechariah 13:9)
56. The one who is called "Sacred Way" (Isaiah 35:8)
57. The God who cannot lie and never will (Titus 1:2; Numbers 23:19; Hebrews 6:18)
58. The One who requires me to walk before You blameless (Genesis 17:1)

59. The God who owns my eyes (Psalm 101:3)
60. The Holy Sacrifice that makes me holy in Your truth (John 17:19)
61. The Lord who is "Holy, holy, holy, Lord of heaven's armies" (Isaiah 6:3)
62. The God who sanctifies the ground, making it holy (Exodus 3:5)
63. The God with a holy Presence (Exodus 3:5)
64. You are the Cloud over Your people Israel (Numbers 9:15–16)
65. The Pillar of Fire over Your people Israel (Numbers 9:15–16)
66. The God who filled the tabernacle with Your holy glory (Exodus 40:35)
67. The One between the two gold cherubs over the ark of the covenant (Exodus 25:22)
68. The Lord who dwells in Your holy temple (Psalm 138:2)
69. The One I bow to, for You are holy (Psalm 99:5)
70. The God of beautiful, sacred clothing (Exodus 39:1–43)
71. The God whose dwelling is holy (Psalm 68:5)
72. The Holiness of Your temple (Psalm 65:3)
73. The Goodness of Your house (Psalm 65:4)
74. The God with an utterly incorruptible and holy nature (Isaiah 6:3; Psalm 99:9)
75. The God of the Most Holy Place (Hebrews 9:8)
76. The God who counts the times we murmur or complain (Numbers 14:22)
77. The God whose ways are holy (Psalm 77:13)
78. The Lord who grants the desires of those who fear You in reverence (Psalm 145:19a)
79. The One who creates a clean heart in me (Psalm 51:10)
80. The One who renews a loyal spirit in me (Psalm 51:10)

A PRAYER DECLARING HIS HOLINESS

Father God, I come before Your holy throne in Jesus' Name and through Your Holy Spirit. I bring You holy worship on this day, for You are pure and You have an utterly incorruptible and holy nature. You are worthy to be praised and adored. You are *Elohim Kedoshim*—the Almighty Holy One. Your Name is holy. Your Presence is holy, and wherever You manifest, the place becomes holy ground.

You are the God of the holy prophets. You are the Holy One who anoints me to be part of Your royal priesthood. You are the Holy of Holies. Lord, You are the holy Fiery Cloud and Pillar of Fire over Your people Israel. The same Holy Cloud and Pillar of Fire over my life. You are the God who filled the tabernacle of Moses with Your holy glory. You are the One between the two golden cherubs over the ark of the covenant. Lord, You dwell in Your holy temple and fill my earthly body with Your glorious Presence. Jesus, You are the Holy One of God, the Holy One of Israel, the Most Holy God.

Lord, You are the holy God enthroned in the midst of Your people's praises. You are *Ruach Hakodesh*—God the Holy Spirit. You are the God of holiness. You are the God of the sacred altar; the God of reverence and respect. You are glorious in holiness, awesome in splendor. You are the God who is to be feared, I tremble in Your Presence.

Jesus, You are the Lamb that was slain without blemish, the sinless and spotless Lamb of God. Lord, You are the incorruptible God. You are the God of the pure in heart.

You are the Lord who sanctifies me, anoints my head with oil, and makes my cup overflow with blessings. You are the God who commands me to "be holy, for You are holy." Therefore, I must walk in holiness every day of my life. You are the Lord who detests the proud, but You favor the humble with grace. Holy Spirit You sanctify me and make me holy in Your Word of truth. Your eyes are upon the faithful so they may dwell with You. You choose only those who are above reproach to serve You.

You are a God of truth, without iniquity; no evil is found in You, Lord. You cannot lie and will never lie. You are the Rock of my life; Your work is perfect, and Your ways are just. You are the Holy One, the God of faithfulness. You are Just, Fair, Upright, and You never Do me Wrong.

You are the God whose utterances are in righteousness; there is nothing crooked or perverted in You. You are the God who delights in pure words, but You hate abomination and haughty eyes. You hate a lying tongue and hands that shed innocent blood. You hate a heart that devises wicked plans and the feet that make haste to run to evil. You hate a false witness who breathes out lies and sows discord among brothers. Lord, guard my heart so I may never practice these sins.

Lord, You own my eyes, for I have decided to refuse to look at anything vile and vulgar. You are the God of my heart, and I will not allow perversity in my heart, nor will I have anything to do with wickedness. You are my Purifier, purifying and refining me like gold and silver. You are the Way of Holiness, in which I must walk and be perfect. Sanctify me and purify me from all my sins. Wash me so I may be whiter than snow and be blameless before You. O God, create in me a clean heart; give me a loyal spirit.

Thank You, Lord, for You are the Holy Sacrifice that makes me holy in Your truth. You are the Lord who is "Holy, holy, holy, Lord of heaven's armies, the whole earth is filled with Your glory!" I worship You with holy devotion for eternity! Amen and amen!

HIS WORD AND COMMANDMENTS

The grass withers and the flowers fade, but the word of our God stands forever.

Isaiah 40:8

When we obey God, we are sure that we know him. But if we claim to know him and don't obey him, we are lying, and the truth isn't in our hearts. We truly love God only when we obey him as we should, and then we know that we belong to him.

1 John 2:3–5 CEV

You are:

1. The Lord whose Word is flawless (2 Samuel 22:31)
2. The Lord whose word burns like fire (Jeremiah 23:29)
3. The Lord whose Word is like a mighty hammer that smashes a rock to pieces (Jeremiah 23:29)

4. The God whose words are always true and correct (Psalm 119:160)
5. The Lord whose Word is truth (John 17:17)
6. The Truth that sets me free (John 8:32)
7. The God who will not hold the guilty innocent (Numbers 14:18)
8. The God whose precepts are right and makes my heart rejoice (Psalm 19:8)
9. The One who makes unbreakable covenants and pacts with humans (Genesis 17:7)
10. The God of ordinance (Psalm 81:4)
11. The God of the law (Psalm 119:138; Matthew 5:17–18)
12. The God of statutes, and I must walk in them (1 King 2:3)
13. The God who made an eternal decree on the sand as a boundary for the sea (Jeremiah 5:22)
14. The Lord, the Sword (Deuteronomy 33:29)
15. The Lord who tests me to see if I walk in Your law or not (Exodus 16:4)
16. The Lord whose Word is sweeter than honey (Psalm 119:103)
17. The God who puts Your laws in my mind and heart (Hebrews 8:10)
18. The One who wrote Your laws in my heart (Jeremiah 31:31–34)
19. The God who fulfills Your words (Joshua 21:45; Lamentations 2:17)
20. The God whose holy commandments bring freedom (Psalm 119:45)
21. The Lord Your commandment is pure and illuminates my eyes (Psalm 19:8)
22. The Lord whose commandments are right and bring joy to my heart (Psalm 19:8)
23. The Lord whose commands are clear and give me insight for living (Psalm 19:8)
24. The God of the Ten Commandments (Exodus 20; John 14:15–16)
25. The God who commands me not to depend on my own understanding (Proverbs 3:5)
26. The God of commandments to be kept (Leviticus 22:31; Deuteronomy 11:1; 1 Corinthians 7:19)

27. The Lord whose decrees are trustworthy and make the simple to be wise (Psalm 19:7)
28. The God of the Tree of Life (Genesis 2:9; Genesis 3:22–24; Revelation 22:2)
29. Christ, the Word who is with God, and You are God Yourself (John 1:1)
30. The Word that gave life to everything that was created (John 1:4)
31. The Lord, Your title is the *Word of God* (Revelation 19:13)
32. The One whose word is a seed in me (Luke 8:11)
33. The One whose word endures forever (1 Peter 1:25)
34. The One who injects me with faith through Your Word (Romans 10:17)
35. The One whose word is upright (Psalm 33:4)
36. Jesus, the Word of Life (John 1:4; 1 John 1:1; Philippians 2:16)
37. The Faithful One and Promise Keeper (Psalm 71:22; Deuteronomy 7:9; 1 Corinthians 1:9)
38. The One who is merciful to thousands of generations (Deuteronomy 7:9)
39. The God who opens my eyes to see the wonders of Your instructions (Psalm 119:18)
40. The Power behind my faith (Romans 10:17)
41. The God who swears by Your own Name and makes decrees of blessing (Genesis 22:16-18)
42. The God of just decrees (Psalm 33:4)
43. The God who does everything fair (Psalm 33:4)
44. The Lord who decrees Your loyal love over my life (Psalm 42:8)
45. The Lord who decrees You loyal love and gives me a new song each night (Psalm 42:8)
46. The Word I dwell in (Colossians 3:16)
47. You are my psalm, my hymn, and my song from the Spirit (Colossians 3:16; Isaiah 12:2)
48. The One whose spoken words are spirit and life (John 6:60–65)
49. You are the Bread of Life and my Daily Bread (John 6:35; Matthew 6:11)
50. You are my spiritual Food (1 Corinthians 10:3)
51. You are my Manna (Revelation 2:17; John 6:48–51)

52. You are the Word that purifies me as I obey You (Psalm 119:9)
53. The LORD with a flawless Word (Psalm 18:30)
54. The Lord whose instructions and laws are perfect (Psalm 19:7)
55. The Lord who revives my soul (Psalm 19:7; 119:154)
56. The LORD with true, fair, and altogether righteous rules and laws (Psalm 19:9)
57. The One who makes the simple wise (Psalm 19:7)
58. The Finger that writes on walls and stones (Deuteronomy 9:10; Daniel 5:5, 24–28)

A PRAYER DECLARING HIS WORD

My beloved Father, Mighty One, perfect in everything, I come before You in Jesus' Name and through the help of Your Holy Spirit. Lord, thank You for Your marvelous Word of Life. You are the Tree of Life from where all pure and true wisdom comes. You are the God of the Ten Commandments who commands me not to depend on my own understanding. God, Your commandments illuminate my eyes to see what is right before You. Your holy commandments bring freedom to my life.

Thank You because You open my eyes to see the wonderful truths in Your instructions. Your Word is sweeter than honey.

Your Word is flawless and perfect. God, all Your words are true and correct. Father, You are the God of ordinances, the law, and the statutes; help me walk in them. Your Word is the Sword of the Spirit. You test me to see if I walk in Your law or not. You are a God of just decrees. Lord, Your Word is the absolute truth that sets me free from bondage, darkness, and even myself.

Lord, I know You are slow to anger and filled with unfailing love towards me. You are the God who will not hold the guilty innocent because there are consequences for our sins. But, Jesus, I know Your magnificent, unfailing love covers and forgives us of our sins if we repent wholeheartedly. You are the Word that purifies me as I obey You willingly. Lord, Your precepts are right, and they make my soul rejoice. You put Your laws in my mind and write them in my heart.

You are the Power behind my faith; when I listen to Your Word, my faith revives, and I can see what You want to reveal to me. Your Word makes me grow spiritually; Your Word is Your love letter to me.

Father, You are the God who swears by Your own Name and makes decrees of blessing over me. You decree You loyal love over me and gives me a new song each night. You sing over me when I am asleep. You are my psalm, my hymn, and my song from the Spirit.

You are the Word I dwell in every day of my life. Your spoken words are spirit and life. You are the Bread of Life and my Daily Bread. You are my spiritual Food and my heavenly Manna.

Padre, You make unbreakable covenants and pacts with humans because You are so faithful to Your word. You always fulfill Your words because You are the Faithful One and Promise Keeper. I know Your promises over my life are trustworthy and true, and they will be fulfilled in Your time.

Lord, Your instructions are perfect to revive my soul; Your decrees are trustworthy and make wise the simple. Your commandments are right and bring joy to my heart. Lord, Your commands are clear and will give me insight into living.

You are Christ, You are the Word, You are with God, and You are God Yourself. You are the Word that gave life to everything that was created. Lord, Your title is the *Word of God*.

Lord, Your Word is a seed that will give me a bountiful harvest. I know Your Word endures forever. Your Word is upright. Lord, You inject me with faith through Your Word. You command me to dwell in Your Word and to use it as a sword to fight against our enemy. You instruct me to obey it and to meditate on it day and night. Your Word is what makes me intelligent and fills me with wisdom.

Your Word is a lamp unto my feet. Your Word makes me glad. Your Word is my daily bread. Thank You, Lord, for Your Word is the blueprint of my future in You. In Jesus' Name, amen.

29

HIS GLORIOUS CHARACTER

Though he was God, he did not think of equality with God as something to cling to. Instead, he gave up his divine privileges; he took the humble position of a slave and was born as a human being. When he appeared in human form, he humbled himself in obedience to God and died a criminal's death on a cross.

Philippians 2:6–8

When he saw the crowds, he had compassion for them because they were harassed and helpless, like sheep without a shepherd.

Matthew 9:36 ESV

You are:

1. The God of meekness, patient and humble of heart (Colossians 3:12; Ephesians 4:2)
2. The God of invisible attributes and qualities (Romans 1:18–21)

3. The God of divine nature (Romans 1:18–21)
4. The God who never fails me (Hebrews 13:5)
5. The God whose will is good, pleasing, and perfect (Romans 12:2)
6. God, the absolute Truth (John 14:6; 8:32; 2 Corinthians 13:8)
7. God, the Righteous (Psalm 119:137)
8. God, the eternal, immortal, invisible One (1 Timothy 1:17)
9. The God who is the same with me every day (Malachi 3:6)
10. The God who is Spirit (John 4:24)
11. The God who examines both the righteous and the wicked (Psalm 11:4)
12. The God who hates those who love violence (Psalm 11:4)
13. The God with eyes like a flame of fire and feet like polished bronze (Revelation 1:14–15; 2:18; 19:12)
14. The Lord my God, a consuming fire (Deuteronomy 4:24; Isaiah 33:14)
15. The Lord my God; Your Name is Jealous (Exodus 34:14; Deuteronomy 5:9)
16. The Lord whose voice raises flames of fire (Psalm 29)
17. The God of relationship (John 1:18; Romans 5:11)
18. The God who endured opposition from sinners (Hebrews 12:3)
19. The God of humility (Luke 22:26; Matthew 20:28)
20. The Lord, the Wonderful Counselor (Isaiah 9:6)
21. The Lord, a mighty God (Isaiah 9:6)
22. The Everlasting Father (Isaiah 9:6)
23. The Great Prince of Peace (Isaiah 9:6)
24. God, the Blesser of all generations from the beginning (Deuteronomy 28; Numbers 6:24–25)
25. The God of grace and peace (Nehemiah 9:31; Judges 6:24)
26. God, the Lord of gentleness (Psalm 18:35)
27. God, the Intimate One (James 4:8; Isaiah 55:6)
28. The God of the inexpressible and glorious joy (1 Peter 1:8; Romans 14:17)
29. God, the One who never makes a mistake (Genesis 18)
30. The God who is the same today, yesterday, and forever (Hebrews 13:8)
31. *El Kanna*—Lord, a jealous God (Exodus 20:5; Deuteronomy 5:9)

32. The One who is always the same and lives forever (Hebrews 1:12)
33. The Lord whose love remains the same forever! (John 15:9; Psalm 136; Lamentations 5:19)
34. The God of big and small details (Exodus 25:9; Exodus 26:1)
35. A kind God (Titus 3:4–7)
36. The God who laughs at the wicked (Psalm 37:12–13)
37. The God of eternal power (Romans 1:18:20)
38. The God who never changes or casts a shifting shadow (James 1:17; Numbers 23:19; Malachi 3:6)
39. *Yahweh-Shalom*—Lord, You are peace (Judges 6:24)
40. You are the very definition of the fruit of the Spirit (Galatians 5:22–23)
41. The Lord, a good God (Psalm 34:8)
42. The God of love (1 John 4:7–21; Galatians 5:22–23)
43. The God of joy (Galatians 5:22–23)
44. The God of peace (Galatians 5:22–23)
45. The God of patience and longsuffering (Galatians 5:22–23; Exodus 34:6; Numbers 14:18; Psalm 86:15)
46. The God of kindness (Galatians 5:22–23)
47. The God of goodness (Galatians 5:22–23)
48. The God of faithfulness (Galatians 5:22–23)
49. The God of gentleness (Galatians 5:22–23)
50. The God of self-control (Galatians 5:22–23)
51. A Friend of those who fear You (Psalm 25:14)
52. The Grace that made me right in Your sight (Titus 3:7)
53. The One who did not think of equality with God as something to cling to (Philippians 2:6)
54. The One who gave up Your divine privileges (Philippians 2:7)
55. The One who took the humble position of a slave (Philippians 2:7)
56. The One who was born as a human being by the Father's will (Philippians 2:7)
57. The One who humbled Yourself in obedience to God (Philippians 2:8)
58. Jesus, the faithful Servant (Mark 10:45)
59. Jesus, humble and gentle at heart (Matthew 11:29)
60. The Lord, a holy God (Revelation 4:8; Isaiah 6:3)

61. The Perfect One (Matthew 5:48)
62. The God of time and eternity (Ecclesiastes 3:11)
63. The Immutable God who never changes (Hebrews 6:17; Malachi 3:6; 1 Peter 1:25)

A PRAYER DECLARING HIS GLORIOUS CHARACTER

Father, in Jesus' Name, I come before You and through the help of Your Holy Spirit. I come with a hungry heart to discover more about You. It is a delight to know you deeper and learn from your glorious character. The more I get to know you the deeper my worship grows. You are the God who is Spirit and must be worshiped in spirit and truth. Your character traits are so inspiringly beautiful. The more I know you the more I love you. You are the God of humility; You are patient and kind. You are the God of invisible attributes and qualities, the God of divine glorious nature. The God of eternal power.

You are the God with eyes like a flame of fire and feet like polished bronze.

Lord my God, You are a consuming fire. Lord, Your voice raises flames of fire. Your Name is Jealous. You are *El Kanna*—Lord, a jealous God.

You are the God who never lets me down. You never make a mistake, God.

Lord, Your will is good, pleasing, and perfect. You are the Immutable God who never changes. Every day, You are the same with me, You never stop loving me. You are a relational God. Lord, You are the all-powerful Blesser of all generations from the beginning. You are my Blesser, my Benefactor. You are the Intimate One, Lord. You are the God of both big and small details. You are a gracious God. You are the epitome of the fruit of the Spirit. You are patient, loving, joyful, kind, good, gentle, faithful, self-controlled, and meek.

Lord God, You are the absolute Truth.

God, You are righteous. You are the eternal, immortal, invisible One. You are the God of humility. God, the Wonderful Counselor, Mighty God, Everlasting Father, Great Prince of Peace. The God of grace. God, You are gentleness. The God of the inexpressible and glorious joy. The Perfect One. You are the God of time and eternity who controls the course of all world events.

You are the God who examines both the righteous and the wicked. You hate those who love violence. You are the God who endured opposition from sinners. The God who laughs at the wicked.

You are the same today, yesterday and forever and you live for eternity.

The One who is always the same and lives forever. Your love remains the same forever. The God who never changes or casts a shifting shadow. *Yahweh-Shalom*—Lord, You are peace, my eternal peace. Thank you for Your goodness oh Lord. You are such a good God for ever!

In Jesus Name, Amen and Amen!

30

HIS WORTHINESS, GLORY, AND MAJESTIC PRESENCE

My prayer is that as you continue to grow in your understanding of who God is and as you experience encounters with the Almighty I AM, your heart will be increasingly filled and ignited with a deep devotion and worship toward Him.

Let us now pause for a moment to express our sincere declaration of worship, lifting our hands high in honor and reverence to the magnificent God we serve.

DECLARATION OF WORSHIP

Lord, You reign as the Sovereign King over all the earth. Your Name alone deserves to be exalted and worshiped, for You alone are God and Lord. From the break of dawn to the setting of the sun, I will raise my voice in joyful praise of Your mighty Name, O Lord. With reverence, I bow before You, recognizing Your worthiness of all honor. The heavenly beings themselves honor You, Lord, for Your unparalleled glory and matchless strength. They honor You, O Lord, for the splendor of Your Name, which surpasses my understanding.

In the splendor of Your holiness, I offer my worship, O Lord. The heavens rejoice, and the earth is filled with gladness because of Your presence! The vastness of the sea and all its creatures join in proclaiming Your praise. The fields and their bountiful crops burst forth with joy! The trees of the forest sing harmoniously before You, O Lord.

O Lord, the righteous Judge of all the earth, Your arrival is imminent. You will judge the world with perfect justice and truth, according to Your divine wisdom. *Yeshua,* Your testimony embodies the very essence of prophetic revelation.

I will forever extol Your Name, for You possess infinite wisdom and eternal power. All glory, honor, worship, and praise belong to You alone, perpetually and without end! Amen.

(See Zechariah 14:9; Revelation 19:9; Judges 13:17–18; Psalm 29:1–2; Psalm 96:11–13; Psalm 113:3; Daniel 2:20).

FEATURED SCRIPTURES TO PONDER

Great is the LORD, *and greatly to be praised, and his greatness is unsearchable.*

Psalm 145:3 ESV

Sing praise to the LORD, *You His godly ones, and give thanks to His holy Name.*

Psalm 30:4 NASB1995

You are:

1. The Lord with a glorious Name (1 Chronicles 29:11–13)
2. The Lord whose glorious Name is worthy to be praised forever (Psalm 72:19–20)
3. The Lord whose heavens proclaim Your glory (Psalm 19:1)
4. The Lord whose voice is powerful and full of majesty (Psalm 29:4)
5. The Lord and King of glory (Psalm 24:8; 29:3; Ephesians 1:17; 1 Peter 4:14; James 2:1)
6. God; Yours is the Kingdom, the greatness, the power, the glory, the victory and the majesty (1 Chronicles 29:11; Psalm 62:11)
7. The One who owns all dominion, and authority before all time, now and forever (Jude 25; 1 Chronicles 29:11)

8. The One who is worthy to receive glory, honor, and power (Revelation 4:11)
9. The King of heaven who is worthy to be praised, glorified, and honored (Daniel 4:37)
10. The God with the crown of glory (Isaiah 62:3)
11. God, the Glory in the midst of city (Zechariah 2:5)
12. The God who keeps me from falling away (Jude 24)
13. The God who will bring me faultless with great joy into Your glorious Presence (Jude 24)
14. The God who called me by Your own glory and goodness (2 Peter 1:3)
15. God, the fullness of greatness, power, glory, victory, and majesty (1 Chronicles 29:11)
16. Jesus, who is worthy to receive power, wealth, wisdom, might, honor, glory, and blessing (Revelation 5:12)
17. Christ, the Hope of Glory (Colossians 1:27)
18. God, the Rock of my strength and my glory (Psalm 62:7)
19. The God who calls me to Your kingdom and glory (1 Thessalonians 2:12)
20. The God who made the light shine in my heart so I could know the glory of God (2 Corinthians 4:6)
21. God, the Mighty Shield around me, my Glory (Psalm 3:3)
22. Jesus, the brightness of God's glory (Hebrews 1:3)
23. Jesus, crowned with glory and honor (Hebrews 2:9)
24. Jesus, the radiance of God's glory (Hebrews 1:3)
25. The Lord whose glory fills the skies (Psalm 19:1; 108:5)
26. The Lord who will give me a crown of never-ending glory and honor (1 Peter 5:4)
27. The God of glory thunders (Psalm 29:3)
28. The God of lightning and thunders (Revelation 16:18)
29. God, the glory of Your people (Luke 2:32)
30. The God who makes me Your crown of glory (Isaiah 62:3)
31. The God of marvelous glory and excellence (2 Peter 1:3)
32. The One who deserves honor and glory to Your Name eternally (1 Timothy 1:17)

33. The One who fills the whole earth with Your glory (Psalm 72:19–20)
34. The Lord whose glory is higher than the heavens (Psalm 8:1)
35. The Lord whose glory will shine over all the earth (Psalm 108:3–5)
36. The God who created me for Your glory (Isaiah 43:7)
37. The God of my praise (Psalm 109:1, 30)
38. The God who thunders over the mighty sea (Psalm 29:3)
39. The Lord whose voice thunders like the mighty ocean (Revelation 4:5; Job 40:9)
40. The God of honor and reverence (1 Samuel 2:30; Exodus 3:5)
41. The God surrounded by light (Daniel 2:22)
42. God, the Spirit of worship (John 4:23–24; Psalm 99)
43. God, the Incomparable (Colossians 1:13–20; Isaiah 46:5–9)
44. God, You are my beauty, shine, and splendor (Psalm 50:2)
45. The Lord whose strength and beauty fill Your sanctuary (Psalm 96:6)
46. God, the Origin and Epitome of beauty (Psalm 50:2; Ezekiel 27:3)
47. The God who shines in glorious radiance (Psalm 50:2)
48. The definition and embodiment of beautiful perfection (Psalm 50:2; Psalm 27:4)
49. The God whose splendor covers the heavens; the earth is full of Your praise (Habakkuk 3:3)
50. God, worthy of being greatly adored (Psalm 96:4)
51. God, my supreme Worship (Romans 12:1–2; Deuteronomy 10:17)
52. The God who builds Yourself a lofty palace in the heavens (Amos 9:6)
53. The God who sits in the heavens and upon the circle of the earth (Isaiah 40:22)
54. God, the Majesty in the heavens (Psalm 29:4; 93:1)
55. God, the magnified One (Philippians 1:10; Daniel 11:37)
56. God, *Adonai*—the Lord, my great Lord (Psalm 18:1–3)
57. God, the Master and majestic Lord (Psalm 8; Isaiah 40:3–5; Ezekiel 16:8; Habakkuk 3:19)
58. The God of all flesh (Jeremiah 32:27)

59. The Lord, worthy of supreme worship and praise (Psalm 96:4; Revelation 4:11)
60. The God who is Spirit; I worship You in spirit and truth (John 4:23–24)
61. The God of perfection and completion (Matthew 5:48)
62. Christ Jesus, my Lord (1 Timothy 1:12)
63. Jesus, the Light, the luminous, glowing, and radiant One (Psalm 76:4)
64. My *Hosanna* in the Highest (Matthew 21:9)
65. The Lord my God, and there is no other like You (Joel 2:27)
66. The Lord with the seven eyes that are the seven Spirits of God (Revelation 3:1; 1:4; 4:5; 5:6)
67. The One who is, who always was, and who is still to come (Revelation 1:4)
68. The God who is enthroned from ages past (Psalm 90:2; 93:2)
69. The God who is enthroned on my praises (Psalm 22:3)
70. The God who is sitting upon the great majestic throne (Revelation 5:13)
71. The mighty God of Jacob (Psalm 132:2)
72. Jesus, the One exalted above all (Psalm 97:9)
73. God, the Lord of majesty on high (Psalm 93:4)
74. God, my hope in the day of evil (Jeremiah 17:17)
75. God, my Portion forever (Lamentations 3:24)
76. God, my Portion in the land of the living (Psalm 142:5)
77. God, my Rock of Refuge to whom I will continually go (Psalm 71:3)
78. God, the Rock of Ages (1 Corinthians 10:4)
79. My Father, the Potter; I am formed by Your hand (Isaiah 64:8)
80. God, the Portion of Jacob (Jeremiah 10:16)
81. God, the Possessor of heaven and earth (Genesis 14:19)
82. God, the Rivers of Water in a dry place (Isaiah 32:2)
83. God, my *Shiloh*, my Peaceful Place (Jeremiah 41:5; Joshua 18:1; Genesis 49:10)
84. God, the Sword of excellency and majesty (Deuteronomy 33:29)
85. Jesus, the Amen (Psalm 41:13; Romans 11:36)
86. Lord, the Living God (Hebrews 10:31)

87. God, the Most High, Great and Mighty One (Psalm 145:3–7)

88. God, the Pearl of Great Price (Matthew 13:46)

89. God, my Mantle of Praise (Isaiah 61:3)

90. God, the Beautiful One (Isaiah 33:17; 28:5)

91. God, my Beautiful Crown, and a Glorious Diadem (Isaiah 28:5)

92. The Lord whose Presence is the home of my spirit (Acts 17:28)

93. The God whose Presence fills me with joy (Acts 2:28)

94. The God who turned my weeping into a joyful dance (Psalm 30:11)

95. The God who clothed me with gladness (Psalm 30:11)

96. The Lord who is Worthy of all my dance (Psalm 149:3; 150:4)

97. God, the reason for my *Yadah*, יָדָה (*yāḏā(h)*)[1]; I praise You aloud! (2 Samuel 22:50)

98. God, my *Towdah*, תּוֹדָה (*tôḏā(h)*)[2]; I give thanks to You, my Lord (Leviticus 7:12)

99. God, my *Halal*, הָלַל (*halal*)[3]; my highest praise and hallelujah (Psalm 146:1; 2 Chronicles 20:19)

100. God, my *Barak*, בָּרַךְ (*bārăḵ*)[4]; I kneel before You with reverence (Ephesians 3:14; Judges 5:2)

101. God, my *Tehillah*, תְּהִלָּה (*tăhᵒlā(h)*)[5]; my spontaneous new song (2 Chronicles 20:22; Psalm 33:3; 40:3; Ephesians 5:19–20)

102. God, my *Shabach*, שָׁבַח (*šāḇăḥ*)[6]; the loud praise of my heart (Psalm 63:3; 117:1)

103. God, my *Zamar*, זָמַר (*zāmăr*)[7] the singing and praise of my soul (Psalm 21:13; 144:9)

104. God, Your Name is a strong tower (Proverbs 18:10)

105. The God worthy of eternal worship (Revelation 5:1–14; 19:1–8)

106. The Lord God of Hosts (Amos 4:13; Isaiah 5:16; Jeremiah 31:23)

107. God, my prophetic Mantle (2 Kings 2:13–14)

108. The magnificent God who can never be praised enough (Psalm 145:3–12; Deuteronomy 4:34; Psalm 48:2)

109. The God with no boundaries to Your greatness (Psalm 145:3–12)

110. The One who deserves reverence and respect (Leviticus 26:2; Psalm 119:15)

111. Jesus, the One who will come with the clouds of heaven (Revelation 1:7; Daniel 7:13)

112. The God who exalts Yourself as Head over all (1 Chronicles 29:11)
113. The God of the psalmists and Levites (Exodus 28:1)
114. God, my Delight (Psalm 37:4)
115. The One with a majestic Name (Micah 5:4; Psalm 8:1)
116. The Lord whose majestic Name fills the earth (Psalm 8:1)
117. The God with majestic power (Isaiah 63:12 NET)
118. The God who dwells on high (Isaiah 57:15; 33:5; Psalm 91)
119. The Lord in whose Presence there is peace (Psalm 29:11)
120. Way more than we know of You (John 21:25)
121. The God who fills my mouth with praise (Psalm 71:8)
122. The God of my heart (Psalm 73:26)
123. The God of my hands (Nehemiah 6:9)
124. God, my Eternal Hope (Titus 3:7)
125. God, my Confidence (Philippians 1:6)
126. God, my Divine Health and Well-being (John 5:11; Luke 11:28)
127. The God of my life (Psalm 146:2; 27:1)
128. The Most High God (Hebrews 7:1; Psalm 87:5)
129. The God who deserves to be praised for Your great love (Psalm 107:8)
130. The Lord worthy of praise among the nations (Psalm 108:3)
131. The God whose unfailing love is infinite and profound (Psalm 108:3)
132. The Lord whose faithfulness reaches to the clouds (Psalm 108:4)
133. The Lord exalted above the highest heavens (Psalm 108:5)
134. The God in our midst when we gather in Your Name (Matthew 18:20)
135. The God who is enthroned in heaven (Psalm 123:1)
136. A great and awesome God (Daniel 9:4)
137. The Lord who I praise with all that I am (Psalm 103:1)
138. The One with a magnificent reputation (Isaiah 63:14)
139. The Lord who established Your throne in the heavens (Psalm 103.19)
140. The Lord who owns greatness (1 Chronicles 29:11)
141. The Lord who owns the power (1 Chronicles 29:11 Psalm 62:11; Proverbs 8:14)

142. The Lord who owns the victory (1 Chronicles 29:11)
143. The Lord who owns the majesty (1 Chronicles 29:11)
144. The Lord who owns the riches (1 Chronicles 29:12)
145. The Lord whose majestic Name fills the earth (Psalm 8:1)
146. The Lord who is worthy of praise (Psalm 18:3)
147. The One who is my pleasure forever (Psalm 16:11)
148. God, the Presence that brings me fullness of joy (Psalm 16:11)
149. The Lord; there is none like You (Jeremiah 10:6)
150. The Lord; You are great (Jeremiah 10:6)
151. The Lord; great is Your Name in might (Jeremiah 10:6)
152. The God who reigns eternally (Psalm 93:1)
153. The Lord robed in majesty (Psalm 93:1)
154. The One who established the world (Psalm 93:1)
155. The Lord whose strength is Your belt (Psalm 93:1)
156. The Name that is to be praised forever and ever (Daniel 2:20–22)
157. Jesus, whose Name is wonderful (Judges 13:17–18)
158. The One who taught children and infants to give You praise (Matthew 21:16)
159. The One who deserves to be praised (Psalm 30:4)
160. The Lord, the King of all time (1 Timothy 1:17)
161. The Lord, the Wonderful Counselor (Isaiah 9:6)
162. The Lord, Almighty God (Isaiah 9:6)
163. The Everlasting Father (Isaiah 9:6)
164. The great Prince of Peace (Isaiah 9:6)
165. The God of the Psalms (Psalm 1–150)
166. The God who is worthy of my shouts of joy with psalms (Psalm 95:2)
167. The burning Flame of Fire that shines with glorious splendor and radiance (Ezekiel 1:27)
168. The Lord, glorious and strong (Psalm 96:7)
169. The Lord, filled with holy splendor (Psalm 96:9)
170. The Lord who reigns (Psalm 96:10)
171. The Lord King (Psalm 97:1)
172. The Lord who is supreme over all the earth (Psalm 97:9)
173. The Lord who is exalted far above all gods (Psalm 97:9)
174. The Lord with a holy Name (Psalm 97:12)

175. *EL*, the strong One! (Mark 15:34; Exodus 15:2; Deuteronomy 7:9; Numbers 23:22)

176. The Lord whose throne continues from generation to generation (Lamentations 5:19)

177. The One who rides the clouds (Psalm 68:4)

178. The Name I sing loud praises to (Psalm 68:4)

179. The God with glorious, unlimited resources (Ephesians 3:16)

180. The God who empowers me with inner strength through Your Spirit (Ephesians 3:16)

181. The One who makes me complete with all the fullness of life and power that comes from You (Ephesians 3:19)

182. The One who is able, through Your mighty power at work within me, to accomplish infinitely more than I might ask or think (Ephesians 3:20)

183. The One who deserves the glory through all generations forever and ever, amen (Ephesians 3:21)

184. The One who speaks to us from heaven (Hebrews 12:25)

185. The One I must be thankful to in all circumstances (1 Thessalonians 5:18; Hebrews 12:28)

186. The One I must please by worshiping You with holy fear and awe (Hebrews 12:28)

187. The holy Name my soul must bless and minister unto (Psalm 103:1–4)

188. The One I must praise with my whole heart (Psalm 103:1–4)

189. The Fountain of my eternal youth (Psalm 103:5; Titus 3:5)

190. The One who redeems my life from the pit (Psalm 103:1–4)

191. The God of the seven feasts and celebrations (Zephaniah 3:17; Leviticus 23)

192. The God of the feasts (Deuteronomy 16:15; Nehemiah 10:33)

193. *El Elohe Yisrael*—God, the God of Israel (Genesis 33:20; Exodus 5:1; Psalm 68:8; 106:48)

194. God, *Jehovah-Sabaoth*—the Lord of Hosts the Holy One (Isaiah 47:4; 2 Samuel 5:10; Psalm 80:4, 7)

195. The Lord who is glorious, so majestic! (Psalm 45:3)

196. God, the true God (Jeremiah 10:10)

197. Lord, the living God (Jeremiah 10:10)

198. The God with a holy and awesome Name (Psalm 111:9)
199. The One who is enthroned above the cherubim (Isaiah 37:16; Genesis 14:18–23)
200. The God who filled the tabernacle with Your holy glory (Exodus 40:35)
201. The God with a great and awesome Name (Psalm 99:3)
202. The God who is great, O Lord (Psalm 96:4)
203. The Most Worthy of praise (Psalm 96:4)
204. The Lord to be feared above all gods. (Psalm 96:4)
205. The God who is surrounded by honor and majesty (Psalm 96:6)
206. The God whose strength and beauty fill Your sanctuary (Psalm 96:6)
207. The Lord who is recognized by all nations (Psalm 96:7)
208. The God with a holy Name (Psalm 99:3)
209. The Lord who is my strength and my song (Exodus 15:2)
210. The Lord, my inheritance (Lamentations 3:24)
211. The Name that is too wonderful for me to fully understand (Judges 13:17–18)
212. The Lord, my mighty and awesome God (Deuteronomy 10:17)
213. The LORD who is highly exalted; You dwell on high (Isaiah 33:5)
214. The One who will fill Zion with justice and righteousness (Isaiah 33:5)
215. The Stability of my times, my Abundance of salvation, wisdom, and knowledge (Isaiah 33:6)
216. The One who is Zion's treasure (Isaiah 33:6)
217. The One sitting on the throne, who is brilliant as gemstones like jasper and carnelian (Revelation 4:3)
218. My new song (Psalm 144:9)
219. The God who is dressed in a robe of light (Psalm 104:2)

A PRAYER DECLARING HIS WORTHINESS, GLORY, AND MAJESTIC PRESENCE

Lord, Omnipotent God and Great I Am, I come before You in Jesus' Name, to give You honor and glorify Your mighty Name.

The heavens resound with the proclamation of Your magnificent glory and breathtaking beauty. Your voice resounds with immense power and radiates majestic authority. You are the God of unfading glory, the God of all flesh and possessor of heaven and earth.

You are the Sovereign King of glory, Yours is the kingdom, the power, and the fame. Lord Your Name is a glorious Name, full of power and honor. You are the God with unparalleled and majestic power. You build Your lofty palace in the heavens. You sit in the heavens and upon the circle of the earth.

The heavens proclaim Your glory and shining beauty. Your voice is powerful and full of majesty; You are the God of glory.

Jehovah-Sabaoth—the Lord of Hosts, the Holy One of Israel. You are adorned with unparalleled splendor, grandeur, and awe-inspiring majesty. As the true and living God, Your Name is sacred, exalted, and filled with wonder.

Lord, You are worthy to receive glory, honor, and power, for You own it all and you have supreme dominion over all. You are the very essence of glory within the heart of my city. You are the Spirit of glory, the source of prophecy, and the inspiration behind my worship. You are worthy of the highest adoration and praise. You are the God of honor and reverence. Your throne is established above the cherubim, and Your presence fills the tabernacle with divine holiness and glorious splendor. You are the God of the seven feasts, worthy to be celebrated with great joy.

God, Your sanctuary is filled with your strength and beauty. You are the exalted and majestic One over this place. My God, Adonai—my great Lord God. Lord, I am grateful for how You transformed my sorrow into joyful dancing and clothed me with gladness. My Master and King, You deserve all the holy dances and praise.

Father, You are Spirit, and I worship You in spirit and truth because that is what You seek and find pleasing. You desire my genuine response to You and Your truth.

You are the God who guards and preserves me, ensuring that I do not fall away, and brings me flawlessly into Your glorious presence through the blood of Jesus Christ. Your faithfulness extends to the heavens.

O Lord, all the glory, power, greatness, victory, majesty, and dominion belong to You, both now and forever. You are the epitome of greatness. You are worthy to receive power, wealth, wisdom, might, honor, glory, and blessing.

You are the Rock of my strength. O God, You are the one who illuminated my heart with the light to see You. Jesus, You are the splendor of God, adorned with honor and surrounded by light. You are the God of marvelous glory and eternal excellence. You are the God of glory, whose voice thunders and flashes like the mighty ocean. Your glory encompasses the heavens, and the earth resounds with Your praise. You are unmatched and deserving of great adoration. Jesus Christ, You are my Lord, the radiant light within my heart. Lord God, You are the mighty Shield that surrounds me, my Hope of Glory. You are my eternal Crown of glory.

You are my *Hosanna* in the Highest; You came from heaven to save and deliver me. I praise and bless Your Name. You are my God, and there is no other like You.

Lord, I know You deserve to be honored eternally; help me honor Your Name the way You deserve. Help me walk perfectly before You with the help of Your Holy Spirit. Help me walk in a way that will honor Your Name in everything I say and do. Protect my name and reputation, as my testimony speaks of You and represent Your great Name.

You are the one who is, who always was, and who is still to come; the God with a sevenfold Spirit with seven eyes and seven aspects. The Omnipresent God. You are the God of perfection and completion. You are enthroned from ages past. You are the God who is enthroned on my praises. The God who is sitting upon the great majestic throne. God, You are the Portion of Jacob. The mighty God of Jacob. Jesus, You are the One exalted above all. The Lord of majesty on high.

Most High God, You are my Hope in the day of evil, my Hope of Glory. Lord God, You are the mighty Shield that surrounds me; the One who redeems my life from the pit. You are my Portion forever; my Portion in the land of the living, my strong Habitation to which I may continually come. You are the Fountain of my eternal youth. You are my perfect Companion. The God of my heart. Your Presence is the home of my spirit. Your Presence fills me with joy and makes me dance joyously before You. You are the reason for my *Yadah*, and I praise You reverently. You are my *Towdah*; I give thanks to You, my Lord.

God, Your Name is a strong tower; You are the eternal Rock of ages, my *Shiloh*, my Worship, the Rivers of Water in a dry place, the Light in Darkness, the Sword of excellency and majesty. Jesus, My Amen, the living God, the Most High, great and mighty One, the Pearl of Great Price, my Mantle of Praise, the Beautiful One. You are my Crown and Glorious Diadem. O LORD,

You are my Father. I am the clay, and You are the Potter. I am formed by Your hand.

God, my *Halal*, my highest praise and hallelujah, my *Barak*, I kneel before You with reverence, my *Tehillah*, my spontaneous new song, my *Shabach*, the loud praise of my heart, my *Zamar*, the singing and praise of my soul. The God worthy of eternal worship. The Lord God of Hosts, You are my prophetic Mantle. The magnificent God who can never be praised enough. The God with no boundaries to His greatness. Lord, the One who deserves reverence and respect. Jesus, the One who will come with the clouds of heaven. The head over all.

God, You are the Origin, the Source, the essence, and the epitome of beauty. You embody flawless perfection, and Your majestic Name permeates the entire earth. Lord, Your glory surpasses even the heavens. You are the God of majestic power, dwelling in the highest realms as the Most High God. Your glory extends to every corner of the earth. Your magnificent Name deserves resounding praise. Your love is boundless and profound, never ceasing to amaze. Thank you for your unfailing love. Among the nations, You are worthy of all praise. Your greatness far surpasses our comprehension. You fill my mouth with songs of praise and thanksgiving.

Lord, in Your Presence, there is peace. You are my Eternal Hope, my Confidence, my Delight, my Divine Health and Well-being, and the God of my life. Lord, You are my pleasure forever. You are Lord, worthy of praise. You are my New Song everyday!

You are Lord, exalted above the highest heavens. Your glory will shine over all the earth. You are in our midst when we gather in Your Name. You are enthroned in heaven. You are a great and awesome God. The One I praise with all that I am. You are the One with a magnificent reputation. You established Your throne in the heavens. You are the Lord who owns greatness, power, victory, majesty, and riches.

Lord, Your Presence is fullness of joy. There is none like You. You are great and Your Name is Mighty. You are the God who created me for Your glory. You created me to worship You eternally. The God who reigns eternally in majesty. It was You who established the world. You are the burning Flame of Fire who shines with glorious splendor and radiance over me. You are filled with holy splendor, and You are glorious and strong. You are the Lord King who reigns supremely over all the earth and is exalted far above all gods. You are the King of all time who rides the clouds. Your throne continues from generation to generation. You are the Lord with a holy Name. You are *EL*—the Strong One! Strength is Your belt. Jesus, Your Name is wonderful, the Name that is to be praised forever and ever. You are the One who deserves honor and glory to Your Name eternally.

God, the Wonderful Counselor, Mighty God, Everlasting Father, great Prince of Peace.

The One who taught children and infants to give You praise. You deserve to be praised. You are the God of my praise. The God of the Psalms. The God who is worthy of my shouts of joy with psalms.

The God of the psalmists and Levites. You are my Adoration, my Delight. The Name I sing loud praises to. You are the God with glorious, unlimited resources. You empower me with inner strength through Your Spirit. You make me complete with all the fullness of life and power that comes from You.

Lord, You are able, through Your mighty power at work within me, to accomplish infinitely more than I might ask or think.

You are the One who speaks to us from heaven. The One I must be thankful to in all circumstances. The holy Name my soul must bless and minister unto every day. You are the One I must praise with my whole heart. The One I must please by worshiping You with holy fear and awe. You deserve the glory through all generations forever and ever, amen!

---

1. James Swanson, *Dictionary of Biblical Languages with Semantic Domains : Hebrew (Old Testament)* (Oak Harbor: Logos Research Systems, Inc., 1997).

2. Ibid.

3. Pedro Ortiz V., *Lexico Hebreo–Español Y Arameo–Español* (Miami: Sociedades Bíblicas Unidas, 2000).

4. Swanson, *Dictionary of Biblical Languages with Semantic Domains : Hebrew (Old Testament)*.

5. Ibid.

6. Ibid.

7. Ibid.

PART 3

PRAYING AND DECLARING YOUR IDENTITY IN CHRIST

GOD, WHO AM I TO YOU?

Finding our true identity in Christ is finding our purpose and reason to live.

We have spent a lot of time getting to know who God is to us, and will continue this journey to the end of our lives on earth and into eternity. With all the revelation you've received so far from God,, I am confident that you have caught a glimpse of His love for you and the significance you hold in His eyes. Redirect your attention now towards hearing the voice of God and listening to His message about your true identity.

Your identity is not based on your past or even your present. Your creation was a historical one. Therefore, most of the time, I say to a birthday person, "Happy Historic Day of Your Birth—because it was historic!" Your creation was spectacular! Everything that God creates is remarkable and stunning. You might have thought that your life was an accident, but nothing could be further from the truth. You were carefully planned by God. You are a precious piece of a majestic puzzle. You are a crucial part of a bigger and eternal plan. This plan started the day of your creation and continues into eternity with our divine Counterpart, the Almighty I AM.

The Lord answers your question regarding what *He says about your identity*. Each of the following statements is being said by God about you. This is what He says and believes about you in the different areas of your life. As you start reading the following powerful declarations from God, listen to Papa's voice telling you how much you mean to Him and what He thinks of you.

Perhaps no one has ever said anything pleasant or positive about you or even believed in you, but God has a lot of wonderful things to say about you because He believes in you. He believes in all His creation, He made you in His image and likeness, and you carry His majestic seal of love. Everyone He created was made with a special plan and purpose. Everything He created comes already with certain abilities and anointings for the function for which it was made.

For example, birds were created and anointed to fly. Fish were created and anointed to swim and live inside the waters. Horses were created and anointed to run with strength and even carry heavy loads. Water was created and anointed to sustain and maintain life, and also for cleanliness. Fruitful trees and plants were created to provide fruits, vegetables, and even medicine for humans and animals. You, too, were created with a specific and divine purpose. You were created to worship our God and live in relationship and communion with Him for eternity. You were created for greatness through Christ.

Jesus died and resurrected so that you can have the kind of life intended from the beginning of creation by our heavenly Father (see Isaiah 43:21; Psalm 29:2).

He does not see you the way others see you, and He does not think of you as you think of yourself. The enemy does not want you to know this because it will ruin his evil plans for you. He does not want us to know the truth about our identity.

Declarations of faith and truth are very powerful tools against the enemy of our souls. Speaking out loud biblical declarations renews your mind, declares God's truth over your life, and tells the enemy what you believe. It establishes Abba Papa's truth and life over your present and future destiny. Once you know and understand your true identity through Christ, no devil can stand in your way.

Your mindset will change, and you will have a paradigm shift. Your life will be filled with hope, joy, peace, and love. Your self-esteem will be healed and set free, and you will gain a fresh, healthy perspective about yourself and others. When you go through difficult times, no matter how your faith may tremble, you will be anchored, knowing the truth of God about your identity in

Christ. It is time to discover more of who you truly are through your loving Creator's eyes.

As you read through, I want you to put your name in front of each declaration. For example, "Yolandita, you are blessed. Yolandita, you were fearfully and wonderfully made by My hands. Yolandita, you are healed by My stripes." Declare these truths over your life every day, and watch what God will do in your life.

You can read the chapters in the order they are written or choose the area that best matches you at any given time in your life. You can take a whole chapter and ponder it for a day or even for a week. Make those declarations every morning and every night over your life and your family.

Words have power, but they are even more powerful when they are synchronized with God's Word. It is our spiritual arsenal of weaponry against darkness (see Hebrews 4:12; Ephesians 6:10–18). I dare to say that this practice of declaring the powerful words of God over your life can even bring mental healing and emotional restoration to your life. I know firsthand that this really works. It has worked for me and my family.

31

WHEN I HAVE PHYSICAL AND MATERIAL NEEDS

When you are going through financial trouble or physical illness, listen to what your heavenly Father is saying to you:

1. You are in good health (3 John 1:2; Jeremiah 30:17; Proverbs 3:7–8)
2. You are healed by My stripes (1 Peter 2:24; Isaiah 53:5)
3. You are strong; you can do all things with My strength and power (Philippians 4:13; Ephesians 6:10)
4. You are blessed (Ephesians 1:3; Proverbs 10:6)
5. You are wealthy in Me (Proverbs 8:18–21)
6. You are rich (Philippians 4:19)
7. You are prosperous (3 John 1:2)
8. You are well taken care of by Me (Genesis 22:13–14; Matthew 6:25–34; Philippians 4:19–21)
9. You are an overcomer by My blood and through My power (John 16:33; Revelation 12:11)
10. You are blessed with every spiritual blessing (Ephesians 1:3)
11. You are a woman/man of faith in Me (2 Corinthians 6:7; Hebrews 11:1; Mark 11:24; Psalm 23; Mark 10:52)

12. You are strengthened with power through my Spirit in your inner being (Ephesians 3:16)

PRAYER

Lord, thank You for taking care of my physical and material needs. You take great care of me, and I have nothing to worry about. Thank You for good health because I am healed by Your wounds. You have made me strong, and now I can do all things with Your strength and power. You have made me an overcomer through Your blood and Your power. Because of You, I am blessed, wealthy, and rich in You and through You.

The world's wealth belongs to You; from You comes all I need. For You not only own the cattle on a thousand hills, but You own the entire world. You always supply all my needs from Your glorious riches. You created me to be prosperous in all areas of my life. I bless Your Name, Father, because You have blessed me in Christ with every spiritual blessing in the heavenly places. Thank You because according to the riches of Your glory, You have granted me to be strengthened with power through Your Spirit in my inner being. I am important to You; I mean a lot to You. My faith is in You, and I trust You, Lord. In Jesus' Name, amen.

32

WHEN I HAVE SECURITY AND PROTECTION NEEDS

When you are going through a situation where you need security and protection, listen to what your heavenly Father is saying to you:

1. You are delivered from the power of darkness (Colossians 1:13)
2. You are transferred into the kingdom of Christ (Colossians 1:13)
3. You are empowered by My Spirit (Acts 1:8; 1 Corinthians 12:11)
4. You are destined to heaven (John 14:2–3)
5. You are confident in Me (1 John 3:21; 4:17; Hebrews 4:16; 10:19)
6. You are clothed with My power (Luke 24:49)
7. You are forgiven (John 8:12; 1 John 2; Colossians 1:13–14)
8. You are redeemed by My blood (Ephesians 1:7; Isaiah 43:1; 44:22)
9. You are free from condemnation because you belong to Me (John 8:12; Romans 8:1; 31–39)
10. You are free from the law of sin and death (Romans 8:2)
11. You are cared for by Me (1 Peter 5:7; Matthew 6:26–30)
12. You are protected by Me (Psalm 34:7–9: 91; Exodus 14:14; Job 1:10)
13. You are more than a conqueror (Romans 8:37; Revelation 12:11)
14. You are an heir of God and co-heir with Christ (Romans 8:17)

15. You are saved by my grace, and you will be with Me eternally (Ephesians 2:8–9)
16. You are free from the power of sin (Romans 6:22)
17. You are justified and made righteous (Romans 5:1; 8:30; 1 Corinthians 6:11)
18. You are victorious through Christ (1 Corinthians 15:57)
19. You have authority through Me (Matthew 18:18–20)
20. You have eternal life (John 10:27)
21. You have power, love, and self-discipline (2 Timothy 1:7)
22. You are covered with My feathers (Psalm 91:4)
23. You are sheltered under My wings (Psalm 91:4)
24. You are protected by a wall of fire (Zechariah 2:5)
25. You have right standing with Me (Romans 8:33)
26. You have My protection against your enemies (Romans 8:31; Isaiah 54:17)
27. You have My secured, unconditional love no matter what (Romans 8:38)
28. You are empowered to stand firm in Christ (2 Corinthians 1:21)
29. You are established, anointed, and sealed with My Spirit (2 Corinthians 1:21–22)
30. You are held secured by Me; the evil one cannot touch you (1 John 5:18; Psalm 91:7)
31. You have fellowship with Me (1 John 1:5–7)
32. You have everything you need to live a godly life (2 Peter 1:3)
33. You have been enabled to share My divine nature in you to flee this evil world (2 Peter 1:4)
34. You have all my great and precious promises (2 Peter 1:4)
35. You are a woman/man with spiritually mighty weapons of warfare (2 Corinthians 10:4)
36. You are bold as a lion (Proverbs 28:1)
37. You are strong and courageous (Joshua 1:9; Psalm 18:32)
38. You are covered with My faithful promises (Psalm 91:4)
39. You have My armor and protection (Psalm 91:4)
40. You are protected by My angels wherever you go (Psalm 91:11–13)

41. You are empowered to trample and crush fierce lions and serpents under your feet (Psalm 91:13)
42. You are God-begotten and God-protected (1 John 5:18)
43. You have boldness and access with confidence through your faith in Me (Ephesians 3:12)
44. You are not afraid, nor dismayed, because I am with you wherever you go (Joshua 1:9; 2 Timothy 1:7)
45. You are not afraid of dying, for I AM eternal life (Matthew 10:28; John 11:25–26)
46. You will not slip or fall, for I have your back (Psalm 55:22)
47. You are the apple of My eye (Zechariah 2:8)

PRAYER

Jesus, thank You, for I know You protect me and make me feel secure in You. I am the apple of Your eye; anyone who touches me touches the apple of Your eye. Thank You for delivering me from my enemies and the power of darkness. Now, You have empowered me with Your Spirit. You have destined me to be with You in heaven. Lord, I know that through Your Spirit, I am strong and I can do all things through Christ who gives me strength and power. You have made me bold as a lion, and You have made me an overcomer through the power of Your blood. I am covered by Your faithful promises.

You are my armor and protection. You order Your angels to protect me wherever I go. They hold me up with their hands so nothing can hinder me. You empower me to trample upon lions and cobras; with Your power I am able to crush fierce lions and serpents under my feet. Now I have boldness and access with confidence through my faith in You, O Lord. I am not afraid nor dismayed, because You are with me wherever I go and I am safe.

I am confident in You, O Lord, for You have made me more than a conqueror. I am clothed with Your power, and I have been forgiven of all my sins. Thank You, Lord, for You have set me free from the power of sin and death. You saved me, and I will be with You eternally.

Thank You for giving me eternal life. I will not fear death, for You are my Eternal Life. Your blood redeems me; therefore, I am free from condemnation because I now belong to You, my King and Lord. You have justified me, and You have made me righteous. Father, You have made me an heir.

Thank You because I am victorious through Christ. You have given me authority through Christ Jesus. I know You care for me and protect me, Lord. You have given me a spirit of power, love, and self-discipline. You cover me with Your feathers and shelter me under Your wings. You have put a wall of protection around me. I am protected and secured in You, and I have nothing and no one to fear. In Jesus' Name, amen.

33

WHEN I NEED EMOTIONAL SUPPORT

When you are going through an emotionally unstable time and you are in need of love and support, remember that God is greater than your feelings. Listen to what Your heavenly Father is saying to you:

1. You are not alone, be strong and courageous (Joshua 1:9)
2. You are My daughter/son whom I love (Mark 1:11)
3. You are My daughter/son, and I am well pleased with you (Mark 1:11)
4. You are My daughter/son who brings Me great Joy (Mark 1:11)
5. You are loved unconditionally (Romans 5:8; John 3:16)
6. You are accepted in the beloved (Ephesians 1:6:)
7. You are called My friend because you obey Me (John 15:14–15)
8. You are valued (Matthew 12:12; Exodus 19:5; Luke 12:24; Isaiah 60:1)
9. You are empowered to pray according to My will (Philippians 2:13)
10. You are empowered with desire and the power to do what pleases Me (Philippians 2:13)
11. You are successful (Proverbs 16:3; Philippians 4:13)

12. You are delivered and freed by the power of My life-giving Spirit (Romans 8:1–2)
13. You are free from the power of sin that leads to death (Romans 8:2)
14. You are adopted through Jesus Christ (Ephesians 1:3–5)
15. You are a carrier of My Holy Spirit, your first installment of My promise of love (2 Corinthians 1:22)
16. You are dead to this life and hidden in Christ (Colossians 3:3)
17. You know your feelings are not greater than My knowledge (1 John 3:20)
18. You have a peaceful heart which leads you to health (Proverbs 14:30)
19. You have My divine peace (John 14:27; Philippians 4:7)
20. You pray about everything with thanksgiving (Philippians 4:6–7)
21. Your heart and mind are guarded in My peace as you live in Christ Jesus (Philippians 4:7)
22. You have a clean and pure heart (Psalm 51:10)
23. You have a loyal spirit in you (Psalm 51:10)
24. You are a poured-out offering unto Me and my body (2 Timothy 4:6–8)

PRAYER

Father, thank You, for I know You care for my emotional need of love and support. I know You are greater than my feelings because You know everything. Because You have given me Your divine peace, I have a peaceful heart which leads me to health. I don't need to worry about anything. Instead, I pray about everything I need, and I thank You for all You have done. My heart and mind are guarded in Your peace as I live in Christ Jesus.

Lord, I know I am not alone, and You want me to be strong and courageous because You are always with me, by my side. I know You love me unconditionally as Your daughter/son. You say You are well pleased with me, and I bring You great joy because I love You. I know I am accepted in the beloved, for You have adopted me through Jesus Christ.

Lord, I am Your friend because I obey You willingly. I know that even if others don't value me, You have valued me since the day of my creation. You empower me according to Your will. You empower me with the desire and the power to do what pleases You. I am successful because of You. I am dead to this life, and I am hidden in You. Everything I do for you is an offering and a loving sacrifice unto You. I am a poured out offering unto you and your body. Thank You, for I am delivered and freed by Your life-giving Spirit. I am a carrier of Your Holy Spirit, which is the first installment of Your love promise over my life. Thank You, my Lord. In Jesus' Name, amen.

34

WHEN I HAVE NEEDS OF IMPORTANCE AND BELONGING

When you feel your dignity is devalued or you need a sense of belonging, listen and remember what your heavenly Father is saying to you:

1. You were fearfully and wonderfully made by My hands (Psalm 139:14)
2. You are My masterpiece, planned long ago (Ephesians 2:10)
3. You are My prized possession (James 1:18)
4. You were born of Me (1 John 3:9)
5. You have My seed abiding in you (1 John 3:9)
6. You are important to Me (James 1:18)
7. You belong to Me (1 Corinthians 6:19–20; 7:23; 1 Peter 2:9; John 8:47; Romans 8:1–2; Job 33:6)
8. You are beautiful (Song of Solomon 1:15)
9. You are My dear child (Romans 8:16; John 1:12; 1 John 3:1–2)
10. You are My Counterpart (Revelation 21:3)
11. You are one with Me (1 John 4:4; John 10:30; John 17:23)
12. You are in Me, and I am in you (John 14:20; 17:23; 26)
13. You are My own image and likeness (Genesis 1:27)
14. You originated in Me (Genesis 1:26; Genesis 2:7; Genesis 5:1)

15. You are My invention (Psalm 139:13–16; Genesis 1:26; Genesis 2:7; Genesis 5:1)
16. You were My idea from the beginning (Genesis 1:26–27; Isaiah 42:5; Job 33:4)
17. You look like Me, your original Daddy (Genesis 1:27)
18. You were created perfect in Me (Genesis 1:27; James 1:4; Mathew 5:48)
19. You are a free, valuable soul (John 8:32)
20. You are the daughter/son of the King of kings (Revelation 19:16)
21. You are known to Me (Psalm 7:9; 139:3; 1 Corinthians 8:3; John 10:27)
22. You are Daddy's princess/prince (1 Peter 2:9; Psalm 45:13)
23. You are chosen by My own will (Colossians 1:1; 1 Peter 2:9; Ephesians 1:4–5)
24. You are My royal priesthood (1 Peter 2:9)
25. You are My holy daughter/son (1 Peter 2:9)
26. You are My own treasured possession (1 Peter 2:9)
27. You are precious in My eyes (Isaiah 43:4)
28. You are honored (Isaiah 43:4)
29. You are dearly loved by Me (1 John 4:10–11; Colossians 3:12; 1 Thessalonians 1:4; Isaiah 43:4)
30. You are Mine (Isaiah 43:1)
31. You are My intimate friend forever (John 15:14–15; James 2:23)
32. You have My full tenderness and affection (Philippians 1:8)
33. You are significant and important to Me (John 3:16; Romans 5:8)
34. You are My Temple, My Dwelling Place; I live in you (1 Corinthians 6:19–20)
35. You are bought with a high price; you belong to Me (1 Corinthians 6:19–20)
36. You have access to My throne of mercy and grace (Hebrews 4:16)
37. You are to Me the fragrance of Christ (2 Corinthians 2:15)
38. You are sealed by My Holy Spirit (Ephesians 1:13)
39. You are raised up and seated with Christ in heavenly places (Ephesians 2:6)
40. You are complete in Christ (Colossians 2:10)

41. You are all I want; you are all the world to Me! (Song of Solomon 7:9–10)
42. You are a member of Christ's body (1 Corinthians 12:27)
43. You are a citizen of heaven (Philippians 3:20)
44. You are My righteousness (2 Corinthians 5:21)
45. You are hidden with Christ in God (Colossians 3:3)
46. You know the love of Christ that surpasses knowledge (Ephesians 3:19)
47. You are filled with all the fullness of God (Ephesians 3:19)
48. You were My idea long before anything else was created (Jeremiah 1:5)
49. You are known by Me since before your conception (Jeremiah 1:5)
50. You are sanctified and *made holy by Me* (Hebrews 10:10)

PRAYER

Lord, thank You because I find my eternal significance and belonging in You. You created me fearfully and wonderfully with Your own hands and made me a masterpiece planned long ago. I came out of You and will go back to You. I carry Your breath. You are my Origin. You made me Your prized possession. I am important to You, and I belong to You. You made me beautiful, for I am Your child, Your counterpart, and I am one with You, my Lord. I am in You, and You are in me. I am Your own image; I look like You.

You are my original Daddy. I am Daddy's princess/prince. I was created perfect in You, not necessarily according to people's eyes or opinions but according to Your eyes. I am a free, valuable soul. I am a child of the King of kings and Lord of lords. You know me. Your will has chosen me. I am now a royal priesthood, Your holy daughter/son. I am Your very own treasured possession. I am precious in Your eyes. You honor me and say to me, "I love You. You are Mine."

Lord, You are my Lover, and You tell me that I am all You want. You desire me because I am very special to You. I am all the world to You! O Lord, You are my Intimate Friend forever. I know I have Your full tenderness and affection; how warm and sweet this feels. You give my life significance and importance. Lord, I am Your temple. You have sanctified me and made holy by the sacrifice of the body of Jesus Christ, once for all. Now You live inside of me and I am inside of You. And because You live inside of me, I am secured, protected, and empowered by You. I am Your righteousness, O Lord. I am dead to this life and fully hidden with Christ in God. I am complete in Christ.

I am a member of Your body, Lord, and a citizen of heaven. I was bought at a high price through Your very own blood. Thank You for giving me access to Your throne of mercy and grace. You have raised me and seated me with Christ in the heavenly places. Now I release the fragrance of Christ. Now I am sealed by Your Holy Spirit.

I love You so much, Lord. In Jesus' Name, amen.

35

WHEN I NEED A SENSE OF PURPOSE

When you feel that you are living a life with no purpose or vision for your future, listen and remember what your heavenly Father is saying to you:

1. You were created for My eternal purposes (Jeremiah 1:5; Romans 8:28)
2. You were created to glorify My Name (1 Peter 4:11; Psalm 57:5; Isaiah 43:7)
3. You are more than a conqueror through My love (Romans 8:37)
4. You are smart and wise through Me (James 1:5; Proverbs 1:7)
5. You are creative like Me (Job 35:10; 2 Chronicles 2:13)
6. You are purified by My blood (Hebrews 10:22; 1 Peter 1:2; Titus 2:14)
7. You are set apart and appointed for My divine plan (Jeremiah 1:5; Ephesians 1:9)
8. You are filled with My Holy Spirit and fire (Luke 3:15–16; Acts 2:17–18, 2:33, 10:45)
9. You are called and appointed (John 15:16; Luke 8:15)
10. You are chosen by Me before the foundation of the world (Colossians 3:12; 1 Thessalonians 1:4; Ephesians 1:4)

11. You are holy and sanctified (1 Corinthians 1:2; Colossians 3:12; 1 Thessalonians 1:4)
12. You are filled with the fruit of My Spirit (Ephesians 5:9, 22)
13. You are My holy vessel, a saint (2 Timothy 2:20–21; Ephesians 1:1; 1 Corinthians 1:2; Colossians 1:2)
14. You are a carrier of My Presence (Exodus 33:14)
15. You live, move, and exist in Me (Acts 17:28)
16. You live through Me (1 Corinthians. 8:6)
17. You are My disciple (John 15:8; 13:35)
18. You are a disciple maker (Matthew 28:19, 20)
19. You are My beloved bride, My radiant church (Ephesians 5:27)
20. You were created for My glory (1 Peter 2:9; Isaiah 43:7)
21. You were created to worship Me eternally (Isaiah 43:1–7)
22. You are My true worshiper (John 4:23–24; Isaiah 43:21)
23. You are My servant (Psalm 119:125; Isaiah 43:10)
24. You are the salt of the earth (Matthew 5:13)
25. You are the light of the world (Matthew 5:14)
26. You are the temple of My Holy Spirit (1 Corinthians 3:16; 6:19)
27. You know Me because you obey Me (1 John 2:3–5)
28. You have chosen to know Me (Isaiah 43:10)
29. You have chosen to believe in Me (Isaiah 43:10)
30. You have been pruned and purified by My Word (John 15:3)
31. You are a peacemaker (Proverbs 12:20; Matthew 5:9)
32. You are fruitful through Me (John 15:16; Mark 4:20; Luke 8:15; John 15:5)
33. You have the mind of Christ (John 15:16; 1 Corinthians 2:16)
34. You are called by Me to My eternal glory in Christ (1 Peter 5:10)
35. You are united to me; you are one spirit with Me (1 Corinthians 6:17; John 17:20–23; Romans 6:5)
36. You are a new creation (2 Corinthians 5:17; 1 Peter 1:23)
37. You are a new person; your old life is gone (2 Corinthians 5:17)
38. You are capable; I have given you capacity (Philippians 4:13; Psalm 40:6; Matthew 19:11; Mark 4:33; Luke 12:47–48)
39. You were made complete through Christ (Colossians 2:9–10)
40. You dwell on whatever is honorable (Philippians 4:8)
41. You dwell on whatever is truth (Philippians 4:8)

42. You dwell on whatever is right (Philippians 4:8)
43. You dwell on whatever is pure (Philippians 4:8)
44. You dwell on whatever is lovely (Philippians 4:8)
45. You dwell on whatever is of good repute (Philippians 4:8)
46. You dwell on excellence (Philippians 4:8)
47. You dwell on whatever is worthy of praise (Philippians 4:8)
48. You are My ambassador of reconciliation (2 Corinthians 5:19–21)
49. You are led by My Spirit (Romans 8:14)
50. You were made for such a time as today (Esther 4:14)
51. You are setting your mind on things that are above (Colossians 3:2)
52. You are Christ's representative (2 Corinthians 5:20)
53. You are a channel of My glory (John 15:5)
54. You are blessed because you hear My Word and keep it (Luke 11:28)

PRAYER

Lord, thank You for creating me with purpose. You created me with an eternal purpose for You. I was made for such a time as today. You created me to glorify Your Name. You enabled me to be more than a conqueror through Your love and power. You made me smart and wise through Your wisdom. You gave me the ability to be creative just like You. Your blood purifies me. You have set me apart.

You have called me and appointed me for Your divine plan. You have chosen me for Your purpose. I am setting my mind on things that are above. Jesus, I am your representative on this earth. I am a channel of Your glory. You have made me holy and have sanctified me for Yourself. Father I know You love me profoundly. You fill me with the fruit of Your Spirit.

I am Your holy vessel; I am a saint before You. I am a carrier of Your Presence. I live, move, and exist in You. I live through You. I am Your disciple. I am a disciple maker. I am Your beloved bride and radiant church. I was created for Your glory. I was created to worship You eternally in Your holiness. I am Your true worshiper because I worship You in spirit and truth.

I am Your servant. I am the salt of the earth and the light of the world. I am the temple of the Holy Spirit. I have come to know You because I obey You, and I have chosen to believe in You and get to know You deeply. I am pruned and purified by Your Word. I am a peacemaker. I am fruitful through You. I have the mind of Christ. I am united to You, and we are one. I am a new creation. I have what it takes, I am capable, and I have the capacity because You have enabled me through Your Spirit.

You have enabled me through Your Spirit to dwell on whatever is honorable, true, right, pure, lovely, of good repute, of excellence, and on whatever is worthy of praise. Father, thank You for making me complete through Christ; I will lack nothing. Thank You, Lord; I love You. In Jesus' Name, amen.

36

LORD, WHAT KIND OF PERSON AM I TO YOU?

When you don't truly know who you are because of the effect of other peoples' opinions on you, listen and remember what your heavenly Father is saying to you:

1. You are an awesome mom/dad.
2. You are a great wife/ husband.
3. You are an awesome daughter/son; I am proud of you.
4. You are a successful man/woman.
5. You are an influencer.
6. You are a great role model.
7. You are intelligent.
8. You have what it takes to be successful.
9. You are elegant/pretty/handsome.
10. You are healthy and whole.
11. You are a joy to be around.
12. You are godly.
13. You are talented.
14. You are My intercessor.
15. You love Me with all your heart.
16. You are loving.

17. You are celebrated by Me.

PRAYER

Thank You, Lord, for empowering me to be an awesome mom/dad. You bless my motherhood/ fatherhood. You enable me to be a great wife/husband. You bless my marriage. You empower me to be a successful woman/man according to Your will. Through Your loving wisdom and power, You make me an influencer of my family, friends, and the world.

You have made me a great role model. You have given me Your wisdom and intelligence; I make intelligent decisions and choices. I have what it takes to live a successful life on this earth. You have made me elegant, pretty/handsome before Your eyes. I am healthy and whole.

I am an awesome daughter/son, and You are proud of me. You say that I am a joy to be around. I am godly. You have equipped me to be talented. I am Your intercessor. I love You with all my heart. I am loving because You are loving to me. I am celebrated by You! Thank You, Lord. I love You. Amen.

37

A PRAYER OF THANKSGIVING AND WORSHIP

Knowing and understanding the reality of how God sees us and what He says to and about us should drive us to our knees in thanksgiving and worship every day. So let us praise our God!

But let the godly rejoice. Let them be glad in God's presence. Let them be filled with joy. Sing praises to God and to HIS NAME! Sing loud praises to Him who rides the clouds. HIS NAME is the LORD—rejoice in his presence!

Psalm 68:3–4

PRAYER

God and merciful Father, You are my Abba Papa. Jesus, You are my Redeemer, my Savior and my Beloved. Holy Spirit you are the gentle and kind Spirit of God who brings forth the fruit of love, joy, peace, patience, kindness, goodness, faithfulness, gentleness, and self-control. Thank You for saving me, delivering me, and setting me free. I acknowledge You with praise for restoring me and giving me a new sense of purpose.

Thank You for loving me unconditionally. You are now my purpose and reason to live. You are amazing grace and favor; You are sweeter than honey. You are my sense of significance and my sense of belonging. You are my Health, my Comforter, my Happiness. You are my Light, the River of Living Water, my Eternal Life. The King who beautifies me and delights in my beauty. You are my divine and eternal Lover, my divine Counterpart. You are my exciting Future and Destiny.

O Lord, You are so beautiful, the most handsome of all. You are wonderful, awesome, incredible, glorious, splendid, majestic, great, all-powerful, incomparable, mighty, and impenetrable. You are the Triumphant God, the Overcomer, the Conqueror, and the Victorious King. You are the Winner of everything—the universal Champion of all ages, the present, and the future. You are the Great and Almighty I AM; Your Greatness is unsearchable. You are Sovereign, Omniscient, Omnipresent, Omnipotent, Omnificent, and Omnibenevolent.

You are my Creator, my Identity, my Author, my Maker, my divine Origin, my Source and Fountain. You are the One who has all my hairs counted. You are my inheritance and wealth, the Owner of the universe, the Owner of gold and silver, the Distributor of wealth, my most beautiful Possession, my eternal Portion. You take care of every detail of my life and supply all my needs. You are the One who can do far more abundantly than all I can ask or think, according to the power at work within me.

You are the God of the impossible; everything is possible with You. Everything is perfect in You, and I can trust You wholeheartedly. You are the Tree of Life; I get guidance from You and solely depend on You. You are greater than my feelings and emotions, and You know everything, for You own all good and perfect wisdom, knowledge, and intelligence. You are over all and through all and in all.

You are a Rock of Refuge, my very present Help in times of trouble. You are my secret Hiding Place where the enemy cannot find me. You are my Deliverer and Liberator, my Savior, my Restoration, my Healer, my Refuge, my supernatural Strength, my firm Victory, my Maximum Security, the Wall of Fire around me, my Protector, my Defender, and a mighty Warrior that fights for me, for the battle is all Yours.

Worthy of being worshiped and celebrated. You are *Yahweh*, Lord. You are *Adonai*, my Lord and Master. You are *Yeshua*, Jesus, the *El Shaddai*, Almighty and All-sufficient. You are *Shalom*, my Peace, the *El Kanna*, a jealous

God, and a consuming fire. *Elohim* of *Elohim*, the God of gods, Lord of lords, King of kings, and the Maximum Power eternally.

You are just and fair, my great Judge and Vindicator. You are Holy and Worthy, the Lamb of God who was slain. The ultimate Sacrifice for my sins, my Atonement, and my Justifier. You are the God of forgiveness, incomparable and unfailing love. Your love is loyal and faithful. You are worthy of worship, the God of honor, the highest God, Magnificent, the One who rides with majesty toward victory, and the Defender of truth, humility, and justice.

Yours is the power, the wealth, the wisdom, and the strength. You deserve the honor, the glory, and the blessing. For the blessing, the honor, the glory, and the power belong to You forever and ever, O Lord. You are seated upon Your throne, for You are the Lamb of God. You are the One who governs with a scepter of justice and righteousness, the Lord of hosts, the Lord of the heav-en's armies, worthy of being feared with great reverence.

You are the Maker of wondrous works. Glorious in holiness, awesome in glorious deeds, and awesome in splendor. The God of inexhaustible love, my Redeemer, the One who snatches me from the power of the grave. You are the Resurrection Power, the One who resurrects the dead and gives life to the dry bones. You are the God who shines with glorious radiance. You are the God of communion and intimate relationship. You are my best and most intimate Friend. I am Yours, and You are mine eternally.

And now, Lord, may You be merciful and bless us, for You are good. May Your face smile and shine with favor on us. May Your ways and Your saving power be known throughout the earth and everywhere. O Lord, may the whole world know Your glory, and may they praise You and sing with joy, for You are the joy of the nations. May You bless us, Lord, and may the world come to fear Your great Name in reverence forever and ever.

In Jesus' glorious Name, amen and amen eternally!

ACKNOWLEDGMENTS

I humbly present this book as a tribute to the Lord and King of my life, Jesus Christ. Without your relentless pursuit of me with unconditional love and showing me a better way beyond religion, this endeavor would not have been possible. I will eternally worship Your holy and mighty name.

To my beloved husband, Dr. Herman Colón Jr., my lifelong companion and lover, I owe you immeasurable gratitude. Your unwavering passion for God's presence and His Word has profoundly impacted me. Thank you for bringing balance to my life and consistently walking in the guidance of the Holy Spirit, supporting me throughout my journey with the Lord. Your countless teachings filled with profound wisdom and spiritual insight have shaped the pages of this book. It is a testament to your ministry in my life.

David Sluka, a devoted worshiper, servant of God, and an invaluable asset to the body of Christ, I am indebted to you for your numerous contributions and wise counsel during the writing of my last two books. Your expertise and guidance have been immeasurable, and I will forever be grateful for your ministry.

I would like to express my deepest gratitude to Dr. Paul Carlyon, I greatly appreciate your invaluable help in assisting me with the correction of the first version of the manuscript of the book. Thank you from the bottom of my heart.

ABOUT THE AUTHOR

Yolandita Colón is an unconventional prophetic worship leader. She is a teacher, author, ordained minister, realtor and kingdom entrepreneur. With a Bachelor of Science degree in music and a minor in Bible from North Central University, supplemented by extensive coursework at Southwest Missouri State University, her qualifications are remarkable.

However, it is her unwavering passion that truly sets Yolandita apart. She is driven to inspire and raise up genuine worshipers of the Father, particularly for the forthcoming revival in these last days. Together with her husband, Herman, they have dedicated over twenty-four years to ministry and have shepherded two congregations in Minnesota, all while nurturing their two sons.

Yolandita's journey is marked by a profound commitment to the Kingdom and an unwavering desire to equip others for a more intimate and profound worship of the Father. Her multifaceted calling and extensive experience make her a valuable asset to the body of Christ.